READING with
Babies, Toddlers & Twos

A Guide to Laughing, Learning
& Growing Together Through Books

SUSAN STRAUB & KJ DELL'ANTONIA
with RACHEL PAYNE

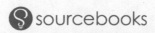

Published by Sourcebooks, Inc.
P.O. Box 4410, Naperville, Illinois 60567-4410
(630) 961-3900
Fax: (630) 961-2168
www.sourcebooks.com

Library of Congress Cataloguing-in-Publication data is on file with the publisher.

Printed and bound in the United States of America.
VP 10 9 8 7 6 5 4 3 2 1

CONTENTS

ACKNOWLEDGMENTS

❖❖❖❖❖❖❖❖❖❖❖❖❖❖❖❖❖❖❖❖❖❖❖❖❖❖❖❖❖❖❖❖❖❖

We are deeply grateful to our contributing families and to all the children's writers and illustrators who make our lives better with their artful work. Among the many kind and book-loving friends who gave us help, we'd like to especially thank Carrie Banks, Delia Battin, Pat Cummings, Michael Fusco, Kathy Kinsner, Deanna Pacelli, Holly L. L. Pierce, and the wonderful children's librarians and materials specialists at Brooklyn Public Library.

And finally, our heartfelt thanks to Joëlle Delbourgo, who believed in the idea of this book from the moment she saw it, and the dedicated people at Sourcebooks who worked so hard to help us transform it into a reality.

Introduction
READ EARLY, READ OFTEN

◆ ◆

Before life presented you with an actual baby, you had a mental vision: a small, cuddly bundle in a blanket, sucking a finger and nodding off to sleep as she listens to you read. As you turn the last page, your voice softens, and you look down—she's out like a light. With a kiss on her soft cheek, you tuck her into her crib whispering, "Good night, Baby."

In reality, that is probably not quite how things played out—it certainly wasn't for us. Reading with a baby, toddler, or two-year-old is not always what you imagine. The barrage of media, the demands of the child as she grows, the requests from family and friends, and the effort of just plain getting through a day mean things don't always go as planned. But reading together should be fun. It's simple, and it can make a real difference to your baby as she grows. We know—sometimes it's hard to see the pleasure or the point. Our goal with this book is to reassure you that it's worth it.

> **TIP: On average, children spend only forty-nine minutes with books per day compared with three to four hours in front of a TV or computer screen. Want above-average kids? Encourage them to read.**

We all want our kids to be readers. We want them to be able to spend private time during which they can slide into another world with a book. As they grow up, we want them to develop big vocabularies, big imaginations, and empathy for other characters. We want them to enjoy reading in every format, from hardcover to paperback to wherever digital books go next. But raising a child who reads doesn't start with *teaching* a child to read—in fact, it doesn't start with a child at all. It starts with a baby.

Do you remember being read to as a baby? Most memories of the reading experience, whether as a parent or a child, begin during preschool. But the building blocks for that experience come from reading with babies, toddlers, and twos. From burpers and droolers, crawlers and cruisers, to walkers and talkers, these little people love reading, too. But, like so many other parts of their development, they can't do it without your help.

Ten Reasons to Read to Your Baby or Toddler

1. It's fun.
2. Reading builds vocabulary.
3. Books stimulate the imagination.
4. Reading increases the chance of later academic success.
5. Books and their characters teach empathy and understanding.
6. Reading entertains, it stimulates, and it lights up the senses.
7. Books are portable and infinitely useful.
8. Reading is an introduction to our culture and our world.
9. It's an inexpensive, richly rewarding way to spend time together.
10. It's fun.

A child who is read to from infancy is a child who knows that books are a source of pleasure and knowledge. She's a baby with a broad vocabulary and a broader experience—a city child who knows cows and a country kid who can hail a taxi. She's an art critic and a connoisseur of rhyme schemes. In short, she's a kid who's going places, because she's a baby who's been places, all in the comfort of your lap.

What's in This Book and How to Use It

Nearly every chapter of this book offers:

1. A thorough consideration of a reading topic.
2. Book lists—a lot of them!
3. Anecdotes and tips from parents.
4. Ages and Stages charts that suggest activities, techniques, and other information on reading with newborns, sitters, crawlers, cruisers, and walkers.

Susan's been choosing books for the READ TO ME Program (designed to encourage teen parents to read with their babies) for twenty years and has learned what grabs a baby's attention. She offers some insight into why babies like what they like. KJ's four children have provided her with oceans of experience of shared reading. Between their demands, her work as a children's book reviewer, and her role as the *New York Times*'s lead parenting blogger, she knows firsthand which books work best and why—and how to experience them with your child.

Together, Susan and KJ wrote the first edition of this book. This new edition brings Rachel Payne into the mix. Rachel, the best imaginable guide to books for this age group, is the early childhood specialist and a librarian at Brooklyn Public Library. She's also the mother of Colin, now two years old and an excellent book-testing laboratory. She knows why some books are carried around, colored on, taken to meals, and slept with, while others are pushed away after a single page.

Rachel has sifted and winnowed through our original book choices, updating lists to reflect the ever-changing children's section in bookstores and libraries. Too many excellent books disappear, often due to poor sales even though the reviews are stellar. Her revised lists are up to the minute, including books available in every format.

The book lists are varied and specific: New Classics, Activity Books,

Pop-Ups, Bedtime Books, and Naming Books (which teach babies and toddlers the names for specific objects). We asked some parents to give us a list of their babies' favorite books at that moment. Book clubs do this for older kids ("If you liked *Little House*, you might also like *Caddie Woodlawn*"), and websites do it for adults ("Customers who bought these selections also purchased…"). We're giving babies equal time. You might be guided to some new favorites.

Finally, all of the tricks, tips, hints, and true confessions you'll find here aim toward one thing: making reading with your baby or toddler fun for you both. We believe it's the best possible gift you can give your baby.

For Teachers, Caregivers, and Librarians

This book directly addresses the concerns and day-to-day lives of parents and other primary caregivers. There's great information here for teachers, professors, librarians, and child-care providers as well. We hope you'll discover some new books for the shelves of your centers, libraries, and classrooms and gain some insight into why certain books can be important or helpful to children at certain times. We also hope you'll use the book as a resource for helping the parents you work with.

A parent who picks up this book is already planning to read to his or her child, but many parents aren't reading at home, or are limiting their reading to bedtime. You are in a perfect position to introduce those parents to the joys of reading with their child by letting them know how much their children enjoy certain books you've read in class, and by including book suggestions or reading tips in your newsletter or on your classroom news board. Other ideas include organizing a book drive for the classroom, suggesting parents buy two copies—one for class, one for home. Teachers in classrooms where not all parents have the resources to purchase books can look to organizations like First Book for help. You could also distribute information on local libraries with children's areas and story times to parents and encourage them to meet at the library for a playdate.

If you are a librarian new to the field or new to working with young children, you might feel baffled about how to advise little ones and their grown-ups on what to read next. We hope the tips, anecdotes, and book lists we've provided can give you insight into the reading lives of babies and toddlers. You are in a unique position to connect children and their parents and caregivers with wonderful books they might never discover on their own in a bin full of board books. It can be hard to figure out which title a toddler is asking for when she says "want turtle book." When you finally decipher the request, there is no more satisfied customer.

Parents turn to a trusted care provider and other professionals in their community for perspective and advice on their child's development as well as for care. We hope we can help you to introduce more parents to the joys of reading with their child.

Let's read!

—Susan, KJ, and Rachel

The Three-Favorites-Each Challenge

KJ challenged Susan and Rachel to come up with one favorite book each—but none of us (including KJ) could do it! Instead, we each chose three: one favorite for each year between zero and three. These are nine books we personally recommend and call "must-haves."

KJ's Favorites

0–1 year: *Clap Hands*, Helen Oxenbury. Short book, short rhymes, catchy rhythm, with enchantingly fat multicultural babies playing on its pages.

1–2 years: *Everywhere Babies*, Susan Meyers, Marla Frazee (illus.). Families of all kinds keep baby's eyes busy while a soothing rhyme draws you through the pages.

2–3 years: *Little Pea*, Amy Krauss Rosenthal, Jen Corace (illus.). A first comedy: to grow up big and strong, Little Pea has to eat all his candy (yuck!).

Susan's Favorites

0–1 year: *This Little Piggy: A Hand-Puppet Board Book*, Little Scholastic, Michelle Berg (illus.). Cloth interactive finger puppet characters wiggle to distract, entertain, and remind us of these classic rhymes. Also try *Old MacDonald*.

1–2 years: *My Aunt Came Back*, Pat Cummings. In energetic and exuberant verse and art, a generous aunt shares souvenirs from her travels with her lucky niece. Unfortunately, this title is out of print, but check online sellers and your library for availability.

2–3 years: *George and Martha*, James Marshall. This launches the exuberant, witty, snarky, friendly, hilarious world of these two best friend hippos.

Rachel's Favorites

0–1 year: *I Kissed the Baby*, Mary Murphy. This delightful, high-contrast book about animals greeting a duckling works for newborns to toddlers.

1–2 years: *Clip Clop*, Nicola Smee. Cat and Dog and Pig and Duck get a ride on Mr. Horse. Great for active toddlers since the story encourages lots of bouncing and clippety-clopping.

2–3 years: *The Wheels on the Bus*, Paul O. Zelinsky. When you're ready for pop-ups, this is the one to get. There are doors to open and shut and wipers to swish, swish, swish. This librarian loves the bus's last stop—the library!

Chapter One
REAL READING, REAL KIDS

•◦•◦•◦•◦•◦•◦•◦•◦•◦•◦•◦•◦•◦•◦•◦•◦•◦•◦•

The Who, What, and Why

Real reading, with real children, is rarely a picture-perfect process. Even a baby who loves to be read to isn't going to curl up in your lap every time. Toddlers tear books. Twos throw them. Trying out an ebook or app? He's all over every button or swipe of the screen, including those that shut the whole thing down or email your boss.

You may think books are for reading. Your baby sees books as infinitely useful for playing peek-a-boo, experimenting with Newton's Law of Gravity, and forming a bridge to allow the giraffe to walk into the plastic barn door.

It seems as if there's an enormous gulf between what the two of you are trying to achieve: you're trying to get to the end of *Harold and the Purple Crayon*, and your baby is trying to taste the book cover. You want to read; he wants to experience. His experience, though, is really akin to your reading. He's learning about the book: as an individual book, a part of a larger set of books, as a hard object, a soft object, a paper object, and, finally, something that causes you to make a given set of sounds.

Whether he's mouthing *Harold*'s cover or using him for a hat, he's happy. Isn't that what you really want—creativity, experimentation, imaginative play, talking and laughing and doing something together? Let go of the goal and savor the experience. You probably already know how it ends, anyway.

Why Read? Because You Like To, That's Why

If you didn't want to read to your baby, toddler, or two-year-old, it's not likely you'd have picked up this book. You've already decided you want to read together, but why? What will either of you take away from the time you spend together, book in hand?

Reading is one of the first activities you can enjoy together. At its best, it's a chance to snuggle in tightly and quietly enter another world. At the very least, it's a distraction from a difficult moment or a difficult day. Sometimes it's a last-ditch way to provide entertainment when you simply haven't got another creative thing left to give.

> TIP: Researchers say that the number of different words a baby hears each day is the single most important predictor of later intelligence, school success, and social competence, if those words come from one of baby's special people—mother, daddy, grandma, nanny—rather than from a box on the wall. Reading counts.

To your child, though, reading is so much more than just fun. The world comes to your baby through his eyes, ears, nose, mouth, and fingers. Reading allows you to bring him even more aspects of that world in smaller, easily absorbed packages. A real truck is a big, scary, noisy thing to a four-month-old or even an eighteen-month-old. A truck on the pages of a book, or even in an app, is small and predictable, something that can be held and controlled or sent away with a turn of the page. The same holds true for monsters and green peas. A book lets a baby take in the world on his own terms.

Books link kids to our world and our culture. *Winnie the Pooh, Curious George, Where the Wild Things Are, Chicken Soup with Rice,* Dr. Seuss—they're a backdrop for our world. A college professor complained to Susan that there's no shared frame of literary reference among her students—she can't assume that they all will have read *Great Expectations* or *To Kill a Mockingbird.* But surely every student had read (or heard) some version of Cinderella! Familiar characters and their stories shape our view of places and things that, as a child, we haven't usually seen yet. Their experiences give us a framework for dealing with our own. As you read to your baby, you welcome him into the culture that will become his own, and you can share other cultures with him as well.

Fun Things Babies Do While You Read

- Fall asleep
- Grab the book
- Pull your hair
- Hold the page so you can't turn it
- Sit on the floor and look at you like you're out of your mind
- Tear the page
- Throw the book on the floor
- Point and demand "what's that?" of every object on the page
- Scream
- Babble out their own stories while you read
- Open and shut the book over and over for a little "peek-a-boo"
- Listen happily for two pages, then head off—and get upset if you stop reading!

"I come home from work as a Head Start teacher exhausted and worried about putting dinner on the table and getting things done. My two-year-old is always tugging at my leg with a book. Finally, I just put everything down, sit on the floor, plop her into my lap, and read her book—and it's usually the best break of my day." —Brenda

Ten Picture Books We Dare You Not to Enjoy

1. *The Adventures of Taxi Dog*, Debra Barracca, Sal Barracca, Mark Buehner (illus.). Even kids who've never seen a taxi will enjoy the bright, graphic adventures of the dog who rides daily with his owner in a New York City cab.
2. *The Everything Book*, Denise Fleming. This is something akin to a Richard Scarry book in the sheer amount of information and entertainment on every page, with gorgeously textured illustrations.
3. *The Hiccupotamus*, Aaron Zenz. There's fun in the colorful, antic illustrations and the travails of the hiccupping hippo as well as the nonsense rhymes.
4. *Higher! Higher! / ¡Más alto! ¡Más alto!*, Leslie Patricelli. A girl begs her father to swing her "Higher! Higher!" on the playground swing with fantastic results. In Spanish and English. Try *Faster! Faster!* for more in the same vein.
5. *I Love Colors*, Margaret Miller. Big baby faces joyfully sport colorful accessories.
6. *Little Night*, Yuyi Morales. Mother Night and her daughter, Little Night, play and prepare for bed in Morales's luminescent art.
7. *Lola at the Library*, Anna McQuinn, Rosalind Beardshaw (illus.). Every Tuesday Lola and her mother spend the day together—at the library. Also *Lola Loves Stories* and *Lola Reads to Leo*.
8. *My Friends / Mis amigos*, Taro Gomi. A little girl learns in very simple ways from animal and human friends. In Spanish and English.
9. *No, David!*, David Shannon. Shannon's illustrations, roughly and childishly drawn, perfectly capture David's amazing knack for trouble as well as his charm. Popular with every kid who's ever heard that sudden shouted, "No!"
10. *Where Is the Green Sheep? / ¿Dónde está la oveja verde?*, Mem Fox, Judy Horacek (illus.). Playful rhymes and droll art introduce us to a variety of colorful and eccentric sheep. Available in both Spanish / English and English-only formats.

Ned's Top Ten

❖❖❖❖❖❖❖❖❖❖❖❖❖❖❖❖❖❖❖❖❖❖❖❖❖❖❖❖❖

"Ned, at two years, two months, is a big fan of books and totally wedded to our bedtime book routine. We usually read four to five books culminating with *How Do Dinosaurs Say Goodnight?* (the current favorite for the past four months!). Recently, I have noticed that he is willing to sit for a bit longer in favor of some wordier books, but we still have our favorite board books that we have been reading since birth. Selfishly, I hope our nighttime ritual continues well into the future because I enjoy his reaction to the books sometimes more than I think he enjoys the stories! Lastly, I noticed as we hit two that Ned was ready for books on tape. This has been a great way to take our favorites (see nine and ten on the list) with us while we are on the go!" —Kitty

1. *How Do Dinosaurs Say Goodnight?*, Jane Yolen, Mark Teague (illus.)
2. *Joseph Had a Little Overcoat*, Simms Taback
3. *Goodnight Moon*, Margaret Wise Brown, Clement Hurd (illus.)
4. *Planes, Trains,* and *Airport,* Byron Barton
5. *Moo, Baa, La La La!* and others by Sandra Boynton
6. *Train Song*, Harriet Ziefert (out of print)
7. *Big Red Barn*, Margaret Wise Brown, Felicia Bond (illus.)
8. *Bark, George*, Jules Fieffer
9. *Chicka Chicka Boom Boom*, Bill Martin Jr., John Archambault, Lois Ehlert (illus.)
10. *Fox in Sox*, Dr. Seuss

Will reading together teach your child to read faster? Will it put him ahead of the curve, get him into the right preschool, help him ace his SATs? No promises, no guarantees—and we don't think you should look for them. We can tell you that nothing shows a baby or a child the importance of reading like a parent with a book in hand. But we can also tell you that if reading becomes medicine (two books a day keeps the bad grades away), it ceases to be fun for either of you. Read together for pleasure, for the fun of shared rhymes, and the excitement of shared worlds. Anything else is just gravy.

Who Reads? Everybody

The amazing thing about books—to a young child—is that every person says pretty much the same thing when they read the same book. In fact, that's one of the ways the baby knows a book *is* a book. It may change a little (Mama laughs at the monkey, and the babysitter always says "zoom!"), but the art and the words and the feeling stay the same. He loves the continuity and the comfort of it. When his parents go out, Grandma or the babysitter can read a special book, and then Mama or Daddy can read it again when they get home. On vacation, the same book can emerge from a laptop, e-reader, or phone app.

"My mother has been reading Hand, Hand, Fingers, Thumb *to two-year-old Brady since he was teeny tiny. Since she lives far away, she doesn't see him as often as we'd like. But I've been holding the phone up to his ear since he was just a few weeks old, and she always quotes it to him. We keep a copy at our house and one at her house, and when we visit her, or she visits us, it's one of the first ways they reconnect—by sitting down and reading 'Dum Ditty Dum Ditty Dum Dum Dum!'"* —Amy

Encourage your babysitter or regular caregiver to read with your baby. Make it clear that books are part of the bedtime and naptime routine, and leave a stack of books in the room they generally play in or next to a bottle or snack.

What Should We Read? Great Literature and Cereal Boxes

Read *everything*. Maybe you're convinced that you only want to read quality stuff to your little one, and you've been avoiding Barney books like the

··

Featured Book

BOOK!
By Kristine O'Connell George, Maggie Smith (illus.)

··

This is the book that proves our point. The baby in this book loves his book. He wears it and treats it like a favorite stuffed toy, taking it everywhere. The Spanish / English bilingual edition, *Book! / ¡Libro!*, is also available.

··

plague. But here's the thing—to some extent, it's all good stuff. Many a reader of *Twilight* moves on to read Jane Austen. Picture books work the same way. Most of the magic is in the act of reading itself, and a few, or even a few hundred, readings of something you consider to be poorly written, plotless, banal, or otherwise offensive to your sensibilities won't hurt anyone but you, and you're tough enough to take it.

That said, not every book works for every child, or at every age. Rachel is constantly asked, "What should I read to my two-year-old? We're outgrowing board books, but most picture books are too long." Some books work better for certain ages. And some books are richer than others and just more fun to read.

While your baby has tastes and quirks from day one, the books you choose can shape those tastes. And since you'll be reading them almost as often as he will, you need books that work and books you'll both love. The rest of this book is devoted to helping you find them.

"I've heard of parents doing the same via Skype, Facetime, and other video chat services. Choose a full-sized picture book with bold art and simple text, and make sure the technical bugs are worked out before beginning. Giving an older child her own copy of the book to hold is great too—and when they visit, Grandma and Grandpa can do a live reading." —Rachel

In the end, reading isn't just about books. Almost everything in our society is covered in words, from cereal boxes to road signs. All make excellent reading in their own way and begin to convey that reading is for fun and for information. Information is powerful stuff to a toddler. When you start thinking about reading throughout your day, don't forget that you already are—at the breakfast table, at the grocery store, in the car, and on a walk as you point out the signs and boxes that describe and direct us.

"My eleven-month-old mostly likes to disrupt other people's reading: pulling newspapers off the table, taking a book out of your hand. His method is to either drop the reading material directly on the floor, or to turn it over in his hands a couple of times before dropping it on the floor. He also favors the inserts that the New York Post *has been putting in the papers. They had a recent series on the Yankees, the Jets, and animal wildlife. They're like magazines, glossy and full of big color photos, but only about six pages. I can tell from the way they are crumpled (and on the floor) that he has been the one enjoying them." —Jennifer*

The Classics
Twenty-Five Picture Books for Every Child's Library

These are great books—books you'll find in every library, every preschool, every bookstore. You've probably heard of many of them; some you may remember from your own childhood and some you may read to your grandchildren someday.

1. *Blueberries for Sal*, Robert McCloskey. This simply illustrated glimpse of the past resonates with any child who's lost sight of Mom as Sal does during a blueberry picking jaunt.
2. *Brown Bear, Brown Bear, What Do You See?*, Bill Martin Jr., Eric Carle (illus.). Many kids can "read" Martin's predictable and comforting text before they even learn their letters. Carle's simple animal collages are iconic.

Irresistible Authors: Helen Oxenbury

It never ceases to amaze us how much a good artist can convey with two dots and a line for a face. Helen Oxenbury is particularly gifted in this regard. Her round-headed babies, with their pants slipping off their chubby waists and their plump hands grasping spoons and drumsticks, look so simple you'll wonder why you can't draw something like that yourself—but you can't. We love her quartet of extra-large board books (*Clap Hands*; *Say Goodnight*; *Tickle, Tickle*; *All Fall Down*) featuring babies involved in their day-to-day activities—reading, eating, bathing, swinging—as well as the books aimed at the slightly older crowd, like *Tom and Pippo* (unfortunately out of print). These books may make a great introduction to narrative for a baby who loves the early books, since his familiarity with Oxenbury's artwork will make the book that much more appealing and comforting. One of her latest works, *There's Going to Be a Baby* (written by her husband John Burningham), is a must-have if there's a second child on the way.

3. *Caps for Sale: A Tale of a Peddler, Some Monkeys, and Their Monkey Business*, Esphyr Slobodkina. A wonderful, timeless tale of copying and cleverness.

4. *The Carrot Seed*, Ruth Krauss, Crocket Johnson (illus.). For more than half a century, this beanie-sporting boy has had faith that his carrot would grow, despite his family's doubt.

5. *Chicka Chicka Boom Boom*, Bill Martin Jr., John Archambault, Lois Ehlert (illus.). In arguably one of the most memorable and playful alphabet books ever, lowercase letters and their parents, the capital letters, cavort up and down a coconut tree.

6. *Clifford the Big Red Dog*, Norman Bridwell. Yes, it's a television series; yes, it's a franchise...but the original books are really good and perfect for babies and toddlers. Big, red dog. Need we say more?

7. *Corduroy*, Don Freeman. A lovely story of a little girl's kindness and empathy for a teddy bear who needs a home, with realistic illustrations.

8. *Curious George*, H. A. Rey. The story of the little monkey, so like a toddler in his curiosity and impulsiveness but so much more capable, is one kids love. You'll probably notice now that George's removal from the jungle isn't the most politically correct thing ever written, but your child won't mind.

9. *Freight Train*, Donald Crews. This multicolored train has been crossing trestles, going by cities, and going through tunnels for over thirty years. Now there is an app that was created with Crews's input.

10. *George and Martha*, James Marshall. The hippos have an admirable friendship, so real that it's full of pranks, hurt feelings, and make-ups. Marshall produced tons more brief stories about them, but this is the first. Arguably the story "Split Pea Soup" is a legend all by itself. Fun for the whole family.

11. *Go, Dog. Go!*, P. D. Eastman. Simple books meant for beginning readers can make great books for beginning talkers. The board book version is a totally different animal, but it still works.

12. *Goodnight Moon*, Margaret Wise Brown, Clement Hurd (illus.). The old-fashioned setting, the simple rhymes, and the cozy illustrations make this a nighttime must-read for many toddlers.

13. *Guess How Much I Love You*, Sam McBratney, Anita Jeram (illus.). Big Nutbrown Hare can one-up Baby Nutbrown Hare's declarations of love every time, but this baby doesn't give up.

14. *Harold and the Purple Crayon*, Crockett Johnson. You may remember Harold, but you probably didn't think of him as a book for babies. In fact, he works very well—simple illustrations and many moons.

15. *Harry the Dirty Dog*, Gene Zion, Margaret Bloy Graham (illus.). Harry needs a bath—and after he's run away from one, he gets so dirty his family doesn't recognize him. His ultimate return and his family's recognition make for a very satisfying resolution.

16.   *Hop on Pop*, Dr. Seuss. A wonderful introduction to rhyme.

17.   *The Little Engine That Could*, Watty Piper, George and Doris Hauman (illus.). This tale still resonates and always will. The original illustrations are fun, but if you find them dated, you can look for Loren Long's 2005 take on this classic. If the words (definitely a little on the sweet and cloying side) begin to get to you, you can always edit a bit.

18.   *The Little House*, Virginia Lee Burton. Most of us remember the poignant illustrations in this story of a little house in the country that becomes surrounded by city before sympathetic owners move it to the country again.

19.   *The Napping House*, Audrey and Don Wood. In this fun, cumulative tale, a nap goes awry due to the antics of a "wakeful" flea.

20.   *Pat the Bunny*, Dorothy Kunhardt. The mother of all interactive baby books.

21.   *The Very Hungry Caterpillar*, Eric Carle. Kids love putting their fingers through the holes and pulling the pages to watch the hungry caterpillar eat his way through an uncomfortable assortment of food.

22.   *We're Going on a Bear Hunt*, Michael Rosen, Helen Oxenbury (illus.). A family, a journey, a bear, and lots of great sound effects from Rosen and lively watercolors from Oxenbury make this read-aloud irresistible.

23.   *Where the Wild Things Are*, Maurice Sendak. Sent to his room for being a wild thing, Max travels to the forest and conquers even wilder things before realizing that home is best.

24.   *Where's Spot?*, Eric Hill. Plump, yellow Spot and his wonder at discovering the world around him have spoken to children for decades. Also available as *¿Dónde está Spot?* in Spanish, and in many other languages.

25.   *Whistle for Willie*, Ezra Jack Keats. A whistle will call Willie the dog,

but Peter can't whistle until practice finally pays off. Refreshingly warm collage illustrations.

Ages and Stages: Getting Started

This chart suggests tips on reading to babies as they develop. Up to a point, these stages are sequential. For example, your baby will sit before he crawls, and crawl or creep or scoot before he walks. Later development is less predictable. Many a baby is madly running off into the parking lot long before he's forming two-word sentences, or piping up with "Why he crying, Mama?" but unable or unwilling to climb a ladder. Verbal and physical development can vary wildly during the toddler years, and we've tried to account for that by suggesting different tips or activities for the wild child and the precocious talker.

The point is to have fun with babies and books. Focus on what the baby CAN do for maximum success.

Newborn

He is absorbing every word…and absorbing is a good way to put it, because for the most part, those words are just sounds to him—sounds that are developing his mind and sparking the synapses he needs to speak English or Chinese (or whatever language he's hearing). But at this age, he's every bit as happy to hear you read aloud from *Sports Illustrated*, although neither the content nor the illustrations will truly satisfy.

Try black-and-white books or books with just a few colors, and leave the page open for as long as he wants to look at the picture.

Find books with texture and help him to pat the bunny or feel the cat's sandy tongue.

Heads Up	Try putting him on the floor with an open book in front of him for "tummy time." Offer him one book to hold (or munch) while you read another.
Sitting	A good time to start "Where is the ____? There it is!" Sit across from each other on the floor and hand books back and forth. Talk about them—"Can I have the book with the doggie? Thank you!"
Crawling / Creeping	Relax—action may win over reading for the next few months. If you find yourselves struggling, save books for quiet moments, like pre-nap and bed. He WILL tire, and he WILL need a break (and so will you). Let the baby crawl to you and a book as you read. Try reading a book with baby in the high chair after a meal.
Cruising / Walking	This is a prime time for insisting on one "favorite" book. Exact repetition is deeply comforting at this stage! This is a big time for throwing books, too. Books are toys but not balls! However, since brain research shows a connection between talking and throwing, you might get a Nerf ball for now, and use the book another time.
Talking (a few words)	Baby may have one favorite word for everything in the book and everywhere else, like boggie. Be patient and try distinguishing cat-boggie, dog-boggie, and gramma-boggie. Try books with animals to let both of you practice making animal sounds.

Talking (a few words) (cont'd)	Baby may want to read to you! Enjoy the reading even though upside down, backward, and unintelligible. Listen, smile, laugh. Look for books that feature a favorite word, like ball or dog or moon. You may be able to bring out something a little longer and more complicated just because it has a moose on every page. Choose one! Let the child decide what to read. This encourages communication and independence. More than two choices can get overwhelming. (Also works with food, clothing items, and toys.)
Talking More	Now you can play "Where is the ____?" and wait for your answer! Be patient—try not to help until he's really stumped. Ask about the less obvious things on the page, too. BABY POWER! WANT BOOK NOW! Well, why not take a little reading break? If you agree right away, it's not giving in to whining, it's just saying yes to a particularly insistent question.
Running (but not talking much)	These little balls of energy can be as hard on books as they are on shoes. Get out the tape and try not to let it bother you too much. If you get really upset over an accidental page tear or the beheading of the pop-up pig, reading may become a game your child won't want to play anymore. Remember that thought processes probably exceed vocabulary if your child is in this stage. Try to choose some more complex books for quiet times, maybe with a focus on something your baby loves to hear about, like farms or trucks.

Running (but not talking much) (cont'd)	Incorporate some physical activity into a reading session. "Can you run and bring me a ball like the one on the page? That bunny is jumping—can you show me how you jump?"
	Serious wigglers may try to interact with the book with their feet, too. We don't know why—something about having the book right where he can reach up and kick it (like when he's reading on your lap or you're lying down together) is too much temptation. If you can, just move the book out of range and ignore it. Try not to turn it into a battle of wills that takes attention away from the book!
Talking ALL THE TIME!	Expand those questions. "Can you find something red? Can you find something the bear could eat? What do you think the mouse will do with the crayons?"
	Try to get your toddler to tell you the stories from his favorite books.
	Try getting something wrong in a book and letting him catch you. Start with something egregious—No! That's not an elephant!
	Don't put aside the baby books just because your baby is talking like an older child. Leave them where he can choose to keep patting the bunny if he wants.
	Try some classic Winnie the Pooh—longer stories, smaller illustrations that don't tell the story. But don't worry if at first it doesn't take.

Chapter Two
START NOW

❖❖❖❖❖❖❖❖❖❖❖❖❖❖❖❖❖❖❖❖❖❖❖❖❖❖❖❖❖❖❖❖❖❖

Question One: "When do I start?" Now. Whether you've got an infant, a baby just sitting up on his own, or a new walker, now is the time to pick up a book and start reading. Reading aloud works at every age and stage.

Reading to the Bump in the Belly

You may laugh, but your baby is listening. Researchers from the University of North Carolina asked mothers to read a selected passage from Dr. Seuss's *The Cat in the Hat* daily to their babies in utero between thirty-two and thirty-seven weeks gestation. Just before and immediately after birth, they tested the babies. Babies recognized the passage. They preferred the familiar passages to unfamiliar ones read by the same voice. (Unborn babies showed their preference with a more relaxed heart rate, newborns by modifying their sucking patterns to keep listening to the familiar part of the story.)

Our conclusion? If it sounds like fun, read away. Dr. Seuss if you'd like, or whatever works. Dads, too. If, on the other hand, this sounds like just one more thing to add to the stresses of getting ready, please—let it slide. Sing to her, talk to her—no matter what you say, she's listening.

"I did read to my belly. I read I Kissed the Baby *to the baby-to-be almost every night and daddy-to-be sang "The Rainbow Connection" to the bump. It was a great way to slow down and connect in all the pre-baby frenzy. We sang the song and recited the book to Colin, as we named him, a few minutes after he was born, which was another great bonding moment. I never noticed that he responded more to this book or this song than others (I didn't have equipment to monitor his heart rate!), but it got us into the habit of reading and singing to him every night."* —Rachel

Newborns: The Perfect Audience

For those few months after birth, your baby is absorbing everything around her. As you read to her, she's taking in all of the sounds and rhythms that make up her native language. Caught in the right mood, she'll gaze at you in worship no matter what you read.

Here are the questions we hear most often about reading with newborns.

Does it matter what I read to a very tiny infant?

Nope! Do you remember the Tom Selleck character in *Three Men and a Baby* reading an account of a boxing match to the tiny baby girl on his lap? It's the wonderful sound of your voice that matters at that age, not the actual content.

Really? We're measuring her age in weeks, and we should read to her?

Should? How about could! With that first baby, it feels good to do something special, something childlike, that isn't just about basic necessities. With successive babies, they'll be in on the reading with older children, and the experience will happen naturally.

> **TIP: Try reading to your older child when you nurse or feed your baby, so she doesn't feel left out of the magic circle. Instead, it can be a special nurturing time for her, too.**

My newborn baby seems calm, content, and happy with the reading one minute, but in the blink of an eye starts wriggling, writhing, and making fussy noises. I can't figure her out. What can I do?

This is classic! There is no clear answer as to what's going on with your baby. Is it hunger, digestion, discomfort, need to shift position, early memories of his birth, annoyance, even wordless rage? Try again another time.

What's she getting out of this, anyway?

She's getting your undivided attention without having to cry or perform for it. She's getting a safe snuggle in your arms unrelated to feeding, burping, or rocking. She gets to be together with you while the words wash over and around her. If she likes being read to, consider it an early investment in a fabulously calming activity you can share for a long time to come.

She's also getting an introduction to books and language. If you want reading, storytelling, and the amazing world of the imagination to be a part of your child's very being, if you want books to be part of the air she breathes, read early, and read often. You'll have a baby who's never known—and can't imagine—a world without books.

"Reading (unlike most things) has made me feel powerful as a first-time mom— especially during those first few weeks when every experience feels brand new. I was amazed by how much is simply 'on the job' training. Reading is something I know how to do. It makes me feel confident as a parent, even when there seem to be so many uncertainties." —Michelle

---

Avital's Top Ten

"Avital is only four months old, but she seems to really enjoy it when we read together—and I know I love it! She responds most strongly to books with clear rhythms, repeated sounds and words, and bold illustrations. We tend to focus on the board or fabric books because she can touch, grab, push, squish, and turn the pages without damaging them. Since she is so young, reading books is kind of like putting on a little performance—which is entertaining for both of us. I chant, sing, or play with voices when we read together to catch and maintain her interest. We have fun lifting up tabs to find various body parts while reading *Where Is Baby's Belly Button?* or singing along with Carole King to "Alligators All Around" from The Nutshell Library. For our nighttime routine, we read *The Runaway Bunny* and *Goodnight Moon*—two books my own parents read to me at bedtime. I have been reading to her since she was born and I can't wait for the time when she will start reading to me!" —Rachel B.

1. *Goodnight Moon*, Margaret Wise Brown, Clement Hurd (illus.)
2. *The Runaway Bunny*, Margaret Wise Brown, Clement Hurd (illus.)
3. *Black & White*, Tana Hoban
4. *The Nutshell Library*, Maurice Sendak
5. *Where Is Baby's Belly Button?*, Karen Latz
6. *Pajama Time!*, Sandra Boynton
7. *Subway*, Anastasia Suen, Karen Katz (illus.)
8. *Chicka Chicka ABC*, Bill Martin Jr., John Archambault, Lois Ehlert (illus.)
9. *That's Not My Pony*, Fiona Watt, Rachel Wells (illus.)
10. *ABC Baby Me!*, Susan B. Katz, Alicia Padron (illus.)

Black, White, and Bold: High-Contrast Books for the Very Young

What kind of books does a newborn like? It's all in the stare. If a book holds his gaze, he's probably interested. While her eyes are learning to focus, she often prefers images with high-contrast colors (black, white, red) and bold, simple patterns (checkerboard). When she's awake and calm, try these titles while she cuddles in your arms or prop them up near her head during tummy time:

- *Black & White*, Tana Hoban. This accordion-fold book is a newborn favorite with simple silhouettes of everyday objects.
- *Daddies and Their Babies* and *Mommies and Their Babies*, Guido Van Genechten. Cat, dog, and even hedgehog parents and their youngsters playfully cavort in black and white.
- *Hello, Animals!*, Smriti Prasadam, Emily Bolam (illus.) Favorite animals cavort in black, white, and sparkly foil.
- *I Kissed the Baby*, Mary Murphy. In black, white, yellow, and pink, each animal shares its joy at a duckling's arrival. Makes a wonderful shower gift.
- *Look, Look!*, Peter Linenthal. The first of Linenthal's inventive high-contrast books depicting animals, everyday objects, and the natural world. Other titles include *Look at the Animals!*, *Look at Baby's House!*, and *Look Look Outside!*
- *My Animals*, Xavier Deneux. Through fun die-cut holes, eye-catching splashes of color, and playful cartoons of animals in black and white, this offering will appeal to newborns and toddlers alike.
- *¡Ñam, ñam! / Yum, Yum!*, Catherine Hnatov. See animals munch on their favorite foods in black, white, and a smattering of other colors. In Spanish and English. Also try *Hop, Hop*.
- *Woof-Woof (Baby Flip-a-Face)*, SAMi. Flip the pages to change the animal faces in bold red, white, and black.

The Surefire Baby Shower Booklist

Even if it doesn't matter what you read to a newborn, it's great to have some good baby books around. These books are the ultimate for baby gift-giving, all guaranteed to please new moms and babies. You can be sure of heartfelt thanks before the first year is over.

- *Baby Cakes*, Karma Wilson, Sam Williams (illus.)
- *Clap Hands*, *Say Goodnight*, *All Fall Down*, and *Tickle, Tickle*, Helen Oxenbury (often sold as a set)
- *Everywhere Babies*, Susan Meyers, Marla Frazee (illus.)
- *Hello Baby!*, Mem Fox, Steve Jenkins (illus.)
- *Hug*, Jez Alborough
- *"More More More" Said the Baby: 3 Love Stories*, Vera B. Williams
- *Quiet LOUD*, Leslie Patricelli
- *Ten Little Fingers and Ten Little Toes*, Mem Fox, Helen Oxenbury (illus.)

Talking with the Author: Vera B. Williams

I remember trying to share a book with my first baby and feeling foolish. But there would be one tiny minute when her attention was caught by the rhythm of some words or by a bit of red or person-like shape on the page. I'd see delight fleet across her ever-changing little face, and was hooked into sharing books with this tiny dawning literacy. Of course the very next minute she'd wrench the book from my hands to suck on the binding. But little by little, we two became a reading pair. I loved that. She would come toddling over dragging a book, plop it down into my lap, put her cheek by mine, and say, "READ ME." The combination is irresistible. The affection in the voice. The singsong of it. The safe sense of an encircling arm (my mother's was covered with fascinating freckles), the snuggle of it, the adventure of turning the pages. My mother worked long hours...worried about money. She had limited time for me, but every now and then I would crawl onto her lap and we would be together with *Here's a Ball for Baby* or *Cantaloupe for Breakfast*, chanting "Honey and a bun..." I'm eighty years old, and I still own the rhythms and images of those little verses from my first times with books and my mother.

Book in Hand, Book in Mouth: Reading with (Slightly) Older Babies

Grasping something in his hand is a big milestone for baby. Once it's in his hand, it seems to go straight into his mouth, quick. This makes reading hard. Feeding, changing, buckling the car seat all become more of a challenge. He's helping; he's hindering; he's making you crazy.

> **TIP: Try a cloth book to distract and entertain baby on the changing mat (and keep his hands out of the mess!).**

It's wonderful to see your baby developing a personality and beginning to engage you. It's also a challenge. Now she can poke a finger into your eye and pinch your skin. She's a lively little person with a very different idea of what to do with that sock. She'll need something to explore with her fingers and mouth while you're reading, too. A pacifier, if you use one, a teething biscuit if she's ready for them, or any of her small toys could work. Another book might be even better. When she takes yours, switch to reading hers. For this reason, we're not big on e-readers with new grabbers—better something you're happy to let her take!

Kendall, mother of Eli, six months, describes the reading scene in Eli's world: "I gave Eli a book the other day in his high chair, and he was sitting there, turning the big pages, and I thought, Oh, he's so advanced! Just then, he grabbed the book in both hands, holding it open, and brought it up— SMACK—into his forehead as hard as he could."

Books with pictures of other babies (photos or simple drawings) usually intrigue babies at this age, as do big, colorful pictures. Of course, if it interests her, she'll just be more anxious to put the book in her mouth. Fabric books with crinkly pages and other textures can be touched, squeezed, chewed, and read, and are easier to hold than the board kind. Read what you can; recite what you recall. You're learning to read to her, and she's learning to be read to. There's no rush.

Starting with Photo Books

Mama's face is arguably the first "book" a baby reads. Photographs of faces are a natural next step.

Some of the best books for babies and toddlers are indeed photo books of faces and daily life. Books of photographs appeal to all ages. Babies like to see other babies, and they can spot a look-alike or a friend early on. Watch your baby mimic the smile or knit his brow in empathy with a miserable little face. Babies become very experienced very soon at reading faces. They pick up a whole universe of information very fast.

If you store photos on a phone or tablet, you may—may!—be able to share those with your baby. Many babies are especially intrigued by a picture you just snapped of—them! Again, there's a stage where he's just going to be more interested in holding whatever you have than may work for you and your fragile technology. KJ put ten photos of baby "friends" in photo sleeves, hooked them together on a teething ring, and gave those to the very young Sam.

Some other books that include fun faces and babies:

- *Baby! Talk!*, Penny Gentieu. Each page shows a set of babies acting out a favorite starter word or phrase, from "Go" to "Uh-oh" to "So big!"
- *Global Babies / Bebés del mundo*, Global Fund for Children. Depicts babies around the world in all their glorious diversity. Text is in Spanish and English. See also *American Babies*.
- *Kiss, Tickle, Cuddle, Hug*, Susan Musgrave. Big photos show off expressive babies.
- *Mrs. Mustard's Baby Faces*, Jane Wattenberg. This accordion foldout is an entertaining gem: happy floating baby heads on one side, and crabby cranky crying babies on the flip.
- *Peekaboo Baby*, Margaret Miller. Baby-face-size photographs of baby

faces with colorful props. See also *What's on My Head?*, *Baby Food*, and *Baby Faces*.

- *Smile!*, Roberta Grobel Intrater. Page-size baby faces flirt with the camera. And also other "Baby Faces" board books: *Peek-a-boo!*, *Eat!*, *Splash!*, *Sleep*, and in Spanish, *¡Cucú!*, *¡Sonríe!*, *¡Qué rico!*, and *¡Al Agua Patos!*

But She's Not Listening!
Reading to Sitters and Crawlers

What you may perceive as "problems" with the reading experience are actually stages of development. Sitting babies are going to grab the book, fall on the book, roll on the book, and drop the book. Crawlers are going to crawl away, crawl back, crawl away, crawl back. This couldn't be better! She can keep your attention and listen to a story while she's on the move.

But the reader may feel frustrated with what seems to be an ungrateful audience. Your first instinct may be to put the book away and wait for a better time. Don't. People of all ages like to keep busy while they listen. Older kids may color during read-aloud time. If you think he's still tuned in, keep going. If he's clearly engrossed in taking apart the remote control, maybe it's time to stop.

Supporting herself and beginning to move are enormous moments for your baby. If she can sit up, she can really use her hands to explore what's in front of her. If a dropped toy skitters away, it's a huge thrill to finally be able to go after it. Make books part of the fun. Spread out a few for her to crawl or roll to while you sit and read from one. Some books focus on single objects: show her *ball* and *dog*. Sit across from her and play *here's a book* or *pass the book*. Bedtime, mealtime, and naptime may provide a quieter reading experience.

At this stage, babies are beginning to understand more about the world around them and to make some simple predictions. When the babysitter shows up, Daddy will leave. When the blanket sleeper goes on, bed is coming. You may find he's beginning to recognize both the reading ritual and certain books, as well.

"Last night, I was reading eleven-month-old Cole But Not the Hippopotamus—*repeatedly. He was enjoying it, but I was getting tired of it. So I started reciting another one of his books,* Snuggle Puppy *(still turning the pages of* Hippopotamus*). Darned if he didn't immediately crawl over to the appropriate book and hold it up for me. Clever boy!" —Doug*

At this point, language is also beginning to seep in. Parents who've been using sign language may begin to see those signs from the baby. Books that identify objects will take on a renewed importance as his understanding increases. You will find—to your joy—that you are beginning to communicate with your baby with words and through shared books.

TIP: Try taking a verbal break and just turn the pages for your baby while she looks at the pictures. Give her time to find her own story in the artwork.

Day-in-a-life books by writer-illustrators like Helen Oxenbury and Rachel Isadora are wonderful for this stage and the next few to come. They create a kind of memory book for a small child. Not very dramatic, and often without a story line, they offer a series of snapshots from a baby's day. Every day is a long day to a baby, full of good times (eating, drinking, nursing, observing, playing) and frustrations (can't pull up, can't reach the toy, can't tell anyone why you're unhappy). These simple little books allow babies to think about their own experiences, which are often strange and new for the baby, no matter how ordinary they seem to us.

Simple Books about Baby's Day

- *The Baby Goes Beep*, Rebecca O'Connell, Ken Wilson-Max (illus.). A baby beeps, booms, smooches, and splashes through his day in this boisterous read-aloud.
- *Baby's Day*, Michel Blake. Each easy-to-open page spread features a black-and-white photo of a baby with one familiar object in full color. See also *Out to Play* and *Off to Bed*.
- *Bathtime for Twins*, Ellen Weiss, Sam Williams (illus.). This pair of toddlers has a good splash in the tub in one of the few board books about twins available. See also *Playtime for Twins*.
- *Bedtime*, Kate Duke. The guinea pig heroes become less and less resistant to bedtime as it grows later.
- *Blankie*, Leslie Patricelli. Blankie accompanies baby through food, nap, and play.
- *Good Morning, Baby*, Cheryl Willis Hudson, George Ford (illus.). A toddler and her daddy enjoy a day together. Also *Good Night, Baby*.
- *Pants Off First!*, Ruth Ohi. A toddler gets himself ready for bed while his clever pets distract him.
- *Peekaboo Morning*, Rachel Isadora. A baby plays a game of peekaboo with his whole household, with the baby peeking out of an activity on one page and a lovely drawing in rich pastels of what he's peeking at on the next.
- *You and Me, Baby*, Lynn Reiser, Penny Gentieu (photos). In Reiser's bouncy verse and Gentieu's rich photos, a diverse group of baby and parent duos eat, play, take a bath, and get ready for bed. Try *My Baby & Me* for a sibling's take on life with baby.
- *Whose Toes Are Those?* and *Whose Knees are These?*, Jabari Asim, LeUyen Pham (illus.). Two really cute "body part" books featuring toes and nose in Q&A rhymes.

The Upright Baby Brigade: Movers and Shakers

Babies who can pull up and walk are *active*. In a child with little language and no self-control, so much mobility can seem like a huge design flaw. It may take all of your energy to protect and divert her. There will be times, however, when your new mover just can't get up and go (at the doctor's office, on an airplane, at a restaurant). A book is the perfect portable toy—it can be read in multiple ways, and it can be the center of a variety of games (some of which have nothing to do with its literary qualities). A book with flaps can provide a fidgety child with a physical activity that doesn't take up much room.

"Henry and Gus (two-year-old twins) add high drama to any reading experience. They play tug-of-war with their board books and rip the flaps off Where Is Maisy? *At this point all the favorite books are taped together, and several have had to be bought anew. I'm on my third copy of* Goodnight Moon. *I loathe that little book, but Henry picks it out of the pile and drags it around with him, going, 'Good-good-good-good-good.'"* —*Judith*

Apps, too, can work at this stage, but they're a very different experience for your baby, and you'll probably want to keep custody of your device. A book can be company for the baby alone in his stroller or car seat. Board books are small, durable, and relatively light; paperback books even lighter, and just one can get your baby through the most boring situations.

So much is happening to babies at this stage physically that they may regress in other areas. They might start waking more often at night and be unable to sit still or calm themselves. This goes for new crawlers as well. Both may become newly frustrated with their inability to communicate their needs or achieve their objectives. A familiar book and a comfortable lap might help to distract them from all those new bodily sensations when

Where Are Baby's Books?

If there are books in every room, you'll read to your baby more often. You can turn to a book when other activities have run out of steam, and she can ask for a book with gestures or words when she needs a little quiet or a cuddle. She'll learn that books aren't just meant to put you to sleep. They're a part of everyday life and can be just as—if not more— fun as any electronic, button-pushing gizmo the toy companies can devise. Best of all, a book is a surefire way to get grown-up participation and attention. Who can resist a request to read?

they're exhausted. If your baby can't hold still in your lap, she can listen as she moves around the room. Make reading a lively, physical activity with rhyming and song books.

Happy Birthday!

The huge birthday party, with games and favors and a pile of presents, is likely to be overwhelming for a two- or three-year-old. Why not hold a "book swap party" instead? Ask each guest (well, the parent of each guest) to bring a gift-wrapped favorite book. Compare notes first, to make sure no one's going to get a duplicate, then give each child a book to unwrap. A willing adult can read the books to an enthralled circle, and each child goes home with a gift book.

Add to a library at your day care or preschool. Each birthday child could donate a book on her birthday, and be the first allowed to borrow it.

Many toddlers will enjoy choosing a favorite book to share, and it's fun to see what other families are reading. You may discover a new favorite. Meanwhile, an approaching birthday calls for topical reading. Try these:

- *The Birthday Box / Mi caja de cumpleaños*, Leslie Patricelli. For a baby, what's the best birthday present? The box it came in, of course. In Spanish and English. For more on the box play theme, try *Big Box for Ben* (Deborah Bruss, Tomek Bogacki [illus.]) and *Not a Box* (Antoinette Portis).
- *A Birthday for Cow!*, Jan Thomas. Pig, Mouse, and Duck make a birthday cake for their friend Cow with hilarious results.
- *Happy Birthday, Moon*, Frank Asch. A story more about giving a gift than getting one.
- *How Do Dinosaurs Say Happy Birthday?*, Jane Yolen, Mark Teague (illus.). Birthday party etiquette from Yolen and Teague's popular dinosaurs. Available in Spanish as *¿Cómo dicen feliz cumpleaños los dinosaurios?*

- *If You Give a Pig a Party*, Laura Numeroff, Felicia Bond (illus.). Whether it's a birthday party or any other celebration, nothing will go quite as expected when this Pig (and her friends Moose and Mouse) are around, except that it will all come full circle. Vividly detailed illustrations and the slightly complicated cause-and-effect story make this good for two-year-olds and up.
- *It's My Birthday*, Helen Oxenbury. A little girl gathers ingredients from her animal friends, and shares both the cooking and the party with them. A gentle, repeating rhythm book about the making of a cake.
- *Max's Birthday*, Rosemary Wells. A very simple story that manages, in just a few lines, to remind kids that what's scary at first can also be thrilling, and then delightful.
- *Little Gorilla*, Ruth Bornstein. Even though he is not so little anymore, everyone in the jungle loves Little Gorilla, and they all gather to celebrate his big day.
- *Mr. Rabbit and the Lovely Present*, Charlotte Zolotow, Maurice Sendak (illus.). A little girl asks for Mr. Rabbit's advice about a present for her mother. As they talk and walk, a basket of lovely and colorful fruits becomes the satisfying answer.
- *Oscar's Half Birthday*, Bob Graham. Having achieved a six months milestone, Oscar's family cannot wait any longer to celebrate. It's a wonderful party.

For older siblings of the birthday kid:

- *The Birthday Swap*, Loretta Lopez. A sympathetic sister offers a wonderful present: to trade her own summer date this year with her sibling's winter-time birthday. Available in Spanish as *¡Que sorpresa de cumpleaños!*

- *Henry's First-Moon Birthday*, Lenore Look, Yumi Heo (illus.). Jenny helps her grandmother with preparations for the Chinese celebration marking her baby brother's one-month birthday.
- *What Will You Be, Sara Mee?*, Kate Aver Avraham, Anne O'Brien Sibley (illus.). At her *Tol*, or first birthday, Sara Mee plays the traditional Korean prophecy game—*Toljabee*—while her older brother excitedly awaits the results.

Tyler's Top Ten

"Tyler loves books morning, noon, and night. We have to take books with us when we go out, and frequently he has me reading to him while he is in the stroller and we are walking around the neighborhood. I can't think of a better gift to a child than giving books, and I am able to see it because now at two years and three months, Tyler can complete most of the sentences in any given book and when he brings them into his crib he narrates the story to himself. For me as a mom, there is nothing better than having him sit in my lap while I read to him, especially since it is the only time he lets me really cuddle with him during the day." —Amy

1. *Crack in the Track* (Thomas & Friends)
2. *Nightbear and Lambie*, Kerry McGuinness Royer, Matt Royer (illus.) (out of print)
3. *Little Blue Truck*, Alice Schertle, Jill McElmurry (illus.)
4. *Are You My Mother?*, P. D. Eastman

5. *Swim, Little Wombat, Swim!*, Charles Fuge (out of print)
6. *Good Night, Gorilla*, Peggy Rathmann
7. *Brown Bear, Brown Bear, What Do You See?*, Bill Martin Jr., Eric Carle (illus.)
8. *The Little Engine That Could*, Watty Piper, George Hauman and Doris Hauman (illus.)
9. *How Do You Hug a Porcupine?*, Laurie Isop, Gwen Millward (illus.)
10. *Another Monster at the End of This Book* (app), Sesame Street

From Those First Few Words to Compound Sentences

Talking is where babies veer off from a consistent development curve. They have to roll before they can crawl and pull up before they can walk, but those first few words could come in almost anywhere. You'll already be seeing signs that she knows what you are saying to her. She may be able to hand you the red book or the dog book or pick out the appropriate book from the box. His vocabulary is growing exponentially, and his understanding increases every day.

"I watched a friend get two kids ready to go out. While her mom was push-guiding the active ten-month-old's arm into the sleeve of his jacket, and trying to prevent him from escaping from his stroller, Ellie, two and a half, noticed her shoelace was untied. 'Oh, Lewis,' she said aloud. Her mother kept working on the baby's wraps but commented, 'Oh dear. What's happened?' She knew Ellie was referring to a favorite book—Oh, Lewis! by Eve Rice. In the book, everything goes wrong for little Lewis, from his mittens to his jacket zipper to his whole day. The refrain 'Oh, Lewis!' is uttered by the exasperated, but understanding, mother at each difficulty. Ellie, describing a potential frustration, used a literary reference." —Susan

Now is a wonderful time to zero in on those first words and start reading slightly longer books that feature those items prominently. Books that

Books for Babies with a Word or Two (Ball! Dog! Cat!)

- *Colors* (Touch, Look, and Learn! series), Emily Bolam. Each vibrantly illustrated page features one word, an animal in a different color, and an embossed textural element to encourage exploration. Also try *Animals Go*.
- *Cradle Me*, Debby Slier. Photographs show Native American babies being carried in traditional cradle boards with one-word captions to describe each of their actions. There is even a space for parents to write a translation of the caption in their home language.
- *Hello Day!*, Anita Lobel. Gorgeous close-ups of farm animals making their iconic sounds.
- *I Can*, Helen Oxenbury. Oxenbury's hallmark babies bend, jump, and more to depict the action labeled on each page. Also in the series: *I Touch* and *I See*.
- *Sam's Ball*, Barbro Lindgren, Eva Eriksson (illus.). Sam is wonderfully insistent, especially when his ball is eyed by the cat.
- *Things That Go*, Sterling Publishing. Clear photos and simple captions of cars, trucks, buses, and more. Check out others in the Say & Play series.

identify objects are useful, but more complex storybooks that introduce concepts like tomorrow and waiting and home do so much more to help your baby understand the things she sees and hears. You may not see the benefit in her speech for months (or even years), but reading together exposes her not just to new words that might not come up in her daily life, but also to concepts and speaking styles. She's absorbing it all.

Book games will expand the baby's vocabulary even further and give her a chance to surprise you with her prowess. You may not even realize she knows the word "bee" until she's pointing at one in a book. Even while you're bringing in more complex books, keep reading the simple ones. A short book with just a few pictures and identifying words will probably be the first book she can "read" to you.

Books also give you and your new talker a shared frame of reference. Getting-dressed books can become favorite jokes as you dress your child.

Quoting from a favorite book as you perform a similar activity helps a child remember the book and draw comparisons between his life and the life the book shows. *You're getting your hair washed just like Elmo!*

"Needing to distract two-and-a-half-year-old Simon, I invented the best game: I recite a line from a story and Simon tells me what the story is. He loves this game, and as I only use books we've read enough to both have memorized, it's fun but not impossible or frustrating. It's pretty gratifying actually—he really knows his favorite stories!" —Rumaan

The New Classics
(And Some Old Ones You May Have Forgotten)

You won't find *Goodnight Moon*, *Guess How Much I Love You*, or *Pat the Bunny* on our list of the new classics. Why not? Because those are the books you already own; the ones you had to return because your baby got three copies as gifts. These are the new classics—books that may not be on your shelves yet but that we think have real staying power, or older books that are still around but aren't necessarily on everyone's list. These are the books and authors that kept appearing over and over again on our parents' lists and were brought up repeatedly by booksellers and librarians.

- *Abuela*, Arthur Dorros, Elisa Kleven (illus.). A young girl and her beloved grandmother take an imaginary flight over the city. Dorros's lyrical text is sprinkled with Spanish phrases, and Kleven's bright paintings evoke the art of Abuela's birthplace. Also available in a Spanish edition.
- *Chugga-Chugga Choo-Choo*, Kevin Lewis, Daniel Kirk (illus.). Introduces a fun concept—that the words on the page aren't necessarily exactly consistent with the pictures. The words describe a real train, but the pictures show a toy train traveling around a

little boy's bedroom. The fact that the little boy shown only at the end is dark-skinned is a bonus—it's always good to see books that can reflect a multicultural society without being *about* a multicultural society.

- *Don't Let the Pigeon Drive the Bus!*, Mo Willems. The Pigeon, in the first of his many adventures, debates the reader on his bus driving capabilities. Toddlers will love the opportunity to say "No!" when the bird demands to drive the bus.
- *Everywhere Babies*, Susan Meyers, Marla Frazee (illus.). Babies are everywhere and are shown at their most babyesque selves. Charming and witty and all-inclusive, showing every kind of family.
- *Fireman Small*, Wong Herbert Yee. Fireman Small (who is indeed small) comes to the rhyming rescue of a town full of animals.
- *From Head to Toe*, Eric Carle. Carle's collages pair humans and animals wriggling, waving, and shaking. The simple text prompts children to join in the fun.
- *Gossie / Gansi*, Olivier Dunrea. Gossie's red boots are missing. When she finds them, she finds an unexpected friend. Clean, bright, and simple line pictures in a baby-hand-size book. In Spanish and English.
- *Good Night, Gorilla*, Peggy Rathmann. The gorilla in this picture book wants to go home with the zookeeper, and he wants all his friends to come too. Any baby who wants to sleep in Mama and Daddy's bed will identify. A nice simple story that baby will quickly want to "read" to herself. *Buenas noches, Gorila* in Spanish.
- *Hug*, Jez Alborough. Beautiful, detailed drawings and a single word tell the jungle version of the lost-in-the-grocery-store story. Try *Tall* and *Yes* for more with these characters.
- *Hondo and Fabian*, Peter McCarty. A dog, a cat, and a baby have a very ordinary day, beautifully but simply illustrated (a Caldecott Honor winner). Baby will like the soothing, repetitive words and

pictures, and adults will like the subtle humor. Small, with (relatively) sturdy pages. *Fabian Escapes* continues the escapades.

- *How Do Dinosaurs Say Goodnight?*, Jane Yolen, Mark Teague (illus.). This is one of those big, fabulously illustrated books librarians read aloud at story times, but it also makes a great bedtime read. Worth springing for because this book will work really well with older kids, too—each dinosaur is different, accurately drawn, and labeled.
- *I Stink!*, Kate McMullan, Jim McMullan (illus.). This is a crashing, banging, disgusting, fascinating, and highly onomatopoeic tale of a city garbage truck making its rounds. Also try *I'm Dirty* for the truck obsessed.
- *I Went Walking*, Sue Williams, Julie Vivas (illus.). A little girl collects a trail of animals on her walk. Simple text, simple pictures, great for babies who love animals. Also available in a bilingual English / Spanish edition.
- *If You Give a Moose a Muffin*, Laura Numeroff, Felicia Bond (illus.). Silly and somehow universally appealing, even though it's fairly complex. Lots of babies really like Moose! (Also *If You Give a Pig a Pancake*, *If You Give a Pig a Party*, *If You Give a Mouse a Cookie*, and several more.)
- *Moo, Baa, La La La!*, Sandra Boynton. Using her signature animals, Boynton illustrates animal sounds realistic and silly. In Spanish, it's *Muu, Beee, ¡Así fue!*
- *Moonbear's Shadow*, Frank Asch. Moonbear tries to rid himself of his shadow in a host of silly ways. With oddly flat outlined illustrations in rich colors.
- *"More More More," Said the Baby: 3 Love Stories*, Vera B. Williams. Three beautiful, multicultural love stories between babies and their caregivers. If you could only have one book, this would have to be

one you'd consider. (We should note that the board book can be hard to read, because the small text in many-colored letters just doesn't stand out as well as it does in the larger versions.)

- *Noisy Nora*, Rosemary Wells. Being a mouse in the middle isn't easy. Nora triumphs with a wonderful technique that goes from noisy to silent.
- *Olivia*, Ian Falconer. Olivia the pig totes around her cat, takes care of her brother, and wears out her mother, all in black and white accented in red.
- *One Hot Summer Day*, Nina Crews. A young girl finds playful and creative ways to beat the heat on a hot city day. Crews's photo collages of her young African-American protagonist are buoyant.
- *Owl Babies*, Martin Waddell, Patrick Benson (illus.). Perfect starter book for separation issues. *Las lechucitas* in Spanish.
- *Pete the Cat: I Love My White Shoes*, Eric Litwin, James Dean (illus.). Pete, the mellowest cat ever, steps in various substances and his beloved white shoes change color to match. With its "Don't sweat the small stuff" message and accompanying song, this one is developing a cult following.
- *Pete's a Pizza*, William Steig. Parents knead their cranky kid into pizza dough, sprinkle him with "toppings," and chase him around the house to "bake" and "eat" him—and turn him from grumpy to giggling in the process. Start reading it to your baby and you'll be tossing your own grumpy toddler pizza before you know it.
- *Silly Sally*, Audrey Wood. Silly Sally, a bouncy, fairy-tale-like creature, goes to town, walking backward upside down, with a pack of upside-down animals trailing behind her.

Ages and Stages: Simple Suggestions and Starting Stories

Newborn	Keep a picture book in the diaper bag. You never know when you will be glad to have something new to share. Prop open books next to the changing table, or tape new images to the wall next to her (or the ceiling, if that's possible). Recite a few simple nursery rhymes or make up nonsense rhymes to see if they get a smile.
Heads Up	Books offer a great incentive to lift the head during "tummy time." Put a soft one down flat for a younger baby and arrange some open board books for the baby who can lift her head, and maybe stretch out an arm to topple them. Direct his chubby hand to touch-and-feel book pages.
Sitting	Substitute baby's name for names in books. Try bringing the world into a book, offering a leaf with a picture of a tree, or a real apple (to hold and smell) to add to an apple illustration. She should be able to "lift the flap," so try a few of those. Be aware that they have a limited life span. Play "book peekaboo." Use your hand to cover and reveal the thing on the page. It's a big hit.
Crawling / Creeping	Pass the books back and forth before you read, saying, "Thank you!" Snap the books open and shut, saying, "Hello! Goodbye!"
Cruising / Walking	Try loading some books into a push-wagon for delivery into the next room. Now is a great time for books with handles, or those little sets of books that come in a cardboard "suitcase."

Talking (a few words)	"Read" a toy catalog or a kids' clothing catalog (we're sure your mailbox is full of them). This won't work so well once she realizes those are things you can *have*, so try it now.
Talking More	Can she start learning the names of a few favorite books? Make sure you're reading the title, too, so she learns how to ask for it.
	Can you play "I Spy with My Little Eye"? I spy something green / round / curvy / soft.
Running (but not talking much)	Try playing "hide-and-seek" with a book, then reading it once it's found.
	Read at mealtime when you have a "captive audience." Offer a book to look at when she's waiting for her lunch, or (and) read to her while she's eating.
Talking ALL THE TIME!	Try getting a new book and seeing if she can "read" you the story from the pictures.
	You're allowed to ignore "Why?" and "What's that?" and "What happened?" after you've answered them three times on a single page.
	Try to set aside a time for reading together, *to yourselves*. You get a book, she gets a book, and you curl up and read. Expect this to last about thirty seconds at this point...but hopefully, you're starting a habit!

Chapter Three
BABY LIT CRIT

❖❖❖❖❖❖❖❖❖❖❖❖❖❖❖❖❖❖❖❖❖❖❖❖❖❖❖❖❖❖❖❖

*Choosing the Best Books
for Your Baby or Toddler*

The acquisition of books is inevitable. Gifts, purchases, and hand-me-downs will accumulate until you're tripping over *Pots and Pans* (Patricia Hubell, Diane deGroat [illus.]) on your way to the kitchen sink. But you and your child will want to choose some (if not most) of the books you share. Since he's not exactly a discerning shopper (most browsing toddlers will go straight for books they already have), you're going to have to choose for him. How to choose? You'll want to

- spot your child's tastes—and choose accordingly;
- stick to what's right for your family;
- search out great libraries and booksellers; and
- start a library that will grow with you and your baby!

Why Does He Like This Book Better Than That Book?

Starting from very early on, babies have distinct tastes: in food, in colors, in activities, and in books. A familiar book may be soothing, but once he can turn his little head away or push at your hand, you're going to know if he likes something new. Granted, you're screening his choices simply by virtue of being the reader and the chooser at this point—but will he like what you choose?

Remember, the artwork is more than half of the book to your baby. He's the reader of the pictures, after all, and the art is very important to his preferences. Very young babies almost all respond to high-contrast images, such as black and white or with just one or two strongly dominant colors.

Most babies like pictures of other babies. (Who doesn't?) Babies who say just one or two words will generally like books with those words or objects in them. Many babies at around a year old go through a phase of being very excited about the moon. Any book where you can point out the moon, like *Harold and the Purple Crayon* or *Good Night, Gorilla*, may thrill him. Beyond that, there aren't many universals among baby book preferences. What you need is help figuring out what your baby does and doesn't like—and here it is.

The Completely Not Foolproof Method of Selecting Books for YOUR Baby or Toddler

Start by putting together a pile of the books he does like. Are there any similarities? This is a zen process—the key word is "notice." Put aside your preconceptions about what the books are "about" and notice the things your baby notices. Be sure to focus on the art as well as the words.

- Are all the pictures very busy, or are they simple?
- How many images are there on each page?
- Is there more than one line of text per page?
- Are the settings familiar or new, and are they drawn in detail or sketched very simply?
- Do all the characters have dots for eyes?
- Are the characters all animals or all human?
- Do the pictures have many colors or only a few?
- Is there a lot of white on the page, or is it all filled in with art?

- Are the pictures drawings or photographs?
- Is the rhythm fast or slow?
- Does the narrative neatly resolve a problem or simply recount a story?
- Do the characters talk?
- Does anything else strike you as you look at all the artwork spread out together, no matter how weird it may seem?

The answers to these questions should help you put together a pretty good list of requirements. As you move your baby into different books—more advanced, longer, or just new to him—you might try changing just one or two elements rather than all of them. For example, add more text, but keep to simple pictures and few colors. Or try wilder illustrations with almost no words at all.

Wild and Colorful Books for Baby

- *Butterfly Butterfly: A Book of Colors*, Petr Horáček. A young girl searches her garden for a butterfly and finds a colorful menagerie. With peekaboo, die-cut holes on sturdy pages, Horáček's art buzzes with vibrancy.
- *Daddy Kisses*, Anne Gutman, Georg Hallensleben (illus.). Rich, soft colors fill foregrounds and backgrounds of the pictures, showing daddy animals loving their little ones. *Mommy Hugs*, *Daddy Cuddles*, and *Mommy Loves* are the companion books.
- *Eating the Rainbow: A Colorful Food Book*, Rena D. Grossman. On these board pages, babies and toddlers enjoy a variety of colorful foods, such as apples, strawberries, mushrooms, and more.
- *Of Colors and Things*, Tana Hoban. Hoban captures photos of bright, familiar objects worth noticing. Also *Red, Blue, Yellow Shoe*.
- *One Some Many*, Marthe Jocelyn, Tom Slaughter (illus.). Slaughter's

bold, deceptively simple cut paper collages of balls, boats, daisies, and more show just how far an artist can take color.

- *Pantone Colors*, Pantone. The international color matching system has created a lovely exploration of color for the very young. Simple images of objects in bold colors are paired with Pantone chips in similar shades.
- *A Red Train: A COLORS Book*, Bernette Ford (ed.), Britta Teckentrup (illus.). Ford and Tenkentrup take us on an unexpected journey as various animals ride a yellow rocket, an orange submarine, and a purple boat.

A Few More Generalizations (That May Help)

- Very active or very sensitive babies (often one and the same) may be overwhelmed if there are too many things on the page, whereas a very calm baby may be pleasantly stimulated by detailed artwork.
- Unless (until) your baby is very verbal, avoid books where there are ideas in the text that aren't pictured on the page. For example, in *Bedtime for Frances*, Frances "started to think about tigers. She thought about big tigers and little tigers…." There are no tigers pictured; in fact, the story isn't about tigers at all, and yet she thinks about them for about five lines of text. Generally, these are books to save for an older toddler or preschooler.
- Don't overlook the obvious—if he likes moose, get *If You Give a Moose a Muffin*.
- If your child likes one book by an author or illustrator, then try other books by the same—but don't count on it. Your son may like that book because of the picture of the balloon on page three, not because of the quality of the writing or the art.
- Repetition, repetition, repetition. Repetition holds kids during longer narratives, like *Green Eggs and Ham* (that, the fabulous

illustrations, and the fact that Dr. Seuss seems to have had a direct line into the mind of small children; but repetition helps).

- Keep it short!
- Keep trying. The pictures that were too much for your son at nine months may delight him at eighteen months—opening up a whole new world of busily illustrated books you'd been avoiding. It's a good idea to go through this exercise pretty regularly, even if all you're doing is a mental review of the shelves or of last night's reading as you enter the library.
- Use what you've learned to add variety. If he likes books about bunnies, that doesn't mean you need to go out and buy six more board books about bunnies.

Remember, your baby isn't interested in the newest books, or the most popular. You will undoubtedly find, as he gets older, that he has a favorite book that not one of your friends has ever heard of, that appeared in print for a few months when he was born and then sank into (undeserved) obscurity. Or you may realize that the bunny characters he seems to love so much have achieved such popularity that they are about to become a TV show—which may take away some of the charm for you, but not for your baby. He has his own inscrutable reasons for liking what he likes. Your job is just to decipher them enough to help him find more and more likeable books.

Five Simple, Clean Books for Baby Purists

1. *I Like It When…*, Mary Murphy. Simple, vivid, and excellent activities to share with your toddler.
2. *My Car*, Byron Barton. Simple, bright, bold, and informative about Sam and his beloved car.
3. *Peekaboo Baby*, Sebastien Braun. A lift-the-flap book with endearing babies and familiar objects.

4. *Playing*, Liesbet Slegers. Slegers's friendly cartoon toddler demonstrates how he plays with a variety of toys. See others in the "Day to Day Board Books" series.

5. *Spot Goes to the Park*, Eric Hill. Irresistibly bright and immediately accessible for all children.

Picking Books for Picky Toddlers and Twos

Things get a little easier with a toddler, and easier still as your child becomes a more articulate two-year-old. While sometimes still inscrutable, the choices become a little less opaque. If he calls a book "doggie book," then he probably likes it because of the dog, which helps when it comes to choosing new books—more doggie books? Additional animal books?

> **TRIP TIP: Don't buy a bunch of new books for a young child right before a trip, even if they are about beloved characters or you're really convinced they'll be hits. For the under-three crowd, novelty is good only in limited doses—and the novelty of an airplane or a new place to sleep means that the bedtime books in particular must stay the same.**

Once your child is enjoying a storybook or two, or using two-word sentences, it's time to stop buying stuff that's too easy. You won't get much use out of it. Word books are still good, as are counting and alphabet books, but look for them to have more complexity. Choose books with lots of objects to identify on a page, like *Richard Scarry's Biggest Word Book Ever!* With counting books, try to find those with a story in the counting, like *Ten, Nine, Eight* by Molly Bang, or that go past ten. Not that you'll find much use for some of this right away, but it's time to start buying books you can grow with.

- Cater to tastes, but don't go overboard. One or two books with identifying pictures of trucks are enough. Try to find books that take the beloved object further—in addition to a book about trucks, try to find one where a truck is driven in the story. If you want a full stack of truck books, hit the library.
- Make reading a new or different book a habit. Try not to repeat the same exact books at bedtime, for example—suggest to your toddler that he pick one (or three) and then you'll pick one.
- Try, try again. Put a book that gets pushed away up on the shelf for a few weeks, or a month, or a year.
- Expand on your toddler's enthusiasms. If he likes a song about whales, try a book about a whale. If he saw a hot-air balloon, look for a book with a hot-air balloon.
- Now's the time when more of the same will probably be a success—more Max and Ruby, more Charlie and Lola, more Maisy. We're firm believers that while you can have too many toys—so many stuffed animals that no one ever becomes special—you can't have too many books. You read them in groups of at least four, after all—read four books, three times a day, and that's eighty-four books a week. So go ahead, get the whole series if you can manage it. Check out fifteen books from the library. Gorge yourselves.
- *Don't* put away the baby books! We've said this before, but it bears repeating—they're comforting. Plus, a really deeply familiar book may be a more satisfying companion in the stroller or the backseat—one he can "read" all by himself.
- Look for books that reflect something your toddler is thinking about or dealing with. Even if he doesn't talk much yet, you know if he's been having trouble sharing or separating. A book could help validate his concerns and ease his difficulties.

TIP: Ask your toddler or preschooler why he thinks baby likes a certain book. His insights may surprise you—after all, he's been there a lot more recently than you have!

Can You Take Your Tastes out of the Equation?

Here's a question—are there more books about cats on your baby's shelf, or more about dogs? Bet the answer corresponds with whether you're a cat person or a dog person. We'll also bet you'd never really thought about it. How else are you unconsciously (or consciously) influencing your baby's library? Would you buy *Angelina Ballerina* for your little boy or *Machines at Work* for your daughter? When you push a book aside, is it because of the art, the subject matter, or just that you don't like snakes? Borrowing a few different books from the library could be liberating. Live a little. Your baby may really like cats.

Nonfiction

When your toddlers and twos become obsessed with a particular topic (likely an animal or a vehicle), don't forget about nonfiction. Most informational books are text-heavy and written for a school-age audience, but the best are also chock-full of great photos or illustrations. You may not be able to read most of these books cover-to-cover with a little one (and unless you share the obsession, you probably won't want to). Look at the pictures together and talk about what interests him. You can look for an app with images of the favorite subject as well. The library or the Internet would be your best bets for the widest selection of books. There are a number of good authors and series to check out:

- The Baby Animals series of board books produced by Kingfisher present animal facts in the simplest of ways with one or two photos per spread. Look for *Baby Animals at Night, Baby Animals in the Grasslands, Baby Animals in the Jungle, Baby Animals in the Snow,* etc.

- Nic Bishop's wildlife photography is unsurpassed. Try his award-winning books titled *Frogs*, *Lizards*, *Butterflies and Moths*, *Spiders*, and *Marsupials*. For informational picture books with a narrative, check out his *Red-Eyed Tree Frog* and *Chameleon, Chameleon* (Joy Cowley, author of both).
- The Busy Books series (Tricycle Press) of board books features playful rhymes by John Schindel and clear animal photos: *Busy Barnyard* (Steven Holt, photos), *Busy Elephants* (Martin Harvey, photos), *Busy Doggies* (Beverly Sparks, photos), and *Busy Kitties* (Sean Franzen, photos), to name a few.
- DK Eyewitness Books is a long-lived series brimming with detailed photos young ones can pore over. Favorites include *Dinosaur*, *Train*, *Car*, *Flight*, *Fish*, and *Jungle*. DK also produces board books with their signature photos.
- Steve Jenkins and Robin Page present information about the natural world in innovative ways using Jenkins's gorgeous, photo-realistic collage. *What Do You Do with a Tail Like This?* (Caldecott Honor), *Move!*, *Time to Eat*, *Time to Sleep*, and *Time for a Bath*.
- Ann Morris creates simple explanations of concepts big and small using photographs taken around the world. Look for *Families* and *Shoes, Shoes, Shoes*, and with Ken Heyman (photographer): *Bread, Bread, Bread*; *Hats, Hats, Hats*; *Houses and Homes*; *On the Go*; and *Tools*.
- National Geographic Little Kids joins the list of series with breathtaking photography and illustration. Try *Little Kids First Big Book of Animals* (Catherine D. Hughes), *Little Kids African Animal Alphabet* (Beverly and Dereck Joubert), and *Little Kids First Big Book of Dinosaurs* (Catherine D. Hughes, Franco Tempesta [illus.]).
- Seymour Simon pens large-format books with amazing photo spreads on a dizzying array of topics, such as *Big Cats*, *Butterflies*, *Dogs*, *Gorillas*, *Horses*, *Penguins*, *Sharks*, *Trains*, and *Whales*.
- The ZooBorns books feature photographs of baby animals from the world's zoos including many critters you've never heard of. Adorable. *ZooBorns!*; *ABC ZooBorns*; and *ZooBorn Cats!*

"A two-year-old and his dad would often come to the library where I worked. As soon as they got in the door, the little guy would yell 'Tiger! Tiger! Tiger!' until his dad or I would bring him a tiger book. After this appeasement ritual, the boy was engrossed and the library was much quieter." —Rachel

What to read when your toddler is obsessed with...

Airplanes

- *Airplane Flight!: A Lift-the-Flap Adventure*, Susanna Leonard Hill, Ana Martín Larrañaga (illus.)
- *Airport* and *Planes*, Byron Barton
- *Everything Goes: In the Air*, Brian Biggs

Babies

- *American Babies*, Global Fund for Children
- *Baby Food*, Margaret Miller

Ballerinas

- *Ballerina!*, Peter Sís
- *Bea at the Ballet*, Rachel Isadora

Boats

- *Boats*, Byron Barton
- *Busy Boats*, Susan Steggall
- *Busy Boats*, Tony Mitton and Ant Parker
- *Little Tug*, Stephen Savage
- *Toot and Pop*, Sebastien Braun

Bugs

- *Bugs! Bugs! Bugs!*, Bob Barner
- *I Like Bugs: A Touch and Feel Board Book*, Lorena Siminovich
- *The Very Quiet Cricket*, Eric Carle

Cars

- *Beep, Beep*, Petr Horáček
- *Everything Goes: On Land*, Brian Biggs
- *My Car*, Byron Barton
- *Toot Toot Beep Beep*, Emma Garcia

Cats

- *Busy Kitties!: A Busy Animals Book*, John Schindel and Sean Franzen
- *Cookie's Week*, Cindy Ward, Tomie dePaola (illus.)
- *There Are Cats in This Book*, Viviane Schwarz
- *Posy*, Linda Newbery, Catherine Raynor (illus.)
- *Touch and Feel: Kitten*, DK Publishing

Construction Vehicles

- *Digger Man*, Andrea Zimmerman and David Clemesha
- *Goodnight, Goodnight, Construction Site*, Sherri Duskey Rinker, Tom Lichtenheld (illus.)
- *Machines at Work*, Byron Barton
- *Machines Go to Work* and *Machines Go to Work in the City*, William Low
- *Road Work* and *Demolition*, Sally Sutton, Brian Lovelock (illus.)
- *Tip Tip Dig Dig*, Emma Garcia

Dinosaurs

- *Dinosaur Roar!*, Paul and Henrietta Stickland
- *Let's Look at Dinosaurs*, Frances Barry
- *Oh My Oh My Oh Dinosaurs!*, Sandra Boynton
- *Simms Taback's Dinosaurs: A Giant Fold-Out Book*, Simms Taback

Dogs

- *Busy Doggies!: A Busy Animals Book*, John Schindel, Beverly Sparks (photos)
- *Dogs*, Emily Gravett
- *Doggies*, Sandra Boynton
- *Hello, Puppy!*, Jane Cowen-Fletcher
- *Walk the Dog: A Parade of Pooches from A to Z*, Bob Barner

Dressing Up

- *Brownie & Pearl Get Dolled Up*, Cynthia Rylant, Brian Biggs (illus.)
- *What We Wear: Dressing Up Around the World*, Maya Ajmera, Elise Hofer Derstine, Cynthia Pon (illus.)

Fairies

- *Alice the Fairy*, David Shannon
- *The Complete Book of the Flower Fairies*, Cicely Mary Barker

Fire Engines

- *Fire Engine Man*, Andrea Zimmerman and David Clemesha
- *Fire Engines*, Anne Rockwell
- *Fire Truck*, Peter Sís
- *Firefighter Frank*, Monica Wellington
- *Maisy's Fire Engine: A Maisy Shaped Board Book*, Lucy Cousins

Fish and Ocean Life

- *Baby Beluga*, Raffi, Ashley Wolff (illus.)
- *Deep Sea Dive: Lift-the-Flap Adventures*, Salina Yoon
- *Hooray for Fish!*, Lucy Cousins
- *I'm the Biggest Thing in the Ocean*, Kevin Sherry

Moon

- *Kitten's First Full Moon*, Kevin Henkes
- *Moon Plane*, Peter McCarty
- *Papa, Please Get the Moon for Me*, Eric Carle
- *Red Knit Cap Girl*, Naoko Stoop

Shoes

- *Baby Shoes*, Dashka Slater, Hiroe Nakata (illus.)
- *Whose Shoe? A Shoe for Every Job*, Stephen R. Swinburne

Trains

- *All Aboard! A True Train Story*, Susan Kuklin
- *Choo Choo*, Petr Horáček
- *I Love Trains!*, Philemon Sturges, Shari Halpern (illus.)
- *Train Man*, Andrea Zimmerman and David Clemesha
- *Trains Go*, Steve Light

Trucks

- *I Love Trucks!*, Philemon Sturges, Shari Halpern (illus.)
- *Little Blue Truck* and *Little Blue Truck Leads the Way*, Alice Schertle, Jill McElmurry (illus.)
- *Tough Trucks*, Tony Mitton, Ant Parker (illus.)
- *Trashy Town*, Andrea Zimmerman, David Clemensha, Dan Yaccarino (illus.)
- *Trucks*, Byron Barton
- *Trucks Go*, Steve Light

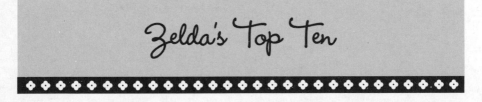

Zelda's Top Ten

"Looking at this list, what most of them have in common is that they have nice rhythms to the language (except for the Ladybug one, which has plastic ladybugs, so nothing else matters). I think the rhythms help her remember the words, and she likes to know what's coming." —Kelly

1. *I Love You, Stinky Face*, Lisa McCourt, Cyd Moore (illus.)
2. *The Three Bears*, Byron Barton (who actually does some of the only really little kid read-aloud versions of those classic stories)
3. *All of Baby Nose to Toes*, Victoria Adler, Hiroe Nakata (illus.)
4. *Mommy Is a Soft, Warm Kiss* and *Daddy Is a Cozy Hug*, Rhonda Gowler Green, Maggie Smith (illus.) (My daughter *loved* these books. I got the Daddy one first because we had sort of a dearth of Daddy stories, and it was such an enormous hit that I bought the Mommy one, too, and oh my gosh we are so very sick of these books that just looking at them makes me restless, but she really, really liked them for a while.)
5. *Ten Little Ladybugs*, Melanie Gerth, Laura Huliska-Beith (illus.)
6. *Each Peach Pear Plum*, Janet and Allan Ahlberg
7. *The Quiet Book*, Deborah Underwood, Renata Liwska (illus.) (another one she was obsessed with)
8. *So Many Days*, Alison McGhee, Taeeun Yoo (illus.)
9. *Ten Little Fingers and Ten Little Toes*, Mem Fox, Helen Oxenbury (illus.)
10. *This Is the Way*, Charles Fuge (out of print)

Your Child's Choices: Living with Supercat

KJ lived with Supercat for months. *Supercat to the Rescue* (out of print), to be precise—a truly adorable first comic book for a toddler, with a sturdy rectangular shape perfect for holding open and turning pages. For what seemed like an interminable period when Sam was three, it became his absolute favorite—the one book he would always choose above any other.

Your child will have favorites, and these will be the books you read over and over again. Sometimes you can hide a book you don't like before it becomes a favorite, but other times, you won't have the heart or the opportunity. You may not realize it wouldn't be your choice until it's too late, or you may actually think the book is cute, the first thirty times. And there you'll be, exclaiming, "Meowie Wowie!" into eternity. Inevitably, you're going to ask yourself: Why? What are you getting out of my reading this book over and over again? Why this one? Unfortunately, any book your child wants to hear at every single reading session is going to become boring to you, no matter how much you liked it in the first place. So, why? Why? WHY?

Quite simply, nearly every child does this at some point or another. Susan's son Ben, starting at twenty months, made her read *The Story of Ferdinand* repeatedly for days and weeks on end. One particular passage seemed to resonate with Ben. When Ferdinand's mother showed her concern about his un-bullish ways, Ferdinand reassured her. "His mother saw that he was not lonesome, and because she was an understanding mother, even though she was a cow, she let him just sit there and be happy." Every time Susan read this, Ben would remove his thumb or bottle from his mouth and say, firmly, "Good!" Susan knew he identified with Ferdinand and was doing his best to get her to be as understanding as Mrs. Cow.

Five Books that Trigger "Again! Again!" Again and Again

1. *Belly Button Book*, Sandra Boynton. One of Boynton's trademark chants features hippos and their beloved belly buttons.
2. *Is Your Mama a Llama?*, Deborah Guarino, Steven Kellogg (illus.). Clever rhymes and riddles keep kids turning the pages and then starting all over again.
3. *One Fish, Two Fish, Red Fish, Blue Fish*, Dr. Seuss. Will you or your baby memorize it first?
4. *Sam Who Never Forgets*, Eve Rice. Every day Zookeeper Sam remembers to feed every single one of the animals. This comforting book may get as worn as your child's blankie from repeat readings.
5. *Who Said Moo?*, Harriet Ziefert, Simms Taback (illus.). Lift the flaps to discover who answered Rooster's morning crow, then to make sure the answer never changes. (Also *Where Is My Baby?*)

Why are you rereading your book noir over and over again? There are several possible answers. Your child may really need to hear this story (and may need you to hear it) like Ben with Ferdinand. Part of the reason for Sam's fixation on Supercat turned out to be that Supercat brings Bitsy a comforting night-light, and Sam wanted one, too. Or maybe he just wants to hear it again because you didn't linger long enough on the page with the fireflies, or adequately perform the Boo Boo dance. Even if you read the book perfectly, saying "read it again" assures that you will once again perform. For once, he's in control (at least until you balk). And he knows what will happen next. For a baby or a toddler, that's big. You're just going to have to learn to live with it, and even try to learn to love it. And make sure the babysitter reads it a few hundred times, too.

It's also true that if you're a book lover, you know that you never want a really good book to end. Your baby doesn't, either. He's still learning about books. It's comforting that they really are the same, every single time. Today, Supercat will always bring the night-light. Tomorrow, Charlotte will always die in the end—but Wilbur will never become bacon.

> **TIP: Once he can understand the suggestion, have your toddler choose a book to take along every time you go out. You'll be starting a habit that will help him get through countless car rides, long waits, and tedious (to him) adult chats. It will serve you both well!**

And the Moral of the Story Is...

Lots of baby books have messages about sharing and friendship and the like. Messages that, surprisingly enough, you may dislike. *The Rainbow Fish* is a book that engenders strong reactions. Is it about sharing, or buying popularity at the price of individuality? *The Runaway Bunny* is another "controversial" book—is the mama bunny smothering her little one, or making him feel safe and protected?

People have also had strong reactions to *Love You Forever*. Does the mother show unconditional love or is she a stalker? *The Giving Tree*: is it another story of unconditional love or is the boy / man taking advantage of the tree?

If you're reading along and suddenly find you don't like the turn the story's taken, it's fine to voice your emotion—"Hey, I don't think that's what she should have done at all!" You're hoping to pass your values on, after all—there's no time like now for opening the discussion, whether your baby can talk back or not!

"Jack, twenty months, is such an active kid, it really is magic the way he can be 'stilled' by a book. Without question it is my favorite thing when he comes over with one he has selected, hands it to me, and commands, 'Read,' as he plops himself into my lap (usually with the pronouncement, 'Sit down'). The books have become part of his emotional life, helping him to sort out new feelings. The Runaway Bunny (by Margaret Wise Brown) is an all-time favorite…an obsession, really. I wasn't sure how I felt about the story line—the mother's practice of following the bunny wherever he goes may be somehow comforting to the toddler who is ambivalent about his independence, but to me it borders on stalking ('If you become a sailboat and sail away from me, I'll become the wind and blow you where I want you to go.')!

But Jack loves it. When still a new walker just beginning to quicken his pace to a run, he'd speed down the hallway yelling, 'Run away, run away.' Then soon after, it seeped into our morning routine, which had been for me to bring him milk that he would drink in his crib, allowing me another ten minutes or so of rest. One morning he began to cry when I left the room. When I rushed back to ask him what was wrong, he said desperately, 'Mommy go away,' and I knew that he meant he felt abandoned—unlike the stalker bunny mommy, I had left." —Kate

---

Featured Book

Yummy Yucky
Leslie Patricelli

A first glimpse of any cover of Leslie Patricelli's books will fill you with glee. Big clear opposites words, and smiling babies with dots for eyes. *Yummy Yucky* features paired babies enjoying or hating various foods. Patricelli's appreciation for the fun and mess of babyhood is evident. We are huge fans. Have fun with *Quiet LOUD*, *Baby Happy Baby Sad*, and the slightly longer books *Higher! Higher!*, *Faster! Faster!*, and *The Birthday Box*.

"I HATE The Rainbow Fish! Although some say its premise is about sharing, I think the message is more about buying friendship and not appreciating the fact that each fish is different and uniquely beautiful in its own way. It also seems to encourage the concept that in order to be viewed as 'good / nice,' you have to give away that which is most precious to you. It seems very socialist in concept." —Melissa

One More Choice: Hardcover, Paperback, Board Book?

Board books are wonderful for babies who rip pages, for moms with tired arms, and for throwing into the bag with all the other supplies. Some books—especially those designed for very little babies, like baby face pictures and naming books—only come in this format, and it's likely to be all you use from the time baby starts grabbing until he's ready to move on to longer stories. When buying a book that's available in several formats, it's a good idea to check to see whether the board book omits anything. Some board book editions of *Chicka Chicka Boom Boom* cut off the second half, leaving out half the fun. Other books may combine text from two pages onto one and drop an illustration. The art often gets shrunk down and some details can be hard to make out. In *Good Night, Gorilla*, it is hard to see what the mouse is doing on each page. If you can, opt for the larger "lap-size" editions of some board books.

Some board books that stem from popular series, like Olivia and Curious George, are not really books by the author at all—they're the author's original illustrations with simple, usually non-narrative text, like counting or opposite books. Some of these can be very good, like the Llama Llama board books. The shorter board books are true to the spirit of the longer picture books and deal with a toddler's everyday experiences. Others are definitely riding on the strength of the franchise. Generally, if you know the author's dead, the spin-off books based on his or her work may also be lifeless.

Once your baby has really started to enjoy the ritual of reading (you'll know because you'll find yourself actually finishing the majority of books you start), it's probably time to stop purchasing board books. Paperbacks are often cheaper and just as beautifully illustrated as board books and hardcovers, and they're wonderfully light for travel. Hardcover books, though, have a magic of their own—a smell and a feel that can create a sensory memory even apart from the pictures and the story—and they're likely to stand up to more wear. (But don't forget to stock up on tape.)

How Do You Want Your Book?

One title of a children's book can come in a variety of formats. These different formats can be confusing, particularly with online shopping. Here is a book format primer to help you sort it all out:

Board Book: With stiff, sturdy pages of heavy-duty paperboard, these books are ideal for babies and toddlers. Some board book editions are shrunken down or condensed versions of their full-size editions, but most of them were originally published in the board book format.

Hardcover: Most folks know what these are, beautiful editions with dust jackets and all. More expensive, they make wonderful keepsakes of well-loved titles. You may see some hardcovers listed with a "reinforced" or "library and school" binding, which just means they are extra sturdy.

Paper-over-Board: These books look like hardcovers (and most online sellers list them as such), but they don't have dust jackets. Some titles in this format are created specifically with toddlers in mind, with stiffer-than-normal pages and rounded corners.

Paperback: Many picture books also come in paperback, which is an inexpensive and lightweight format that is great for travel.

Mass-Market Paperback: Probably the cheapest and least expensive of all formats. The printing quality is not as good and the pages are thin, but you can't beat the price.

Ebook: While adult ebooks have taken off, things are moving a little bit slower in the children's ebook world. A growing number of the titles listed in these pages are available in ebook, which is great for heavy fairy tale anthologies or for taking multiple titles on the road.

Book App: Many publishers, writers, and illustrators are creating apps based on their popular books or characters. These can be similar to ebooks and include the full text and illustrations of the book, but there are interactive components. You can make animals say "moo," "baa," or "la la la" with a tap or open up each car of the *Freight Train*. (More on ebooks and apps in chapter 8.)

Where to Get Them

We love all bookstores. We love our local independent bookstores: labors of love, each and every one. We support them with visits and dollars. Barnes & Noble continues to offer a place to review selections plus coffee and treats. However, paying full price for every book gets expensive. We especially love libraries. Here you'll find treasures old and new all for free! So here's a quick rundown on what else is out there and why you might want to give it a try.

TIP: Look for a bookstore with a basket of toys and a small enough kids' area that you can keep one eye on a mobile baby or toddler as you browse, and you'll be able to preview the books but still make the bookstore a family outing. Beware the toddler making a break for the cookie case in the coffee shop!

Libraries

It's amazing how many new moms forget the library entirely, yet there's no better way to taste-test books and feed your hunger for something new. Even the smallest community libraries usually have a children's room with a specially trained children's librarian, and the selection won't be limited to books that are currently in print. If there's a problem with even the most knowledgeable bookstore staffer, it's that he's probably slightly biased toward the newer books because he may be more familiar with them. Librarians can lead you to authors and books you might never find otherwise.

Independent Bookstores

If you have a local bookstore specializing in children's books or an independent bookseller with a large children's section, use and support it. It's a great resource. The owners and staff of these stores devote a considerable amount of time to all forms of children's literature, and they'll know what you mean when you request a book about farm animals with simple illustrations and no more than one line of text per page.

Toy and Baby Stores

The smaller stores often have a small, but lovely, selection of books, and these kinds of stores are often your best bet for cloth and plastic books.

Book Clubs

Some child-care centers participate in book clubs operated by publishers like Scholastic. You will periodically get a circular from your child's teacher

Ten Tips for Using Your Library

1. Find your local library here: www.publiclibraries.com.

2. Get your baby a library card! Yes, babies can have their own library cards at most libraries, which your nanny or babysitter can also use.

3. What's available beyond books? Most libraries have DVDs, CDs, and download-able materials like ebooks, audiobooks, and music. A few libraries even circulate toys, e-readers, and tablets!

4. Know the children's librarian. He can let you know what's new at the library in the way of books and programs. He also appreciates feedback, either con-cerns or accolades.

5. Don't see what you want on the shelf? Request the book you want from another library. Do it yourself online or ask library staff to help you.

6. If your child is old enough, encourage him to check out his own books. Some libraries have self-checkout machines and return slots that toddlers love!

7. Concerned about losing or damaging library books? Keep them in a special library bag to transport the books to and from the library.

8. Worried about overdue fines? If you request it, many libraries will send you an email reminder a few days before the due date. You can usually renew your items online if no one else has requested them.

9. Embarrassed that your child has damaged or lost a book? Don't worry; the li-brary staff has seen it all. You may have to pay for the book, but the library is still the best deal in town.

10. Go to story time at your local library. Many libraries have a free story time geared to your child's age. It is a great way to meet local families and learn songs and rhymes.

and you can order hardcovers, board books, or mass-market paperbacks—often below retail prices. The books can range in quality, since the clubs sell everything from award winners to TV tie-ins. Your child's teacher may get some free books for the classroom as a thank-you from the book club. If you're interested, consider setting it up as a parent volunteer. Scholastic will also help centers and schools set up one-shot book fairs.

Used Bookstores, Secondhand Shops, Garage Sales

Book conditions vary greatly, and you'll probably find some that are practically new. Some libraries host ongoing book sales to sell their discarded titles on a regular basis. Your local library, along with neighborhood schools, churches, and other community groups, will often hold annual book sales as a fundraiser. You'll have to do some digging, but nothing beats that serendipitous moment when you find a treasure. Since you hope they'll become worn with use, why shouldn't the books start out a little tattered?

Discount Stores

TJ Maxx and similar stores receive regular shipments of overstocked children's books. They can have some wonderful deals on books, particularly if you ask when they expect to receive new shipments and plan accordingly. Stores like Target or Buy Buy Baby may also offer a small discount on current titles.

Street Vendors

In major cities, you'll find street vendors with tables full of books you've never heard of, from publishers you've never seen before. These vendors are a great source for naming books, alphabet books, coloring books, and those laminated placemats with educational facts and such on them. (If you do find a vendor selling one or two copies of a popular title, unused, or selling books you recognize from the bookstore, beware. The New York City Police Department warns that these books are often stolen or off the gray market. You want to be sure to support the authors, illustrators, and publishers who have brought your family so much pleasure!)

Online Shopping

So convenient, but with one problem—unless you're looking for specific titles, it's hard to tell what you're getting. Many sites include reader (parent) reviews, which can be helpful. There are even online independent bookshops, like Jay Bushara's onepotato.net, that offer a curated selection that's easier to browse.

Online Auctions

If you're in the market for a lot of books, and you don't mind sorting through them once you've got them, try eBay or one of the other auction sites. Parents trying to make room for older kids box the baby books up and sell them in lots. Some will list every title they're selling, others just a select few. A box of twenty books may go for as little as $12. Don't forget that shipping is added on after the bidding stops. It's not a bargain if you find yourself paying $5 or $10 more in shipping costs!

Where to Keep Them
Shelves, Baskets, and Piles

Your baby wants to be able to get to his books at all times, for easy chewing, perusing, and reading with his grown-ups. You want them neat and out of the way. It's time for a compromise—after all, if he can't get to the books, how will he be able to read them, play with them, or use them for building blocks? For the most part, traditional book storage won't work well. If his books are lined up tightly on the shelf with only their spines showing, he won't be able to pick which one he wants or pull it out. You need a solution that allows him easy access but allows you to get to his crib without stepping on *The Foot Book*.

For starters, try not to keep the books all in one place. You want to be able to read at any time of the day without having to go to one specific location, and you want the constant presence of books to suggest reading activities to both of you. Different rooms may call for different solutions. You might have room for a special children's bookshelf that allows the books to be displayed with their covers showing in the nursery or playroom, and for other rooms you might consider baskets, boxes, or magazine racks. All are more easily accessible for baby than a regular shelf.

If you are using shelves, try stacking the books up or keeping the shelves loose so that it's easy to pull them out (and keep in mind that pulling them out may be the part your baby likes best!).

Can't-Put-Them-Down Storybooks
Blockbuster Fiction for the Younger Set

No library is complete without books that tell a story, but many babies who are just starting to sit still and really participate in the reading aren't ready for much of a narrative. They need very short stories. Plot development is not that important to them. You may even find that your more verbal or more patient baby is really ready for some longer tales—but many of the beautiful hardcovers in the store have a whole paragraph of text on each page. That's too much for most babies and toddlers. We've provided some starter storybooks that can ease your baby gently into longer listening times. Older toddlers may be ready for longer stories, and we've included our favorites here, too.

Irresistible Author: Rosemary Wells

Rosemary Wells's contribution to the world of books for very young children is incalculable. We all see ourselves and our children in her Max and Ruby series of sibling rivalries, or Noisy Nora's plight as the middle child, or McDuff the dog's experiences with a new baby in the house. Ms. Wells has an immediately recognizable aesthetic and seems to have remembered childhood's trials perfectly. Although her characters are little animals (kittens, bunnies, and woodchuck-like dogs), they burst with human life and foibles.

- *Angus and the Cat*, Marjorie Flack. Angus the dog accepts a cat into his home, with simple pictures, few colors, and a fun twist told only in the illustrations.
- *Bark, George*, Jules Feiffer. Mama dog takes her puppy, George, to the vet to see why he can't bark. Great simple illustrations that are fun for you both.

- *Duck on a Bike*, David Shannon. The title says it all. All the farm animals eventually appear on bikes. Good for the toddler with a new tricycle or seat on Dad's bike.
- *Giggle, Giggle, Quack*, Doreen Cronin, Betsy Lewin (illus.). A little easier to understand for a toddler than this author's other popular book, *Click Clack Moo*. A duck types messages from the barn.
- *Have You Seen My Duckling?*, Nancy Tafuri. The "lost" duckling can be seen hiding on each page as the mother queries the other animals around the pond.
- *Hop Jump*, Ellen Stoll Walsh. Betsy the frog, tired of hopping, encourages her brethren to dance, and soon all but one join in. That's okay, because there's room for both dancing and hopping in this world. Walsh's collage frogs are a treat. Available in Spanish as *Salta y brinca*.
- *Mr. Gumpy's Outing*, John Burningham. Mr. Gumpy takes a group of farm animals on a raft. Disaster ensues, which is handled quite calmly. Burningham's quiet pencil drawings meld perfectly with the text. See also *Mr. Gumpy's Motor Car*.
- *Sheep in a Jeep*, Nancy E. Shaw, Margot Apple (illus.). Clever rhymes in every line. Sheep make mistakes but clean up their messes. There are many more sheep books by Shaw and Apple to peruse.
- *Wemberly's Ice Cream Star*, Kevin Henkes. Worried Wemberly mouse comes up with a creative way to eat her ice-cream star so it won't drip on her dress and she can share it with her stuffed pal Petal.
- *We're Going on a Lion Hunt*, David Axtell. In this rhythmic and interactive romp, two girls search for a lion on the African Savanna.

Longer Stories

- *Beatrice Doesn't Want To*, Laura Numeroff, Lynn Munsinger (illus.). Beatrice, a visibly stubborn pencil-and-ink canine little sister, doesn't want to do anything that might make it easier for Henry to take care of her, including a visit to the library. But once she gets there, she's so captivated by story time that she doesn't want to leave.

- *Cold Little Duck, Duck, Duck*, Lisa Westberg Peters, Sam Williams (illus.). Baby Duck arrives too soon for spring but soon dreams a glorious spring into being for all the animals.
- *The Complete Adventures of Big Dog and Little Dog*, Dav Pilkey. Five delightfully simple stories about two mismatched canine buddies.
- *Gilberto and the Wind*, Marie Hall Ets. In this quiet classic, a young Latino boy discovers the playful properties of the wind through a toy sailboat, a pinwheel, soap bubbles, and more. Available in Spanish as *Gilberto y el viento*.
- *The Great Gracie Chase: Stop that Dog!*, Cynthia Rylant, Mark Teague (illus.). Gracie the dog runs away accidentally and finds herself being chased by the whole town. Lots of repetition and a surprise ending.
- *Green Eggs and Ham* and *The Cat in the Hat*, Dr. Seuss. Rhyming story classics suitable for all ages.
- *How to Catch a Star*, Oliver Jeffers. Flat, whimsical images show a boy sitting on a beach, waiting for the stars to drop, to no avail…until a starfish washes ashore.
- *Leaves*, David Ezra Stein. A young bear worries that the leaves are falling from the trees in the autumn, but he revels in the spring after a long winter's nap. An Ezra Jack Keats New Author Award winner.
- *Lola Loves Stories*, Anna McQuinn, Rosalind Beardshaw (illus.). Lola loves it when her father reads her stories, and his tales become the spark of her imaginative play.
- *Little Bear's Little Boat*, Eve Bunting, Nancy Carpenter (illus.). When Little Bear gets too big for his beloved little boat, he searches for someone who will appreciate it as much as he does.
- *Little Bunny on the Move*, Peter McCarty. Soft, luminous watercolors in a nearly black-and-white palette follow Little Bunny as he resists all other destinations and heads for home.

- *Max and Ruby's Bedtime Book*, Rosemary Wells. Grandma tells Max and Ruby three stories featuring their favorite characters— themselves of course!
- *The Story of Ferdinand*, Munro Leaf, Robert Lawson (illus.). Susan's son Ben's favorite book as a toddler. Black-and-white illustrations. A bull stays true to himself—even if he's not exactly the bull anyone expected.
- *Umbrella*, Taro Yashima. A young Japanese American girl can't wait for a rainy day so she can use her birthday present, red rain boots and an umbrella. The 1959 Caldecott Honor-winning art is still lovely.

Ages and Stages: What to Look for in a Book at Every Stage

Newborn	Starkly contrasting images in black and white or primary colors are most likely to catch an infant's attention. If he's interested, give him plenty of time to look.
Heads Up	Cloth and rubber books are great for babies just gaining more control over their bodies. Look for the simplest and brightest.
Sitting	Photographed or drawn pictures of baby faces, ideally nice big ones, look like familiar friends.
Crawling / Creeping	In addition to the baby pictures, simple lift-the-flaps are wonderful for babies practicing using their hands.
Cruising / Walking	Newly minted toddlers love silly rhymes and animal sounds.
Talking (a few words)	Look for any book with those first words in it. Nothing's more exciting than a chance to point and yell, "Dog!"

Talking More	Nursery rhymes can allow a child who's getting more verbal to fill in the blanks with the "punch rhyme."
Running (but not talking much)	Books with lots of action sounds or songs set to music can provide an opportunity to move around while still enjoying the reading.
Talking ALL THE TIME!	Get out those storybooks and talk about what happens, or turn the tables with a wordless book he can "read" to you.

Chapter Four
STORIES

◆◇◆◇◆◇◆◇◆◇◆◇◆◇◆◇◆◇◆◇◆◇◆◇◆◇◆◇◆◇◆◇◆◇◆◇◆

Reading Aloud, Making It Up, and Fairy Tales

Human beings are hardwired for stories. It's a fact that in our lives we will hear and tell tales of our life experiences as we roll along. Give us the opportunity for constant contact with one another, and what's one of the first things we will do? Share and read stories together.

But maybe you haven't read aloud since you were in high school, nor had a wriggly listener on your lap since you babysat the neighbor's child in eighth grade. Now, suddenly, you're reading out loud, talking your way through picture books, trying to remember fairy tales, and then comes the command: "Tell me a story." It's a little daunting. You can start with the easy stuff, reading aloud from picture books, where characters, story, and images are all before you and your only job is to bring them to life. Telling stories from wordless picture books, relating fairy tales, and making up your own can come a little later. By the time your baby is really listening to the stories you tell, you'll be relating them with ease.

What's So Important about a Story?

At their best, simple early storybooks tap into the emotional and imaginative experience of childhood for both the baby and the reader. The baby sees and hears that there is an arc to experience; that most things—days, meals, diaper changes, stories—have a beginning, a middle, and an end; an introduction, a crisis, and a resolution. The adult is put in touch with childhood feelings in a fresh, surprising way.

In reading a story to a baby, a toddler, or a preschooler, there is a physical closeness, a joining together as one. It's usually peaceful and calm. Often, the power of storytelling encourages others to sit still and listen, too. The narrative pulls everyone in together. The characters have a dilemma that speaks not just to the concerns of the small child but to some universal, larger concern for us all.

Remember *The Story of Ferdinand*? Young Ferdinand is the classic outsider—seemingly powerless but able, in the end, to remain true to himself and resist the powerful lure of others' expectations. The baby rejoices in Ferdinand's return to home, mother, flowers, and serenity. The adult may value Ferdinand's ability to embrace being different (particularly since that difference takes a nonviolent form) and his trust that his mother will still love him, regardless of what kind of bull he is.

Stories for very young babies don't have to have powerful messages, but they do need a main character. The baby will begin to identify with and root for him whether he's an elephant like Babar or a bull like Ferdinand. Each character resolves his conflict and moves on. Baby, and parent reader, learns at least one way to deal with a dilemma.

Reading Stories Aloud: Basics for Grown-Ups

Not everyone feels comfortable reading aloud, but your child will be delighted, enchanted, and enthralled regardless of your style and skill. Even if you mispronounce the name "Hermione" every single time, she's going to think that's the perfect way to read. If others in the room listening—your partner, your spouse, your mother—make you feel self-conscious, read with just your baby until you feel more comfortable. Above all, don't let any "read-aloud" feature in an ebook or app take over for you every time!

We talk more about this in chapter 8, but studies have shown that babies and children benefit far more from a live reader than from anything else, even if you're sitting with her and turning the pages. Your voice, however you read, is her best conduit into the book. We can offer a few tips, but our most important advice is to just grab a book and go. The rest will come naturally with a very little bit of practice.

Remember, the words and the text are just part of the reading experience for your baby. While you read the words, she's reading the artwork. Without the pictures, there would be no book at all! You are the announcer, the phone line, the television set—the doorway into the world of the book. While you're reading aloud, the book is the world.

Tone and Volume

Obviously, you can read loudly in the middle of the afternoon and softly at night. Even better, you can crescendo when the Cat brings in Thing One and Thing Two and whisper in shock when Mother approaches and the mess is yet to be cleared up. You can also take a tone that's appropriate for the story—excited and happy, yes, for dancing hippos and shopping sheep, but sympathetic and calm for the monkey who's lost his mother and needs a hug,

Library Story Times

Many libraries offer "story times" for designated age groups. They're free! Currently there is even a lively trend to offer programs to very young babies. Some programs are very organized, with a quiet time for reading followed by some playtime. Others are more of a free-for-all, with a higher tolerance for kids running up to see Olivia or away to demonstrate a few marching moves. If you are unsure about your reading aloud skills or don't know any bouncy rhymes, this is a great way to watch how the pros do it and learn some new material. Try out a few in your community and see which type suits you and your baby best. Your baby will get the most out of it if you or your caregiver is engaged, too. You may need to get a free ticket or register in advance for popular programs. There are programs for toddlers, preschoolers, school-age kids, and teens, so your child can really grow up at the library. Some coffeehouses, bookstores, and toy stores also host story times.

or the owl babies who await their mother's return. You are entering into the emotional world of the book.

Letting your voice take on the appropriate emotional tone of the story helps to teach your child about feelings. Your baby hears you responding empathically to the characters' dilemmas. You help her to understand that the dog is sad because he misses his family, and the owls are anxious as they await their mother's return. Your baby will learn from the characters in the books and their experiences, but you and your voice and tone and facial expressions will always be her barometer (and her reminder that, after all, it's only a story in a book).

"My daughter's only seven weeks old, and she's had a terrible time with infant stomach cramps. I just read her a couple of chapters of Winnie the Pooh, *and she listened. She looked at the pictures. She loved the sound of my voice. And it went on like that for more than twenty minutes! Quite frankly, she could have gone on for longer, but I quit because I got tired. I was amazed." —Rita*

Animation and Voices

It's up to you—do Max and Ruby have special squeaky voices? Do the animals each have a real (or silly) animal sound? It doesn't matter—some of the best readers aloud modify their voices only slightly for each character, and others have a repertoire that could offer them a lifetime career with Disney studios. Trust us, their kids love them either way. Sometimes a really, really bad imitation of a lion growling is much funnier than the best copy of the real thing. One caveat—if you do a really special and amazing voice or sound once, expect to be doing it again. And again. And again. Possibly for years. Not that that should stop you!

Rhythm, Rhyme, and Repetition

In some books, the rhythm is the very essence of the book. In others, it's more subtle. Once you've found it you'll want to use it. The rhythm shows you where to put the emphasis and even how long to pause between pages. Rhyming words are usually the ones that get emphasized, and once you're putting a little more force on those words, you'll usually find that you're following the rhythm of the book naturally. Trust yourself, and be aided by the writer or poet. These books can lend themselves to bedtime—no matter how lively the story, the rhythm can always be slowed down to sleepytime levels.

Like advertising jingles, baby books are repetitious for a reason—to better stick in your mind. Repetition focuses the mind by creating patterns. We get the message and learn to predict what's coming next. In reading aloud, repetition of words and phrases gives you the opportunity to be creative. You can make a joke by getting it wrong or adding your child's name to a list in the book.

Great Starter Read-Alouds No One Can Resist

- *The Complete Adventures of Peter Rabbit*, Beatrix Potter. A rich source of storytelling from one of the first, and one of the enduring best.
- *Five Little Monkeys Jumping on the Bed*, Eileen Christelow. Mama calls the doctor and everybody giggles. *Cinco monitos brincando en la cama / Five Little Monkeys Jumping on the Bed* is the Spanish / English bilingual edition.
- *Frog and Toad Are Friends*, Arnold Lobel. Rewarding stories galore about friends. Available in Spanish as *Sapo y sepo son amigos*.
- *The Gruffalo*, Julia Donaldson, Axel Scheffler (illus.). The patterns, repetition, and slightly scary monster in this fable about the power of storytelling make it a great read-aloud for a wide age range. There's no such thing as a gruffalo, or is there? The animated short film of the same name is a wonderful example of a successful picture book adaptation.
- *Horton Hears a Who!*, Dr. Seuss. It's easy to follow the drama and

rhythm of this classic Seuss tale, and even the least comfortable reader will get caught up.

- *This Is the House that Jack Built*, Simms Taback. Taback's house is delightfully full of details with labels, animals, and odors everywhere.
- *King Bidgood's in the Bathtub*, Audrey and Don Wood. The castle is in an uproar when the king decides to rule from the tub. The Woods' buoyant verse and detailed, Caldecott Honor-winning art are perfectly matched.
- *Little Bear*, Else Holmelund Minarik, Maurice Sendak (illus.). Important simple stories about a child-bear and his family. There are several more Little Bear books to enjoy.
- *Please, Baby, Please*, Spike Lee, Tonya Lewis Lee, Kadir Nelson (illus.). In Nelson's radiant paintings, an impish baby gets up to lots of recognizable mischief. After a few readings, your child will be shouting "please, baby, please" in all the right places. Also try *Please, Puppy, Please*.
- *Snuffy*, Dick Bruna. Excellent, concise stories from this internationally renowned storyteller for very young children, the author of the Miffy books.
- *This Little Chick*, John Lawrence. In playful verse, a little chick explores the farmyard and learns to make the sounds of the other residents. Lawrence's prints were recognized on the *New York Times* Best Illustrated list.
- *The Three Billy Goats Gruff*, Paul Galdone. Three trip-trapping goats outsmart a troll.
- *Tumble Bumble*, Felicia Bond. A parade of animals joins a tiny bug on an excursion that ends in a friendly pileup on a little boy's bed.

Wordless Books

Here's the thing about wordless books: the whole story is in the pictures. These books don't need words.

Here's the thing about most parents: we can't read a wordless book without talking. We see a story in pictures and we talk about it.

Reading begins with observing. Many picture books, even those with plenty of words, also tell their story in the pictures. Wordless books (by which we mean pure wordless books like *First Snow* or books like *Good Night, Gorilla* or *Oink* that may have a word or two) can be huge fun. They put you and your baby on the same page, inviting you both to enter into the story visually.

Wordless books also make reading simple. The illustrations are loaded with narrative information, so a story naturally moves along with dramas and development. Even insecure readers or non-English-speaking parents will surprise themselves that they can tell a story just by saying what they notice.

Soon enough a baby will read a wordless book to herself. She develops the ability to interpret what she sees rather than have it interpreted for her through another's words. She begins to comprehend a story line and character interaction, to anticipate what happens next and identify with the character's plight. All these are evident signs of intelligent pre-reading and lead directly to reading.

As children grow into talkers during their second year, wordless books prompt them to tell you what they see, to invent stories, and imagine dialogues. Their renditions are just as valid as yours are. "What do you see?" works equally well for the parent as for the child. "What happens next?" does too. Your version and hers could in fact lead to a lively discussion, a kind of baby book group, fun for you both. See our list of excellent wordless books. You'll be as delighted as your baby. We promise.

A Dozen Wordless Favorites

1. *10 Minutes till Bedtime*, Peggy Rathmann. Dad doesn't notice the hamster tourists visiting the little boy hero at bedtime. Every page is full of details that tell the tale in cartoonesque drawings.

2. *A Ball for Daisy*, Chris Raschka. A dog, a ball, a love affair. Young ones may need help following Raschka's panels, but Daisy's feelings are instantly recognizable in his Caldecott Award-winning watercolors.

3. *A Boy, a Dog, a Frog, and a Friend*, Mercer Mayer. One of the best ever. Through its pictures, it tells the story of a boy and a dog trying to catch a frog. It's fresh, humorous, and full of surprises.

4. *Good Dog, Carl*, Alexandra Day. The soft-focus illustrations belie the absurdity and humor of this tale of a babysitting Rottweiler. Check out Carl's other adventures, one of his latest being *Carl at the Dog Show*.

5. *Jack Wants a Snack*, Pat Schories. A hungry puppy eyes the treats being served at a little girl's tea party.

6. *The Lion & the Mouse*, Jerry Pinkney. In this retelling of Aesop's fable, a lion spares a mouse's life and the mouse in turn comes to the lion's rescue. Pinkney won the Caldecott for his paintings set in the African Serengeti.

7. *Pancakes for Breakfast*, Tomie dePaola. A farmer and her animals produce every ingredient for a pancake breakfast.

8. *Sunshine*, Jan Ormerod. This silent gem follows a very little girl through her day. The companion book, *Moonlight*, is also a treasure, as it follows the same little one through preparing for bedtime.

9. *Truck*, Donald Crews. Like his other books adored by toddlers, this one is bold, clear, colorful, and entertainingly easy to read. The truck encounters lots of weather and real roadside signs and construction as it carries its load of bicycles.

10. *Wave*, Suzy Lee. At the beach, a little girl enjoys a playful romp with a wave. A *New York Times* Best Illustrated Children's Book for 2008.

11. *Where's Walrus?*, Stephen Savage. When a walrus runs away, both the zookeeper and the reader end up playing a game of hide-and-seek with the escapee.

12. *Wonder Bear*, Tao Nyeu. A bear with a magical hat takes two children on a dreamy adventure.

Fairy Tales: Telling the Stories Everyone Knows (or Thinks They Do!)

When you need a story and you need it fast, it's natural to reach into your mind for a "once upon a time" classic fairy tale. *Goldilocks, The Three Little Pigs, Little Red Riding Hood*—they seem to reside in all of us, and we see their echoes in endless books and cultural references. If you haven't thought about Little Red for years, you may find she holds a few surprises. What was she doing in the woods again? And wasn't there something about a wolf eating Grandma? What's that about? And now that we come to think of it, where did this come from anyway? Among all the books we've read and stories we've heard, why do these stick with us?

"When my nephew Luk was young, we used to go out for a family dinner a couple of times a month. He would often get bored after the meal, as most kids do. One night I told him the story of The Three Billy Goats Gruff *using three pieces of bread in graduating size (goats), a butter knife (bridge), and salt shaker (troll). Luk demanded a repeat performance after every family dinner. We always made sure to tip the server well." —Rachel*

Fairy Tales Connect with a Child's Developmental Stage

Fairy tales imply stories of wonder and enchantment. They also resonate profoundly in an emotionally deep place. In some cases they hit the nail on the head at the time a child is squarely in a developmental phase.

The story of *Rumplestiltskin* can be a good fit during potty training, a time when many children seem to feel they're struggling with an impossible task. At the root of the story, there is the challenge for a young girl to turn straw into gold. If she accomplishes this amazing feat, she will please her mother, please the father / husband / king character, and become a queen. Why would such an odd tale continue to have universal appeal if it didn't touch something profound and speak to something beyond a child's ability to put into words?

The story of *Goldilocks and the Three Bears* is a cheerful reversal of something quite scary to a child who feels secure in her family and threatened by outsiders. Just why Goldilocks is lost and wandering near the Bears' house isn't clear, but anyone can see the cozy appeal of the Bears' home, filled with steaming porridge, comfy chairs, and soft beds. It's funny to see the little girl as a threat to the Bears' predictable world, rather than the other way around.

The adventurous appeal of *The Three Little Pigs* speaks to toddlers just able to move away from their secure home base. This is a time when a baby understands that she is really an individual, with her own impulses and the ability to run away and say no. Moving off, however giddy and fun, suggests a degree of danger both real and imagined. In the traditional version, making the wrong choices out in the world leads to disaster. The wolf blows down the houses and then eats the first two piglets. Only the most painstaking piglet succeeds in defeating the wolf. In kinder versions, bad choices lead to second chances. Together, in the solid brick house of the third piglet, the pig brothers turn the wolf into stew and live happily ever after.

Mrs. Pig's parenting skills were pretty good: she taught her sons to be self-reliant individuals and to support each other. That's a great story to hear repeatedly, for both mother and the children. The pigs, like children, are little but capable, innocent and creative; they conquer their fears and actual threats.

And Then What Happened?
Fairy Tales, Classic and Fractured

- *Chicken Little*, Rebecca Emberley, Ed Emberley. Panic ensues when Chicken Little mistakes a mere acorn for imminent doom. Emberley's playfully zany collage fits the wackiness of the tale. Give the Emberleys' *The Red Hen* a try, too.
- *Cinderella*, Barbara Karlin, James Marshall (illus.). As with all of Marshall's quirky artwork, this Cinderella has humor tucked into

every crevice. Also try *Goldilocks and the Three Bears* (a Caldecott Honor winner), *Red Riding Hood*, and *The Three Little Pigs*.

- *Dusty Locks and the Three Bears*, Susan Lowell, Randy Cecil (illus.). Goldilocks is a grubby little tomboy in this modern version.
- *The Gingerbread Boy*, Richard Egielski. Set in New York City, various inhabitants chase the gingerbread boy through the streets, down into the subway, and into Central Park. For a more traditional telling, see Paul Galdone's version.
- *Goldie and the Three Bears*, Diane Stanley. The eternally picky Goldilocks wanders into the Bears' house while looking for a friend who's "just right."
- *Jack and the Beanstalk*, Nina Crews. Things may not be what they seem in this modern, urban version of the famous "Jack" tale. Crews's photo-collage illustrations use a multicultural cast of characters.
- *The Little Red Hen*, Paul Galdone. The Little Red Hen can't get anyone to help her bake a cake, so she makes her cake and eats it, too. Available as an ebook. Byron Barton's version is also a delight.
- *Little Red Hen (Makes a Pizza)*, Philemon Sturges, Amy Walrod (illus.). Little Red Hen makes a truly amazing pizza with no help from her friends, but, in the end, everyone gets a taste and helps with the dishes.
- *Rapunzel*, Rachel Isadora. In this simplified adaptation, the tale is moved to Africa where the heroine sports cascading dreadlocks. Check out Paul Zelinsky's award-winning version when your child can sit for a longer text.
- *The Runaway Piggy / El cochinito fugitivo*, James Luna, Laura Lacámara (illus.). In this fracturing of "The Gingerbread Boy," a Mexican piggy cookie flees from a crowd of would-be eaters. The text is in Spanish and English.
- *Stone Soup*, Jon J. Muth. Zen monks are involved in this retelling of this trickster tale that celebrates the power of generosity. The drawings are painterly and full of atmosphere. A Chinese edition is also available.

- *The Three Bears*, Byron Barton. The classic story simplified, with his colorful blocky illustrations.
- *The Three Little Pigs: An Old Story*, Margot Zemach. Zemach's engaging watercolors illustrate this straight retelling of the story, where the pigs do get eaten. See Marshall's and Galdone's versions as well.
- *The Ugly Duckling*, Sebastien Braun. This simplified version of Hans Christian Andersen's fairy tale is accessible for the very young. When your child is older, be sure to share the version illustrated by Jerry Pinkney.

Irresistible Authors: Paul Galdone

Three Little Kittens, *The Three Bears*, *The Little Red Hen*: These timeless tales are retold and drawn so persuasively by masterful artist Paul Galdone that they invite enjoyable hours of rereading and looking. Once you and your child have gone through them a few times, you will be able to close your eyes and still see and hear the teeny-tiny woman and the three little bears, goats, kittens, and pigs. Galdone's illustrations are easily understood and enlivened with particular details for children looking closely. The wolf in *The Three Little Pigs* has eyes that focus on the pig quite intensely, and their communication is clear. Three different fonts highlight the big, middle, and little wee bears' bowls and chairs. Galdone's pictures never become dated.

Cultural Dimensions to Fairy Tales

All fairy tales deal with conflict. Historically, fairy tales have been women's stories, and were told rather than written. Perhaps that's why so many of the stories concern girls successfully overcoming distressing situations, and often via magical means. The Brothers Grimm collected their tales from peasants; the French writer Perrault collected, embellished, and composed stories to amuse the king and his court. Hans Christian Andersen wrote his own.

Because these stories are so deeply entrenched in Western culture, the most casual reference to them can serve to make a point.

Modern authors seem to love to use them as jumping-off points, creating new versions or picking up where the old story left off. You can do the same, if you want to keep the story going.

But What about the Scary Ones?

It's happened to all of us. You turn the page, and there it is—a scary monster, a burning house, a whipping—something you're just not sure how to handle. Maybe it's the giant in *Jack and the Beanstalk* about to devour the boy. Maybe it's a character trapped in front of an oncoming train. Do you boldly read on or do a panicked, on-the-spot revision? Take a deep breath and read on. It's just a book—and that's just the point. Many parents worry that by reading about scary things, they're introducing them to their child. But the fears are already there. Have you ever thought about how many "giants" there are in a baby's life? Or how a looming face appears to your baby? What if the face says, "I'd love to eat you all up!"?

> **TIP: Got monsters? Try helping your child play with the monsters in different ways. Have her help you draw a monster. She can add the hair or choose the colors. She could pretend to be a monster, with or without a hand-created brown-bag monster mask. Playing leads a child to talking and mastery. Monsters are imaginary. *Go Away, Big Green Monster!* (Ed Emberley), which lets the child control the scariness, is perfect.**

Fears—of the dark, of imaginary monsters, of dogs or puppets or clowns—are natural and ingrained. We pretty much all start with some of them. Seeing the fear represented in a book validates the fear and puts it into context. Other people are scared. Other people come out okay. It's okay to be scared. Fairy tales and other stories put voice to our fears and allow us to conquer them.

You may think it's never occurred to your child that you (or she) could die. You're probably wrong. Making death, or any other fear, into an unmentionable only makes it more frightening. A matter-of-fact reading of a fairy tale—death, teeth, and monsters intact—simplified for the youngest listeners, yet safely removed from reality, lets those fears out in the open and gives them an airing. Fairy tales encourage children to use their imagination to overcome their fears.

TIP: Happy Halloween! Plenty of kids find Halloween both fun and a little anxiety-provoking (thanks, costume aisle at Kmart!). Plenty of Halloween books take the mask off all the scariness. KJ's Halloween-loving family also adores Kazuno Kohara's beautifully illustrated *Ghosts in the House*: a little girl moves into a creepy, dark house with "just one problem: it was haunted." But she's a witch, and she and her cat quickly round up the shiny white ghosts, tuck them all into the washing machine, and they live quite usefully and happily ever after.

Fairy Tale Collections to Make You Happy Ever After

It's rare to find a fairy tale collection truly targeted at babies, toddlers, and twos. Here are a few of the simplest with plenty of pictures. You may find yourself needing to abridge the text a bit for some toddlers and two-year-olds; others will be ready to enjoy them in full. Either way, since you'll be reading from these for years, they're a good investment.

- *The Giant Golden Book of Elves and Fairies*, Jane Werner, Garth Williams (illus.). A beloved treasury reprinted to the joy of all. Williams's illustrations form a basis for what some of us think these little creatures (like the Little Mermaid) actually look like. Squint your eyes and you'll see them again, too.

- *Mary Engelbreit's Nursery Tales: A Treasury of Children's Classics*, Mary Engelbreit. Through her colorful, detailed illustrations and direct narration, Engelbreit has done a masterful job with such favorites as "Jack and the Beanstalk," "The Gingerbread Boy," "Puss in Boots," and eight others.
- *Nursery Classics: A Galdone Treasury*, Paul Galdone. Beautiful illustrations with plenty of detail fill this collection of four classic but simple tales. Currently available only as an ebook.
- *Tomie dePaola's Favorite Nursery Tales*, Tomie dePaola. DePaola illustrates this collection of poems, fables, and stories with his accessible drawings. Featured stories include "The Elves and the Shoemaker," "The Princess and the Pea," and "The Frog Prince."
- *Yummy: Eight Favorite Fairy Tales*, Lucy Cousins. These retellings of "Little Red Riding Hood," "Henny Penny," "The Three Little Pigs," and more are true to older variants. Animals get eaten and violent things happen, but somehow Cousin's colorful and playful cartoons remind us it is all "Once upon a time..." A *New York Times* Best Illustrated Children's Books for 2010.

Folk, Fairy, Legend...What's in a Tale?

Myth: Usually a sacred story that explains how the world came to be, and other mysteries of the universe. (For example: tales of gods and goddesses throughout the world)

Folktales: Fictional stories about people and animals that have been passed down via the oral tradition. For some cultures, there is no distinction between folktale and myth. (Anansi the Spider)

Fairy Tales: Usually European in origin, most fairy tales began their lives as folktales. The most famous were collected and written down (and rewritten) by the likes of the Brothers Grimm and Perrault (*Cinderella*). Other fairy tales are original stories, like those of Hans Christian Andersen (*The Ugly Duckling*).

Legend: The story of a person, a people, or a place that has some historical basis, but has been greatly embellished through the years. (King Arthur)

Tall Tale: A story that has larger-than-life characters performing outlandish feats, all for dramatic effect. (Paul Bunyan, John Henry)

Fable: A short story, often involving animals, written or told to teach a moral or lesson. (Aesop)

Stories Make the World Go 'Round: World Folktales

A great way to explore another culture or delve deeper into your family's heritage is to read folktales together. Every nation and culture has them, and more are being published every year as picture books or in anthologies. Most are written for older kids, but here are a few that are good for older twos and threes.

- *Head, Body, Legs: A Story from Liberia*, Won-Ldy Paye, Margaret H. Lippert, Julie Paschkis (illus.). In this creation story that comes from the Dan people of northeastern Liberia in Africa, individual entities Head, Body, Legs, and Arms must figure out how to unite as one to eat a mango. For more from this team, try *Mrs. Chicken and the Hungry Crocodile*.
- *How Many Donkeys?: An Arabic Counting Tale*, Margaret Read MacDonald, Nadia Jameel Taibah, Carol Liddiment (illus.). While taking his wares to market on several donkeys, a befuddled merchant thinks that he is always one donkey short because he forgets to count the one he is riding on. The text and illustrations include numbers in both English and Arabic.
- *Mabela the Clever*, Margaret Read MacDonald, Tim Coffey (illus.). In this folktale from the Limba people of Sierra Leone, an observant, quick-witted, and quick-footed mouse outsmarts a cat and saves the other mice from her village.

- *Monkey: A Trickster Tale from India*, Gerald McDermott. Monkey must keep one step ahead of a hungry crocodile. McDermott has adapted several other trickster tales from around the world, including *Jabutí the Tortoise*, *Zomo the Rabbit*, *Pig Boy*, *Coyote*, and *Raven*.
- *Moon Rope: A Peruvian Folktale / Un lazo a la luna: una leyenda peruana*, Lois Ehlert. Thinking that worms are plentiful on the moon, Fox and Mole attempt to get there via rope. In Spanish and English. Also try *Cuckoo: A Mexican Folktale / Cucú: un cuento folklórico mexicano*.
- *The Little, Little House*, Jessica Souhami. In this Eastern European Jewish folktale, a family learns to live in their tiny house through Aunty Bella's practical demonstration of how much worse it could actually be. For a longer adaptation with Caldecott Honor-winning illustrations, check out Margot Zemach's *It Could Always Be Worse*.
- *Rabbit's Gift*, George Shannon, Laura Dronzek (illus.). Showing kindness to their friends in the midst of winter, the same turnip is given and re-gifted by a group of animals. A fable from China with lovely art from Dronzek.
- *The Squeaky Door*, Margaret Read MacDonald, Mary Newall DePalma (illus.). In this delightfully silly tale, based on the Puerto Rican folk song "La cama," a grandma comforts her scared grandson at bedtime by putting a bevy of animals (from the cat to the horse) into his bed.

Can You Make Up a Story?

"Tell me a story" is a classic child's plea to stave off bedtime, pass waiting time, or just because it seems like a good time for a snuggle. Of course, if you have an e-reader app on your phone, you may always have a book in your pocket, but why not try flying solo once in a while? So there you sit, child in your arms, and you begin: Once upon a time…

> *"Zelda is almost three. She likes to read to her toys. If you leave her in her room with a bunch of books, you can lurk around a corner and listen to her flipping pages and explaining what's happening in the book to her toys."* —*Owen*

Once upon a time what? Suddenly this is harder than it sounded. A prince? A princess?

You don't know anything about princes and princesses. You don't want this just to be some rehash of something you read, do you? Wait, that's not a bad idea. If there are only seven plots in the world, there's no sense coming up with a new story.

So maybe you tell a story you already know, a truncated version of *The Three Little Pigs* or the book you read last night with an owl for a hero instead of a rabbit. That's fair. Or maybe a story about your child would be best. You relate the events of the day, ending each with *and then... and then...* You might even send your child off in a rocket to the moon, only to discover that you have disappointingly little for her to do once she gets there.

Afterward, she seems satisfied, but you may be feeling a bit inept. Haven't you read interviews with authors who say their books came directly from the stories they told their own children? Yours didn't sound like a book. It sounded, well, a bit bald. No dialogue. Not much adventure.

TIP: There's something about "Once upon a time" that can be intimidating. It sets the bar too high. Start with something different, like "once there was a little boy who..." or "I once knew a dog who..." The story might flow a little more easily.

Why Tell Stories?

When you tell a story rather than reading one, your child listens without any aids to focus her attention. She has to imagine the scenes, the people, the colors, all for herself and remember what's going on without the help of a picture.

When you tell a story, whether it's a personal one or your rendition of a fairy tale, you tailor your words to your baby. Focus on what she knows, where she's been, and what interests her. You can tell her about the three little pigs' mother, or what kind of shoes they like to wear. You can tell her about something you did when you were little that's just like something she did today. She's your baby, and you know what she likes better than anyone else.

Telling stories about your childhood, or even about your day, deepens your connection to one another. Telling fantastical stories about her helps her to dream, to see herself in ways she'd never imagined, and to begin to imagine them. Even putting your own spin on a book she's heard many times is a great way to reinforce her natural creativity (who says the sky has to be blue every time?).

Telling the Stories You Know

You probably have some favorite stories: the time Uncle Ben ate the centerpiece or the one about the fraternity guy who mooned the president of the college. But perhaps something simpler is better for baby. A story that starts with breakfast, crescendos at a garbage truck emptying a Dumpster, and then ends with arrival at day care might be just perfect. A young baby will enjoy a gentle, even droning narration of her day as she falls asleep. No need to reach a high point for her.

Stories about your childhood will also come naturally. "When I was your age," they begin, and go on from there. Toddlers love simple stories about how Grandma made Mommy pancakes every Saturday or soup when she was sick. You may even find she has an unusual fascination with some character and wants to hear more about your childhood dog or even the funny guy at work who dropped a box of paperclips down the stairs.

"I told my daughter a story every night when I got home from work, starting when she was very small. By the time she was three, it was a real ritual for us, and the stories started getting really complicated. I couldn't just wing it—I'd make up something to happen in the car on the way home from work. It's actually really fun for me, too. She's six now, and currently in a hot-air balloon with a monkey and a toaster on her way to Peru (sometimes she helps with the plotting)." —Jim

CAPeR: Making It Up as You Go

At some point in the first three years of raising your child, you're going to find yourself making up a story from scratch. Maybe you've always imagined a child who'd say, "Tell me a story," maybe you're continuing a tradition you loved as a kid, or maybe you're just stuck in traffic, or a waiting room, or at the airport. Most kids love these homemade tales. Maybe it's just the sheer joy of having something they know you're creating just for them.

Making up a story on the fly is harder than it sounds. You're going to need characters, action, a bit of dialogue, and, if you're up to it, a problem and a resolution. We've even come up with a formula: CAPeR. Characters, Action, Problem, Resolution.

So: Big and Little find a ball. "I want it," says one. "No, I want it," says the other. They pull and pull on the ball until it bursts. They cry. "I have some tape," says Big. "I'll hold the pieces together," says Little. So they tape it together. Big blows it up, and they decide to play catch. The end.

Not destined for a starred review in *Library Journal* but enough, with some embellishment, to entertain a baby or toddler in line at the grocery store. If you've got a gift for storytelling, you're golden. If not, maybe CAPeR will help. Either way, you're guaranteed to please your audience—and by the time she's old enough to want a little more action, you can encourage your child to chime in.

Ages and Stages: Storytelling and Fairy Tales

Newborn	Read everything aloud, from the instructions on the back of the instant coffee to *The Daily News*. If you're looking at the words, share!
	Bedtime stories always start the same way (Once upon a time; Once there was a little girl named…) and end the same way (And then they all slept all night through). It doesn't matter what you put in between.
Heads Up	Be prepared to get down on the floor with your tiny one and have a conversation eye to eye. It's such an effort for your child to raise her head, but having Mommy or Daddy's smiling face to greet her makes it worthwhile.
Sitting	Find some clever oven gloves to use for puppet-like stories.
	Act out a silly simple story between two toys. They could play hide-and-seek, or just jump up and down and talk to each other.
Crawling / Creeping	Do read the same books over and over. At this stage, she's just beginning to make a connection between what you say and the pictures.
	If you're condensing a fairy tale, try to keep in the key phrases (Once upon a time, And he huffed and he puffed and he *blew* the house down) so that they'll stay consistent as you read more of the story.
Cruising / Walking	Tell a bedtime story about their day and all of their wonderful accomplishments.
	Choose a few books with a consistent character and try giving that character a special voice.

Talking (a few words)	Ask your child for one or two or three things to put in the story: a girl, a dog, and a ball. Then tell that story!
Talking More	She can start learning the names of a few favorite books. Make sure you're reading both the title and author, too, so she can start learning how to ask for it. Open up a new wordless book and ask her what she can name that she sees.
Running (but not talking much)	Act out fairy tales with lots of action, like The Gingerbread Boy and The Three Little Pigs. Look for books that encourage you to interact, to tickle and grab each other as you read aloud, like *Pete's a Pizza*.
Talking ALL THE TIME!	Get the children to help you read the story by leaving off the last word, or by asking what happens next. Make "mistakes" in reading on purpose. See what happens. Compare and contrast versions of favorite fairy tales.

Chapter Five

HOW TO JUDGE A BOOK BY ITS COVER

❖❖❖❖❖❖❖❖❖❖❖❖❖❖❖❖❖❖❖❖❖❖❖❖❖❖❖❖❖❖❖❖❖❖❖❖❖❖❖

Telling a story through pictures is an ancient tradition for human beings. All art and literature began with early efforts at communication: in French and Spanish cave paintings, Egyptian mummies and tombs, and Eskimo ivory carvings. Written communication came much later. Even today, when we want to be absolutely sure our meaning is understood, we often turn to art. "Let me draw you a picture."

What Can Babies See?

Object and face recognition: At birth, babies can see your face from arm's length, but they seem to prefer borders and often gaze at the hairline. By two months they hone in on your features (like nose and mouth) and by three to five months (if not earlier) can distinguish Mom's face from a stranger's.

Focusing: Infants start life farsighted. By two to three months, most infants focus accurately.

Eye coordination and tracking: Newborns can track an object if it's large enough, has good contrast, and moves slowly. By three months this ability is well established.

Color: By two to six weeks, infants can distinguish a red from a green object. Detecting pastels and other subtle colors will take time to develop.

Pictures Are Worth a Thousand Words

The pictures in children's books absolutely qualify as art. They tell stories, convey emotion, capture attention, and bring pleasure. Where else can you find art that is universally approachable, speaking to young and old and in between? A picture book is itself an art form that fits in your hands.

For babies, toddlers, and twos, picture books are the only books, and in a very real sense, the artwork is the book. For now, he's concentrating on visual literacy. The words are just squiggles—part of the art. But "reading" the artwork now leads to reading words later.

Your baby's bookshelves are already filled with art. Some of it is elaborate and exceptional, some not so great but still much loved and full of communication. Understanding how the artists arrange elements like color, line, shape, and movement to tell the story can make reading with your baby that much more fun.

Baby's First Art

- *A Color of His Own*, Leo Lionni. A chameleon is blue because he can't find a color of his own, until he finds a friend to share his constantly changing shade.
- *I Kissed the Baby!*, Mary Murphy. Brightly colored animals against a black background welcome the baby duck with tickling, singing, and a kiss from Mama.
- *Look at That!: Wild Animals*, Guido van Genechten. Simple, accessible, and delightful paintings of favorite animals.
- *A Magical Day with Matisse*, Julie Merberg, Suzanne Bober. Lilting, rhyming text invites the reader into ten Matisse paintings. Look for other books in the "Mini Masters" series.
- *Out to Play*, Michel Blake. Each page of this easy-to-open board book

features a brightly colored object for a black-and-white photographed preschooler to play with. Also *Off to Bed*.

- *Winter Friends*, Carl R. Sams II and Jean Stoick. Big photos of winter scenes, with small sparks of color, will entrance all ages.

TIP: The dust jacket of any hardcover you buy can make great art for a baby or toddler's room, especially hung in a group with a theme, like trains or a specific illustrator. Any framing place can dry-mount them to prevent wrinkling, or you can trim them yourself and slide them into inexpensive frames with pre-cut mats. Hardcover books may be expensive, but at least you get a bonus gift!

Visual Literacy: Learning to Read the World

So why does this matter? Aren't the pictures just there to give the baby something to look at while you read? Why make such a big deal about "art"?

Visual literacy is important because we live in an increasingly visual culture. The images we see communicate a surprising amount of information. By looking at and talking about what we see, we help our children to understand even more of the world, long before they have words of their own to describe what they see and understand.

Both infants and young children experience the world through their senses rather than words. It's your

Artists and art editors consider each detail:
- Size
- Shape
- End papers and dust jackets in hardcover editions
- Title placement, fonts, and style
- Text color, font, size, placement on the page
- Borders
- Bar codes

Talking to the Artist: Pat Cummings

"In books, it's unfair to mislead readers by showing expressions that don't convey the mood / message. In *Ananse and the Lizard*, the lizard HAS to have a glint in his eye even while smiling. I ask the really little kids if Ananse should trust him, and they shake their heads vigorously because they already know the smile is too sly. No poker faces allowed in picture books. Even if it's merely a raised eyebrow or a crooked smile, something's gotta give a clue to the emotions."

comforting tone, not the words of your lullaby, that soothes him to sleep. When it comes to reading, the words are only beginning to be more than pleasurable sounds. But the pictures, the pictures are everything. Most babies are taking in much of their new world through their eyes, and it all goes by fast. Pictures in books hold still and provide a chance to examine the world and all its many elements in a handy portable format.

The art in books does three things for your baby. First, it holds still and focuses his attention. He can look at a picture of a bowl of cereal without being distracted by a kitchen full of movement and objects, and he can enjoy it visually without anyone trying to feed it to him.

Second, he gets to read. Someone has depicted a bowl of cereal and he's interpreting that picture. He can have time to think about cereal, or notice that the bowl has a small puppy decoration on it. He can even touch the page and move his hand to his mouth, indicating a complete comprehension of cereal as something that one eats.

David's brother gave him a favorite book to read to his six-month-old nephew. "Show him one page at a time," the brother cautioned, "because he goes nuts when you show him a two-page spread." David dutifully began reading the board book of shapes to the baby, and then was overcome with curiosity. When he presented the baby with two pages at once, the little guy began to get agitated and make pre-crying noises. Quickly David turned the page and held one page in front of the baby. Disaster averted; happiness restored.

Third, pictures (just like words) can mean more than they say. He learns to read the emotions in the pictures. He sees that the baby in the picture is angrily pushing the cereal bowl away, or eating happily, and he gets a sense of what is happening.

> **TIP: Find out what art excites your baby. If he's mobile or can sit up and grab, line up two or three strikingly different books at the same distance from him. Which one does he go for first: the colorful or the black-and-white? Busy or simple? (This is going to work best at home, rather than in a new and distracting environment like the library or a bookstore.)**

Behind the Scenes: The Elements of Children's Book Art

Understanding a few basic elements of art can enrich the experience of reading with your child and help you enjoy watching him entering the world of visual communication. You'll see how much the artists' choice of elements such as style, color, and point of view help your baby to read and understand the story better. These are the specifics of visual literacy and they appear whether the artist works in watercolor, collages, cartoons, photographs, drawings, or constructed interactive pop-ups / lift-the-flaps.

Artists use line, color, shape, and space as tools. These elements operate in every piece of artwork, including your child's scribbles. With the exception of color, it's difficult to isolate these elements—lines create shapes that define space. But it's the principles created by the combined elements—balance, spatial relations, emphasis, and patterns—that your baby is absorbing with every picture he examines. Every book he looks at, from picture books to cloth books to books shaped like dinosaurs, will establish and reinforce these basic principles.

TIP: Encourage your child to pick a favorite color among the many in a really colorful book, and don't press him to make the same choice every time. Why did he choose that color today? How do you know it's his favorite and not your choice for him?

Visual Elements and Principles

- Color: All colors are mixed from three primaries: red, blue, and yellow, shaded by the addition of black or tinted by adding white.
- Line: A line is the track made by a point moving in space.
- Shape: Wherever the ends of a continuous line meet, a shape is formed.
- Space: Space can be two-dimensional, three-dimensional, negative (as in background space, or the space between the legs of a chair), or positive (the chair itself).
- Balance: The arrangement of the lines, shapes, and colors on the page creates (or intentionally avoids) a balanced scene.
- Emphasis / Spatial Relationships: The eye of the viewer will focus first on an area of emphasis or center of interest. Includes perspective, proportions, and positional placing of objects in a picture.
- Pattern / Rhythm: Repeated shapes, lines, or colors create movement and rhythm in a composition.

Color

Color is both the most obvious and the most commonly discussed element of visual literacy. Every parent likes to name colors and teach them to their babies. Color saturates most board books and picture books. Bright color focuses the eye and mind.

Babies, toddlers, and two-year-olds all respond to colors and enjoy making some personal interpretation about them. For example, Molly Bang's eponymous ball in *Yellow Ball* (unfortunately out of print) stands out on every page as it travels from one family's beach game out to sea and into the arms of a new welcoming child. The color helps convey an emotion: we root for the bright ball in the actively whirling dark and scary ocean storm. In making her ball yellow, Ms. Bang communicates something wholesome and hopeful. The ball is a glowing orb and a comforting companion. Yellow is a color of happy contentment. A violet ball would make a very different story.

Dark colors in books for very young children are much less common. Books like *Owl Babies*, in blacks, grays, and blues, stand out on the shelves and in the readers' minds. The blues and blacks of the night surround the artist Patrick Benson's white baby owls, and heighten a feeling of anxiety they experience over their mother's absence. These "dark" books aren't necessarily somber or ominous, but the use of darker colors does effectively enhance the mood of the story and contrasts strongly with most other books for kids.

Colorful Books and Books about Color

Books about colors are common, which only makes the uncommonly good ones stand out all the more.

- *Cat's Colors*, Jane Cabrera. This is a cat's colorful search for its favorite color, with enough story line to help grown-up readers go through color choices cheerfully.
- *Color Dance*, Ann Jonas. Four young children in colored leotards dance with joyous abandon, using colored scarves to demonstrate how colors mix.
- *Colores de la vida: Mexican Folk Art Colors in English and Spanish*, Cynthia Weill, folk artists from Oaxaca (illus.). A lovely bilingual exploration of color through a rainbow of wood sculptures created by amazing artists from Mexico.

- *Color Farm*, Lois Ehlert. This board book employs shapes and cutouts in bright colors to create the animals, all with the same bright green eye (created by a cutout to the back page of the book). See also *Color Zoo*.
- *Frederick*, Leo Lionni. While most of the mice scurry about collecting food for the approaching winter, Frederick gathers intangibles like sunrays, colors, and words. His word pictures nourish the downcast mice with warmth and imagination during the dark season. Winner of a Caldecott Honor.
- *Is It Red? Is It Yellow? Is It Blue?*, Tana Hoban. Vibrant photographs capture everyday colorful things seen in the city.
- *Mouse Paint*, Ellen Stoll Walsh. Three white mice hop, mix, and splash dance in their color puddles, mixing new colors as they move. For other concepts, see *Mouse Shapes* and *Mouse Count*.
- *My Colors, My World / Mis colores, mi mundo*, Maya Christina Gonzalez. Desert dweller Maya explores her colorful world, from Papi's black hair to Mami's orange and purple flowers. In Spanish and English.
- *Shades of People*, Shelley Rotner, Sheila Kelley. In accessible language and striking photography, Rotner and Kelley explore the many different colors people come in.
- *Spot the Animals: A Lift-the-Flap Book of Colors*, American Museum of Natural History, Steve Jenkins (illus.). With sturdy flaps, explore the exquisite colors of the natural world in Jenkins's stunning collage.
- *Why Is Blue Dog Blue?*, George Rodrigue. "Artists don't have to paint things the way they really are."

Line

A line is where a drawing starts. Lines, beginning with one dot, lead our eyes and define the shape. The lines can be thick or thin, curved, broken, or wavy, and appear in any color. They can outline a form or create a landscape or a nose in a single stroke.

Featured Book

Harold and the Purple Crayon
Crockett Johnson

In this delightful book by author / illustrator Crockett Johnson, line is everything. Harold draws a thick purple line that becomes each landscape—a tree, the ocean, the city. This line has held the attention of generations of children as Harold draws—and lives— anything he can imagine. Maybe Harold reminds us all that simple creativity can add a lot to life. If you can draw a moon, you need never walk without moonlight.

Line is the foundation of everything: art, design, and alphabet. A child's first drawings are all lines: round scribbles, dark zigzags up and down the page. Later the lines become things, and later still they form letters, words, and full-blown illustrated manuscripts.

What is the impact of line on the readers? We know that line directs our attention and defines the image. But the quality of the line also affects our feelings about the images and pictures. Some lines make us feel the solidity of an object or activity of the person. A character's body sitting stiffly erect, with thick straight balanced lines, conveys one thing; curvy and lightly drawn lines convey another. Angled eyebrow lines show surprise or happiness or anger or fear. Is the character seemingly drawn with a few lines, in a fluid don't-take-the-pencil-off-the-paper way, or are there lots of scratches that might create a feeling of hyperactivity? Line, like color, can carry emotional weight.

Shape

Shapes help us organize our world. Wherever the ends of a continuous line meet, a shape is formed. Shapes come, well, in all shapes: circular, oval,

Featured Book

How Do Dinosaurs Say Goodnight?
Jane Yolen, Mark Teague (illus.)

When ordinary suburban human parents try to tuck their enormous darlings into bed, they need LOTS of room. The artist uses skewed and dramatic perspectives to incorporate the huge dinosaurs that soar up to their ceilings, dwarf their beds, and tower over their shrimpy parents.

square, triangular, and amorphic, which is a non-geometric free-form. Geometric shapes such as circles, triangles, or squares have perfect, uniform measurements and don't often appear in nature. Organic shapes are associated with things from the natural world, like plants and animals.

One fun feature of shapes is that they can become tangible. You can do more than just put them on paper. You can cut them out, hold them in your hand, and share them. Shapes put boundaries on things. It's a way of organizing our world, and recognizing things that are similar and those that are different. And of course, letters are shapes. If children play and have experience with a variety of shapes, it will be easier for them to learn to read.

Why else do we enjoy teaching our children about shapes? Like colors, geometric shapes offer something clear to learn, and there are lots of books (and apps, too, in abundance) to help teach them. It's even more fun to spot the shapes in the books you already have: the round wheel, the rectangular windows.

Books themselves often have interesting shapes or are quite small. Think of those board books of snowmen or puppies. These are generally small enough to be held easily by a baby or toddler. Beatrix Potter designed small books for small hands about one hundred years ago. The shape was classic, the size was not, and it changed the world of books forevermore.

Shapely Favorites

- *Changes, Changes*, Pat Hutchins. This forty-year-old (and counting!) favorite wordless book tells a tale of family hardships and affection by shifting shapes into houses and fire engines.
- *Little Cloud*, Eric Carle. Clouds transform into a plane, a shark, and a clown, and then back into a cloud among clouds.
- *Lots of Dots*, Craig Frazier. A delightful exploration of all the places and things in which dots and circles can be found.
- *My Heart Is Like a Zoo*, Michael Hall. Hall creates an amazing number of animals by using only one main shape: a heart.
- *Round Is a Mooncake: A Book of Shapes*, Roseanne Thong, Grace Lin (illus.). This concept book brings in an Asian sensibility for shaped items and begs us to look around to find circles, triangles, and squares of our own. For an exploration of color, try Thong and Lin's *Red Is a Dragon*.
- *Shape by Shape*, Suse MacDonald. In a fun guessing game, each turn of the page reveals another shape and another section of a dinosaur that is slowly being revealed.
- *Shapes, Shapes, Shapes*, Tana Hoban. Real objects are photographed as the round, square, and triangular—and fun—objects they are.

Space, Balance, and Perspective

For the most part, we all find pleasure in balance. Symmetry is our default setting, and we gain a measure of assured comfort when things conform to our expectations. Babies quickly begin to recognize balance or the lack of it. They'll spot a table with only three and a half legs or a fishbowl balancing on an umbrella and recognize the problem long before they can put words to it.

But asymmetry can be remarkably effective. A slide is a slide, and fun, partly because it's a line on a diagonal, or spiral. A swing at rest is a stable, squared-off shape, but becomes thrilling when moving in an arc. Drawings use balance—or its absence—to engage our emotions so we feel that the character is safe or in danger depending on the pitch of the line.

"At two and a half, Sam is fascinated by airplanes: real ones, toy ones, books, pictures. As he talks about them, it's clear he's struggling to grasp perspective. He points to the picture of the plane about to take off and exclaims, 'It's too big to fly!' On the next page, as the plane recedes into the distant clouds, he tells me, 'See, it has to get little to go up up up in the air!' Later, as a passenger in a real plane, he tells me that we are 'getting littler' as we take off. I explained, but I don't think I changed his mind." —KJ

Think of an empty room. Where do you place the things to maximize the space? Do you pile all the stuff into one corner of the room, or balance things out pleasingly and artfully? The same problem confronts every artist who starts with a blank page.

In general, artists help the baby readers to focus on the one or two important visuals as they read through the book by using and defining space—leaving the background blank, for example, or filling it with a familiar or unfamiliar scene. In her Max and Ruby board books, Rosemary Wells focuses on the characters and important props. The background is just a colored page—negative space that isn't Max, or a bathtub. In her picture books for older toddlers and preschoolers, Ms. Wells elaborates Ruby and Max's background with patterned wallpaper, sofas, and kitchen cabinets—and takes up the whole page.

Dr. Seuss focuses on the characters without much identifying background information, and, in doing so, he skews both balance and perspective. We get the feeling of slight anarchy, even in the simplest *Hop on Pop*. Most Seussean background is white with the characters not needing any particular location. If location is key, it's sized and shaped to suit the scene. A huge train can balance on a tiny, precarious track without concerning the characters at all—although it may concern some readers!

One librarian said she hated the work of Dr. Seuss when she was a child. She liked knowing what things really were. She liked order. Dr. Seuss's worlds seemed chaotic and messy. Anything could and did happen, and she was unable to enjoy his wit. It took years before she understood how other children adored his slip-slapping, pop-hopping, witty art and rhyme.

Artists employ tricks to make things appear to be smaller (or less important) the farther away they are from us. The artist reveals her point of view by placing the objects in the picture frame. One look at Vera B. Williams's lucky babies in *"More More More," Said the Baby* proves the point. Those babies are clearly VIP STARS, and it's not hard to guess Ms. Williams's point of view about the centrality of babies.

Perspective also tells us many things about the relationship of the characters. Who's up close, and what's farther away? Which one is the king or the important character? The artist's perspective can shift us into unexpected places, as in Jon Muth's retelling of *Stone Soup*, where the reader sees all the villagers peering down at her from around the rim of the soup pot. Grasping the picture is a real leap for a child, who may at first be mystified by the perspective from inside the pot.

> **TIP: Have your toddler or older child write and illustrate a book to be read to a new baby. He can dictate the words of the story to you (and even get your help with some drawings) or just read it from his own pictures. No matter where the book stands on the "art" spectrum, baby will be thrilled by so much attention from a big sib.**

Pattern, Rhythm, and Movement

You probably think of rhythm in connection with poems and songs, but what about in art? Pictures have rhythm, and movement, too. The artist creates motion by repeating shapes, lines, or colors. An undulating line suggests movement and flow, like a wave on the shore. Curves and arcs suggest movement, too. As a whole, each picture moves you through the story, or setting, or time.

Patterns are repeated in alternating rhythms of color, texture, shape, or images. "Cumulative" books, which repeat the same pattern of animals and dialogue on each page with a slight variation, are great examples of pattern that appears in both words and pictures. "There Was an Old Woman Who Swallowed a Fly" is an exemplary cumulative song. The predictable pattern is both comforting and empowering—the youngest reader can figure out what to expect.

Cumulative Books that Take Us Along for the Ride

Cumulative stories repeat an element that has come before in the text until there is a long list of characters, props, or actions. Think *The House that Jack Built*. They can be fun, if sometimes exhausting, to read aloud. Their repetition make them ideal for toddlers mastering new words and the cause-and-effect nature of storytelling.

- *The Bridge Is Up!*, Babs Bell, Rob Hefferan (illus.). A raised drawbridge plus a growing line of vehicles with animal drivers equals a delightful read-aloud for your car and truck lover(s).
- *The Cazuela that the Farm Maiden Stirred*, Samantha R. Vamos, Rafael López (illus). In this tale seasoned with Spanish words, a farm maiden and some animals prepare *arroz con leche*. Recipe included.

- *The Doorbell Rang*, Pat Hutchins. The doorbell rings and brings more and more friends coming to share delicious cookies. The Spanish edition is *Llaman a la puerta*.
- *Drummer Hoff*, Barbara Emberley, Ed Emberley (illus.). In a farcical romp, a motley brigade of soldiers assembles and sets off a cannon. Emberley's stylized, colorful, and 1968 Caldecott-winning art still sings.
- *The House that Jack Built*, Jenny Stow. This version of the famous cumulative nursery rhyme uses the Caribbean as a backdrop.
- *Jump, Frog, Jump!*, Robert Kalan, Byron Barton (illus.). A frog attempts to nab a fly without being captured itself. *¡Salta, ranita, salta!* is the Spanish version.
- *Move Over, Rover!*, Karen Beaumont, Jane Dyer (illus.). Rover's doghouse is overrun by his animal neighbors, including a skunk, during a thunderstorm. Winner of a Theodor Seuss Geisel Honor.
- *Mr. Gumpy's Motor Car*, John Burningham. The children and various animals pile into the car with the kindly Mr. Gumpy, and although, as we say when each animal gets in, it's a squash, all goes well until it starts to rain, and every animal has a reason not to get out and push.
- *The Noisy Counting Book*, Susan Schade, Jon Buller. A young boy's fishing expedition builds to a noisy crescendo as various animals show off their vocalizations. The board book is a condensed version of the longer, out of print first edition, but it still sings as a read aloud.
- *Oh, Look!*, Patricia Polacco. When three goats escape their pen and head for the fair, every page brings a new obstacle to overcome in this clever take on the "Going on a Bear Hunt" rhyme.
- *When the Elephant Walks*, Keiko Kasza. This cumulative story reveals we're all afraid of something. The bear scares the crocodile, and the crocodile scares the wild hog, and so it goes.

"My two-year-old Dylan keeps making me turn the page before I'm finished with the words. He's just finished with that picture. It's like he's reading to a different rhythm. I do my best to work with him and follow the story so that we can still enjoy reading together." —Denise

The Art of...Enjoying the Art

Art is enriching, constant, and comforting. While every picture contains certain familiar elements, looking at each new image offers an opportunity for endless imaginings. Taking in whatever is there to see is the baby's whole experience at that moment, his immediate reality. He studies every element on the page, both entering into and taking things out of the artist's world. Adults are quick to turn the page or get the babies to help to do it. Slow down! He's still looking, drinking in the sights and absorbing the information. Although we can't be sure what he thinks of the picture, we have evidence that he's responding. How do we know? Does your child return to a particular picture time and again? Does he smile? Does he lean in to go nose to nose with the character, stroke the pet, or even mimic the character's face? Or wave his arms in excitement when shown a picture of a cow?

For you, a new appreciation of art can make reading together more fun. You'll begin to recognize certain artists. KJ's husband spotted Ian Falconer's style (*Olivia*) immediately on a cover of *The New Yorker*. You may even pick up some technique. Soon enough, your child is going to be begging you to draw pictures for him. It's nice if you can create a recognizable dog. At the very least, trying to figure out what makes Helen Oxenbury's round baby faces with dot eyes and line smiles so much more charming than yours might occupy you during your fourteenth reading of *Goodnight, Baby*.

Talking to the Artist: Lois Ehlert

My mother used to read the same book to all three of us kids. So in the books I create, I try to extend the age levels up and down so that every reader gets something. A beginning reader, for instance, might just read the large text, and an advanced reader might read the subtext or little labels, which have more complicated words. I try to make sure they don't get bored. The really little ones can read the pictures.

I also love music; I love the sounds of the human voice. Although I started out being an artist, I am always conscious of how the words sound, and the rhythm of the sentence structure. I make sure that I lay out the design so it does not break the line for the person reading aloud.

For example, *Feathers for Lunch* features a woodpecker. Not only are some words and labels written in red but so are the sounds important to the story, like the *jingle jingle* of the cat's bell. In one place the woodpecker is pecking on the tree looking for ants, and I have four or five ants walking up the dark bark offering little surprises to test children's visual literacy.

Children don't always want to reread a book. If they only read it once, there's something not quite right.

Great Books for Making Art with Your Baby and Toddler

Your child's first art experiences are going to be all about exploration. Don't worry about masterpieces to hang on the refrigerator just yet. It is all about getting the feel (and sometimes the taste) of the art materials. Not sure how to get started? Let these books be your guide.

- *First Art for Toddlers and Twos: Open-Ended Art Experiences*, MaryAnn F. Kohl, Renee Ramsey, Dana Bowman
- *The Little Hands Art Book: Exploring Arts and Crafts with 2-to-6-year-olds*, Judy Press, Loretta Trezzo (illus.)

- *Mudworks: Creative Clay, Dough, and Modeling Experiences*, MaryAnn F. Kohl
- *Young at Art: Teaching Toddlers Self-Expression, Problem-Solving Skills, and an Appreciation for Art*, Susan Striker

TIP: Try an app for art. There are dozens of apps out there that allow you or a child to draw on a tablet or smartphone. Choose the simplest—just lines and color if you can—and take turns making lines of varying colors and width on the screen, or play "Pictionary" with an older child who can guess what you're drawing, and take a turn at doing the same.

Great Books about Kids Making Art

- *The Dot*, Peter H. Reynolds. "I can't do it" becomes "I'm an artist" when a simple dot, treated like a masterpiece, inspires more. Winner of an Irma Black Award Honor. See *Ish* and *Sky Color* also by Reynolds.
- *Go to Bed, Monster!*, Natasha Wing, Sylvie Kantorovitz (illus.). When Lucy can't sleep, she draws a monster who jumps off the page to become a rambunctious playmate.
- *Harold and the Purple Crayon*, Crockett Johnson. Fueled by imagination, Harold and his purple crayon are going places. The other adventures of Harold (*Harold's Fairy Tale*, *Harold's Trip to the Sky*) are fun, but the first one is the best.
- *I Ain't Gonna Paint No More!*, Karen Beaumont, David Catrow (illus.). When her son paints every bit of the house, Mama declares that he ain't gonna paint no more…but with wild colorful splatters and the gradual obliteration of any white space on the page, he proves her wrong on a new canvas, painting part of his body.
- *Jeremy Draws a Monster*, Peter McCarty. When Jeremy creates a very demanding monster out of his artistic skills, the creature becomes a menace. See also *The Monster Returns*.

Featured Book

A Good Day
Kevin Henkes

The inviting cover artwork radiates pleasure, joy, and satisfaction. There is a set of orderly squares, with animals that flow into a circle. It doesn't matter where your eye takes you first: the yellow bird leads to the white dog leads to the brown squirrel leads to the orange fox. And squarely in the middle is A GOOD DAY. There is color and movement. The four animals seem to be smiling in closed-eye happiness. It's a promising start.

However, opposite a page of brightly colored lines, the first page is a bold downer: It was a bad day... Each of the featured animals experiences a loss. Henkes draws each animal in a side-view with an expressive, simple semicircle eyebrow over a wide eye registering the sadness. We feel empathic, and concerned. We've lost things, too! The text on the left page is simple and clear; the illustration on the right page shows the loss as it happens in nature.

But then...Now, again opposite a page of brightly colored lines, the losses are gains. Things are found, even better than before. Life is improved so much that the little eye of each animal is squeezed closed in exquisite joy. Do the colorful stripes signify all of us in the natural world, animals and people, too? The structure flips, too: the now joyous illustrations are on the right and the text on the left. Aided by Mr. Henkes's pen, we too have switched our orientation to the world. Left is right; down is up!

And then there's more. A free-spirited little girl dances with a beautiful newfound feather. She, like the bird / dog / squirrel / fox, is liberated. She finds a gift in nature; she's part of the circle of life. It's a very good day.

Beautiful Books for Sharing
Showcasing the Elements

These are books that focus on one or more of the individual elements of art: shape and color, line and balance. They tend to be on the simpler side but should remain relevant as your baby grows into a toddler and beyond.

- *Barnyard Banter*, Denise Fleming. Fleming's unique pulp painting medium holds the reader on every page. It's one of the best noisy animal books ever, with a remarkable textural quality.
- *Ben's Trumpet*, Rachel Isadora. Brilliant use of line. The young boy and all the language surrounding him perfectly reflect the zigzag rhythm of this jazzy story in black and white. A Caldecott Honor book.
- *Black Meets White*, Justine Fontes, Geoff Waring (illus.). Imagine creating a book about the colors black and white, and making their relationship entertaining and instructive. The final interactive pull-tab is a stroke of genius.
- *The Day the Babies Crawled Away*, Peggy Rathmann. A preschooler chases the escaping babies at a picnic with the illustrations presented almost entirely in silhouette. Cool and fascinating.
- *It Looked Like Spilt Milk*, Charles G. Shaw. Bold white clouds on bright blue sky suggest shapes of known and inventive creatures and things.
- *The Little, Little Girl with the Big, Big Voice*, Kristen Balouch. A little girl with a booming voice scares away the jungle animals, until she meets a roaring lion. Balouch has a unique color palette and graphic sensibility.
- *Look-Alikes Jr.*, Joan Steiner. This artist uses small found objects from various rooms in the house to create the rooms in miniature, prompting you and your child to spot a bed built with crayons and pasta and other tiny eye-teasers. Try also *Look-Alikes*.

- *Monkey and Me*, Emily Gravett. Gravett perfectly captures the energy and enthusiasm of a young girl and her stuffed monkey companion imitating all the animals she encountered on a trip to the zoo.
- *Mouse Mess*, Linnea Riley. A little mouse with the munchies leaves behind a huge mess. Package labels and other letters and words throughout the art add to Riley's visual experience.
- *Noah's Ark*, Lucy Cousins. Cousins (of "Maisy" fame) offers her trademark childlike drawings, bright colors, and patterns to spark up a familiar story.
- *Owen's Marshmallow Chick*, Kevin Henkes. Owen, a delightful line-drawing of a mouse, gets an equally delightful and colorful Easter basket and makes a friend out of the candy chick.
- *Rap a Tap Tap: Here's Bojangles—Think of That!*, Leo and Diane Dillon. With graphic and energetic page spreads, the Dillons, very simply, tell the life story of tap dance legend Bill "Bojangles" Robinson. Winner of a Coretta Scott King Award Honor.
- *Rosie's Walk*, Pat Hutchins. Hutchins's famous hen outsmarts a fox in perfectly complementary designs and colors. Broad, almost physical humor for all.
- *Seven Blind Mice*, Ed Young. In Young's Caldecott Honor-winning retelling of an Indian fable, seven blind mice visit different parts of an elephant and argue about what it could be. While some of the concepts may be ones your child will grow into, the art is a wonderful first lesson in color and design. *Siete ratones ciegos* in Spanish.
- *The Squiggle*, Carole Lexa Schaefer. A found red ribbon becomes a dragon and a thundercloud for a group of imaginative schoolchildren. Sparse, simple illustrations become richer in the imagined scenes.
- *Swimmy*, Leo Lionni. One black fish in a sea of red fish beckons readers into a remarkable, and meaningful, underwater world.
- *Ten Black Dots*, Donald Crews. What can you do with ten black

dots? Animals, vegetables, and minerals are all represented. Ten black dots are there too for the counting.

- *That's Good! That's Bad!*, Margery Cuyler, David Catrow (illus.). When a boy at the zoo gets a balloon, that's good. When the balloon carries him away, that's bad—and so on in this wild tale of adventure, illustrated with dramatic close-ups and wide-angle drawings for a lesson in perspective.

- *Who Hops?*, Katie Davis. Birds fly. Bats fly. Flies fly. Rhinos fly. NO THEY DON'T! Hilarious, with great use of line, borders, and balance as the animals move across the pages (or don't, in the case of the rhino). The bilingual Spanish / English edition is *Who Hops? / ¿Quién salta?*

Bringing It All Together

These books are full of images you could hang on the wall.

- *All the World*, Liz Garton Scanlon, Marla Frazee (illus.). A poetic exploration, both visually and textually, of our interconnected world. A Caldecott Honor winner.

- *Big Momma Makes the World*, Phyllis Root, Helen Oxenbury (illus.). Oxenbury gets an enlarged story to illustrate here but draws the same bold characters in colorful adventurous activities. It's a great creation myth, as well. Winner of Boston Globe-Horn Book Award.

- *Birds*, Kevin Henkes, Laura Dronzek (illus.). The narrator is fascinated by the variety of colors of birds she sees out her window. Dronzek's paintings are beautiful in their simplicity. Try Helen V. Griffith's *Moonlight*, also illustrated by Dronzek.

- *Close Your Eyes*, Kate Banks, Georg Hallensleben (illus.). Bright watercolors, softly smudged, with few defining lines create a hypnotic bedtime story as a mother tiger reassures her little one about the world of sleep. *Cierra los ojos* in Spanish. The other titles by this team are also lovely.

- *George Shrinks*, William Joyce. Lively, bright, and an amazing adventure in perspective as George tries to complete his chores in spite of being the size of a salt shaker.
- *The House in the Night*, Susan Marie Swanson, Beth Krommes (illus). Swanson and Krommes together have created poetry in both words and images that explore light, love, and home in the striking color palette of black, white, and gold. A Caldecott Award winner for 2009.
- *Machines Go to Work*, William Low. With fun gate-fold pages, Low has authored a book about trucks, boats, helicopters, and trains with gorgeous art created on a computer (you'd swear they were oil paintings, though). Also *Machines Go to Work in the City*.
- *Mufaro's Beautiful Daughters*, John Steptoe. Everything in this African Cinderella story looks realistic and informative, and as personal as if it were a family's artistic scrapbook. This Caldecott Honor winner is a little long for most twos, but your child will grow into it. *Las bellas hijas de Mufaro* in Spanish.
- *Polar Bear Night*, Lauren Thompson, Stephen Savage (illus.). Pastels and soft colors contrast with the defined, linocut style in this story of a baby polar bear's gentle nighttime adventure. A *New York Times* Best Illustrated Children's Book. The sequel is *Polar Bear Morning*.
- *A Sick Day for Amos McGee*, Philip C. Stead, Erin E. Stead (illus.). A zookeeper gets a much-needed, get-well-soon visit from the animals in his care. Stead's Caldecott-winning drawings are winsome and charming.
- *Stone Soup*, Jon J. Muth. Muth's watercolors pull the reader right into the small Chinese village, where the buildings have almost as much character as the people. The sparse Asian style is a revelation to those used to busy American children's art and eases the transition to a longer—and more abstract—story.
- *Two Little Trains*, Margaret Wise Brown, Leo and Diane Dillon

(illus.). In the Dillons' first real book for preschoolers, they create dynamic parallels painting a powerful real train and a child's toy train moving along. There is a feeling of motion in a slightly old-fashioned and yet timeless spaciousness.

Ages and Stages: Art Activities with Readers 0–3

Newborn	Show and Tell: She'll watch and listen to whatever you show and tell. Show: Draw some good fat lines with a marker or crayon. Tell: Talk about colors, shapes, and pictures or anything else you see.
Heads Up	He might be able to hold a fat crayon, although unable to do much with it. Help him to make a mark. Talk about the colors of the things he's holding close. Give him colored paper to crumple.
Sitting	Smearing food might lead to finger paints, or just a mess. He might (like KJ's Sam) have hysterics over his dirty hand. Make a handprint in clay or play dough. Make or buy large shape magnets for the refrigerator or a metal door. Try to make sure they're easy to pull off and on!
Crawling / Creeping	Cut a series of objects in a single color out of magazines and tape them onto cards for added sturdiness. Hand him a series of blue objects to look at and hear about! (If you do several colors and the cards survive, later you can mix them up, lay them out, and use them for "pick something blue.") Invent a point-to or choose-a-shape game.

Cruising / Walking	Play a color-match game with a book. Try one that's focused on color, like one with a different color on every page. Give him a few (two or three) colored squares to choose from and see if he can make a match.
	Make some play dough. Break off some of the flour-white lump and add drops of food dye to create blue, red, yellow, and green balls.
	Draw big shapes on paper that you can lay on the ground and help him to stand inside the triangle, the circle, or the square.
	Draw lines in the sand, lines in the dirt, lines in the snow, and use sticks, fingers, or feet.
Talking (a few words)	She'll love watching *you* try to draw in the style of a favorite book or character. Get the book out and try to come up with a simple but recognizable Max or Clifford, and let him color the results.
	Straws or pretzel sticks can make a line on the ground or along the table—a line, or a path, or a road.
	Play a version of I Spy to spot a color or shape, like where's the red book or where's the round book?
Talking More	With (a lot of) your help, he can make a collage caterpillar like the very hungry one. Cut out circles for him and stick double-sided tape on the back. Show him how they can overlap to form a caterpillar (and draw in eyes and antennae for him).
	Make "puppets" to act out a simple story. You cut out the shape (fish are nice and simple) and make stripes or dots with paper and double-sided tape for him to stick on. Then tape a straw to the back, leaving enough sticking out at the bottom to hold.

Talking More (cont'd)	Try drawing something he commonly requests, but leave the shape incomplete—a train with a gap in it—and see what he notices.
	Squeezable icing is good for drawing. Don't bother with a too-hard-to-squeeze decorative tip. Just take the cap off and squeeze it onto graham crackers. Edible art.
	Playfully change the colors of ordinary objects and see what happens. Draw pictures of the snowman in blue, or the refrigerator green, or the dachshund pink.
Running (but not talking much)	Let the artist stand up. Tape the paper to a wall or easel.
	Weather permitting, take the activities and chalks outdoors.
	Gather a ball and a few small cars you don't mind getting dirty, and let him roll them through paint on paper and look at the lines that result.
	Play "go get the circle / square / triangle" with shapes you've made or found. Vary it by making them in different colors and asking for the red triangle, or the blue circle.
Talking ALL THE TIME!	Have him dictate a story to you. Then one or both of you draw and color the pictures. Write out his words exactly and then punch holes in the book and tie it together with yarn.
	Get a new picture book, and have him tell you the story from reading the pictures. Write it down and read it back to him.
	Talk a little about style—this artist used paper to make these pictures, this one drew, this one painted. When he draws or paints or pastes paper, remind him of favorite books where the technique is the same.

Talking ALL THE TIME! (cont'd)

Have a "shape meal." Cut sandwiches into circles, serve wagon wheel pasta, round cookies, etc. A variant could be to have a "color clothes day."

Play color-spotters anywhere and everywhere. Ask him what color things are now, before he has a firm idea of what color they *should* be. The sky may be white or gray today, and the grass blue. Take a look—he's probably right.

Using balloon stickers, he can draw the strings. Using train stickers, he can draw a line for the track and another for the smoke.

Chapter Six
INTERACTIVE BOOKS MAKE READING "SENSATIONAL"

Babies "read" with their eyes, mouth, nose, fingers, and ears. Physical interactive books put a sensory-filled world easily within baby's grasp. (Their digital counterparts are discussed in chapter 8.) Their textures, flaps, pop-ups, and pull-tabs offer children a chance to reach in and physically engage with them. For babies, the activities are simple: touch the cloth puppy, lift the flap, look in the mirror, feel the bumpy rubber corner with finger or tongue. This is truly the beginning of reading, and it's sensational. In fact all reading is interactive: nothing happens until you turn the page.

Toddlers and twos get wheels to spin and tabs to pull. Pages come in different shapes and sizes or with holes revealing a glimpse of what comes next. Pop-ups in their simplest form can work for an older baby and then, becoming gradually more complex, delight all ages. Some books are devoted entirely to touchable textures or pop-up surprises, but many combine all of these elements for a fully three-dimensional experience. Interactive books are usually favorites for every age.

Hardworking Books for Hardworking Babies

The importance of touch and feel to an infant cannot be overemphasized. Being held, stroked, snuggled, and swaddled helps her feel secure and valued.

Touching, for her, is also an act of discovery. She can use her own sense of touch to explore everything else that's out there. As soon as she can see it, she's going to want to touch it. Have you ever seen a baby trying to pick the paisleys up off a bedspread? One of the ways she learns that the apple on the page isn't real is by putting out her hand.

If It's Not Paper, It Won't Rip

There are plenty of books out there that invite your baby's touch. Cloth books are lightweight, indestructible, and easy for a baby to manipulate. Their soft format makes them nearly as cuddly as a favorite animal or blankie. They're great for distracting your baby on the changing pad or table. You'll see her wave the book about, "talk" to it, and perhaps even try to get it into her mouth to taste whether it's a good read or not. Anyone who's seen a baby grab a book and accidentally stick the corner into her eye can see the advantages of cloth.

Books made from other textures like rubber, foam, or plastic are toylike and bath friendly. Floating plastic tub books are great for a wider range of ages. Foam books, like the Soft Shapes books from Innovative KIDS, usually have removable pieces that become toys to act out the stories (there's even a train with tracks), or stick to tub walls. Try to put the pieces back in after every reading, or eventually there will be nothing left to read with.

All are good additions to a baby's world. Unlike stiff cardboard-paged board books, these books (especially cloth ones) can be floppy, and some-times hard to read. But they are useful.

Susan has a flea market treasure: a one-hundred-seven-year-old cloth book manufactured in 1905 by Dean's Rag Books. The logo shows two dogs tearing away at the book, with the phrase "Quite Indestructible" underneath the tug-of-war. The images are still wonderfully clear after over a century, and the alphabet connections are full of story and poetry, although today's author might replace "G was a gamester who had but ill luck" or "U was an usher who loved little boys" with something a bit more politically correct.

Look, Mom, No Paper!
Books Made of Cloth, Plastic, Foam, and Beyond

Since the availability of specific titles changes regularly, you may find a different selection at your bookstore, baby store, or toy store (for obvious reasons, most of these books don't circulate from libraries). Just look for something you think you and your baby will enjoy. Here is a breakdown of what is available in the non-digital, paperless book world:

Cloth Books: Also called "rag books," these are usually made out of some kind of thick fabric or quilted material. Some have ties so you can hang the book from your baby's crib rail. Most just open like traditional books and some even have interactive flaps. Pros: Almost all are machine washable (but if it has something that makes a noise embedded in it, you may want to think twice) and quite cuddly. Cons: A little floppy when you try to read them with your child.

Plastic / Vinyl Books: With foam on the inside and plastic or vinyl on the outside, these books often have some kind of ocean / boat / water theme for bath play. They are also fun to use at the beach, in the pool, or at mealtimes. Don't buy used plastic books, since you want to make sure they are phthalate and BPA free. Pros: Easy to wipe down and great for distracting a fussy child in the bath. Cons: It can be tricky to dry each page of a wet plastic book when they all cling together. Also, companies are swearing their plastics are safe, but what will be the new chemical we have to worry about?

Foam Books: Both spongy and stiff, these books, which feel like they are made of very thick craft foam, really hold their shape. Pros: This format lends itself to a lot of interesting interactive elements, such as textures, pop-out puzzle pieces, and more. Cons: Your child WILL chew these books and the teeth marks won't disappear. If you have any qualms about synthetic substances in your child's mouth, try another format.

Tyvek © (or something like it): This stuff is a nontoxic "synthetic material made from flashspun high-density polyethylene fibers" (whew!) and is now being used for rip- and waterproof baby books. Think paperback board books. We can only find one publisher who uses this material ("Indestructibles"), but their wordless books with delightful art deserve a shout-out. Pros: They really are rip- and waterproof. They're very lightweight and great for travel. Cons: They will wrinkle.

Fuzzy Wuzzy Was a Book: Textures to Touch and Feel

Dragging your new baby's hand across a "bunny's" fur or a "chick's" feathers is a lovely feeling for you both. Each fur or feathery swatch prompts you to say something about it. What does it feel like? What do you tell your baby as she comes in contact with the velvety patch that stands for a cow's lips? A little piece of sandpaper that represents Daddy's scratchy face? A small rubbery bit that feels like a tractor's tire? Here's something an ebook or app simply cannot do.

You can find "touch and feel" books where the texture is inset into a page or glued on, or with textures sticking off the sides like tags. Foam books may come with different textures to rub. Any of these will probably serve to grab your baby's attention.

> **TIP: Many cloth books come with a hole or ring for attaching to the stroller, and there are some board books with clips attached. These are great for baby to look at on the go and allow you to jump in with a little reading at odd moments throughout the day.**

Babies love touch-and-feel books because they add another sensory element to reading. Parents love them because they give a busy baby something to do with her hands besides grabbing or pounding on the book you're holding! The best of these blend in the texture with the other art on the page.

Seven Fuzzy, Furry, Rough, and Smooth Books for Sticky Fingers

You'll likely want to buy your own copies, but many libraries *do* circulate touch-and-feel board books.

1. *Are You Ticklish? / ¿Tienes cosquillas?*, Sam McKendry, Melanie Mitchell (illus.), Laurie Young (designer). If these textured monkeys, zebras, and elephants are ticklish, are you? In Spanish and English.

2. *Fuzzy Fuzzy Fuzzy!: A Touch, Skritch, & Tickle Book*, Sandra Boynton. Lots of interesting textures on Boynton's signature characters. The duckling really is "incredibly soft."

3. *I Like Vegetables: A Touch and Feel Board Book*, Lorena Siminovich. The Petit Collage series includes some of the most artful touch-and-feel board books on the market with Siminovich's lovely patterned collage. Also try *I Like Bugs*, *I Like Fruit*, and *I Like Toys*, each focusing on a different concept.

4. *Pig-a-Boo!: A Farmyard Peekaboo Book*, Dorothea DePrisco, Treesha Runnells (illus.). With peekaboo flaps, silly animal sounds, and several soft textures, this one will grow with your child.

5. *Tails*, Matthew Van Fleet. Animals here have wonderful large and small tails to touch, feel, slide, and flip. Also try Van Fleet's *Heads*.

6. *Baby Touch and Feel Farm*, DK Publishing. All of the titles in this wonderful chunky board book series work for us. Good sturdy choices include *Pets*, *Wild Animals*, *Home*, *Dinosaur*, and *Fire Engine*.

7. *Touch and Feel Zoo*, DwellStudio. DwellStudio's simple, clean graphic images include large areas for tactile exploration. See also *Touch and Feel Farm* and *Touch and Feel Town*.

Dovid Pinchas's Top Ten

"My son, Dovid Pinchas, loves reading books! He enjoys turning the pages, so much so that I can't always finish reading the words! He loves just sitting by himself on the floor, browsing through the books in his collection, turning the pages, and ingesting / digesting the stories. At this time, there is no specific favorite, though he does like pushing the button in *My Little Noisy Book of Ducklings* to make it 'quack'!" —Chana

1. *Danny Duck Takes a Dive!*, Debbie Rivers-Moore, Nicola Morse (illus.) (out of print)
2. *Ten Little Ducklings*, Jenny Tulip (out of print)
3. *My Little Noisy Book of Ducklings*, Roger Priddy
4. *Gossie*, Olivier Dunrea
5. *Who Am I?*, Ruchy Schon, Ruchela Roth (illus.)
6. *Let's Go to Shul*, Rikki Benenfeld
7. *Boruch Learns About Pesach*, Rabbi Shmuel Kunda (out of print)
8. *Goodnight Moon*, Margaret Wise Brown, Clement Hurd (illus.)
9. *What Do You See? In Your Neighborhood*, Bracha Goetz
10. *What Do You See? At Home*, Bracha Goetz

Tote That Book, Lift That Flap

The simplest, most straightforward interactive book for a baby or younger toddler is the lift-the-flap. The flaps are an extension of peekaboo, the most congenial and universal game. Babies want to know what's in, under, or behind there. Their curiosity makes them want to know what's inside everything, whether it's a paper bag, closet door, or cat litter box. You can play peekaboo with any book, of course, opening and shutting its pages, but the flaps invite baby to experiment on her own.

Lift-the-flap books are also excellent conversation pieces. While your baby lifts flaps to help Spot look for his doggie bowl, you can talk with her about her guesses and her predictions. We love looking for Spot, especially when there's a surprise animal under the flap, like the penguin that answers "NO, he's not here. Try over there." How surreal. How funny. And

You'll Never Find a Used Copy of *Pat the Bunny* (Here's Why)

Pat the Bunny, by Dorothy Kunhardt, is both the original touch-and-feel book and still the most enduring. As popular today as when it was first published in 1940, the book appears in almost every baby's new library. What's so great about it? Why is it irresistible?

There they are, Paul and Judy, two old-fashioned children who can DO things. Judy can pat the bunny, play peekaboo, look in the mirror, feel Daddy's scratchy face, read her book, and wave bye-bye. Paul can smell the flowers and put his finger through Mummy's ring. All of these activities are in line with a baby's natural development. Best of all, Paul and Judy invite the baby to join them, to try it too, to have fun. Babies touch everything and develop the capacity to grab and hold things, like the books we're holding—and here is Judy's book, waiting to be seized. They crave applause, approval, and the bunny in Judy's book teaches them a winning trick. "How big is bunny?" "Soooooooooo big!" Bunny gestures outward with his ears and arms. "How big is baby?" a parent asks. "Soooo big!" gestures baby, stretching her arms wide, too. Applause. Delight. Again.

Real babies face a steady stream of people coming and going to attend to their needs, some of whom wave and say bye-bye. After smiling, waving bye-bye is one of baby's first sociable acts, and Paul and Judy wave bye-bye, too. But they can be brought back with just a flip of the page. Is there an element of nostalgia in *Pat the Bunny*'s continuing popularity? Of course. But your affection for it isn't what pulls out Judy's book, rips Mummy's ring, and yanks the peekaboo cloth right off of Paul. That's baby's job—and she's good at it. If she loves it to death, you may have to buy another copy.

how entertaining for a fifteen- to eighteen-month-old child who delights in saying "no" herself. Once the animal or object is found, there's no end to the discussion you can have with very little toddlers about it. These discussions, which allow the child to become a teller of the story, are an early form of what academics call Dialogic Reading, one of the cornerstones of literacy.

Nine Books of Flaps for Lifting

1. *Dear Zoo: A Lift-the-Flap Book*, Rod Campbell. When a child writes to the zoo to request a pet, a series of animals are sent, flaps are opened, and creatures are rejected as too big, too tall, too fierce, until the perfect pet arrives. It's great fun.

2. *Eggs 1 2 3: Who Will the Babies Be?*, Janet Halfmann, Betsy Thompson (illus.). Lift the flaps to discover what will hatch out of each egg. A great flap and first science book for sophisticated twos and threes.

3. *Fuzzy Yellow Ducklings*, Matthew Van Fleet. A nice combination of touchable textures and flaps.

4. *Good Morning Toucan*, DwellStudio. With inviting graphics and sturdy flaps, various rain forest animals wake up with the sun. Also try *Goodnight Owl*.

5. *I Say, You Say Animal Sounds!*, Tad Carpenter. A delightfully interactive and rambunctious read-aloud where youngsters supply the animal sound effects as they open the flaps. *I Say, You Say Opposites!* is also available.

6. *Spot's First Walk*, Eric Hill. Spot sets out into the neighborhood, and both he and the reader discover several surprises under each flap. If your child loves Spot, there are many more titles available both with and without flaps.

7. *Tuck Me In!*, Dean Hacohen, Sherry Scharschmidt. The reader uses various colorful flaps to tuck in an assortment of baby animals. An inventive delight.

8. *Where Is Baby's Belly Button?*, Karen Katz. This is a bestseller for babies and toddlers because it is really well constructed, entertaining, and leads directly to knowing body parts like belly button, eyes, and hands. Try also Katz's *Where Is Baby's Mommy?* and *Toes, Ears & Nose* (this one's written by Marion Dane Bauer). All three titles are available in *Baby's Box of Fun: A Karen Katz Lift-the-Flap Gift Set*.

9. *Where Is Maisy?*, Lucy Cousins. Maisy is bright, simple, and charming, and Cousins's questioning flaps invite answers. For more of the same, try *Where Are Maisy's Friends?*, *Where Does Maisy Live?*, and *Where Is Maisy's Panda?*

Paper Engineering: Pulls, Pop-Ups, and Whirl-a-Ma-Jigs for Toddlers and Up

Interactive books for toddlers and twos require even more participation of the reader. She must figure out what's expected—pull the tab? Push it? Move it around on the page? Wheels and pulls and levers beg to be touched or tugged. Paper pop-up structures burst from the page. Books that engage multiple senses draw the older baby or toddler in and make reading even more of an adventure.

Tabs and Tugs for Busy Fingers

Books with tabs to pull, wheels to turn, or paper levers to shift are ideal for the curious toddler or two-year-old. Even more than pop-ups, these books, like lift-the-flaps, require reader interaction. Moving the outstretched tab makes the windshield wipers move; lifting the flap moves a passenger in and out of the bus door. It's like magic.

These books offer the excitement of making something happen and provide bonus lessons in the areas of manual dexterity and patience. The tabs and wheels can be frustratingly difficult at first and then too floppy to have much effect unless they're handled just right. The desire to get it right is so strong, the risks—a ripped book, a bent page—bearable, but still there. It makes the book and the reading experience just a little more special when there's something at stake, however small it may seem to you. Maybe because they're almost like toys, maybe just because they're full of thrills and surprises, these books are often favorites, and reading them is even more of a treat.

"I'm reading to my nephew of eleven months every opportunity I get. He has specific favorites even now. One of them is a lift-the-flap Maisy book. Now when he reads a regular board book, he grabs at the pages searching for the flap." —Rachel

Books to Engage Nimble Fingers

- *Farm Animals (Magic Color Book)*, Louisa Sladen, Luana Rinaldo (illus.). Pull the heavy, thick tabs to help the farm animals reveal their colors. Several more available in the series.
- *Hop, Skip, and Jump, Maisy!: A Maisy First Science Book*, Lucy Cousins. Maisy demonstrates running, stretching, and jumping while other animals show off their moves as well. A very simple introduction to movement and the tabs and other moveable parts are so much fun. (Also try *Maisy's Wonderful Weather Book*.)
- *Knick-Knack Paddywhack!*, Paul O. Zelinsky. Zelinsky illustrates the classic nonsense song, with plenty of details and fun movement. The paper engineering in this *New York Times* Best Illustrated Children's Book is breathtaking.
- *Moo*, Matthew Van Fleet. Through up-close photos, pull-tabs, gatefolds, textures to feel, and sound effects, Van Fleet takes us on a fun trip to the farm. Extra-sturdy tabs make this a good investment. Also *Cat* and *Dog*.
- *Peek-a-Zoo*, Marie Torres Cimarusti, Stephanie Peterson (illus.). Animal peekaboo, with nice, big baby-sized faces. *Peek-a-Moo* and *Peek-a-Pet* follow the same format.
- *The Wheels on the Bus*, Paul O. Zelinsky. The wipers swish. The doors open and shut. The people go up and down. The babies go wah, wah, wah. Still one of the best interactive books out there to date.
- *Woody Guthrie's Riding in My Car*, Woody Guthrie, Scott Menchin (illus.). In this version of Guthrie's famous song, a family of dogs takes a trans-American road trip. There are plenty of flaps and tabs on this journey.

Boo! Pop-Ups to Startle, Tickle, and Thrill

Pop-ups, unlike pulls, flaps, and twirls, happen automatically when you open the book or turn the page. The image pops up. It jumps out of the book's pages at you or toward you. Depending on what pops up, these books can be very funny or even very scary. There's a bit of the charm of the unexpected—most books stay flat, after all—which makes a pop-up book just a little more exciting.

> **TIP: There is no sob louder than that of an older child whose pop-up has been ripped out by the baby, unless it's the baby when the older child won't let her have the pop-up book. Try designating a few special pop-ups for the older child alone. When the inevitable disaster strikes, involving her in the repair work may dry her tears.**

Pop-ups range from the simple and relatively solid work of the Snappy series to the intricate spinning fantasies of Robert Sabuda and Matthew Reinhart. Again, this is where ebooks can't compete. These books may seem a little less participatory, but it's the page turn that makes it happen. One result of a pop-up surprise could be a scream from the baby. On the second reading, the anticipation of the page turn is like the baby version of a horror movie, where organ music crescendos signal the approach of a creeping, crawling thing. For some kids, this might be too much. For others, it's great to do it again and again, a monster well within their control.

Talking to the Artist: Paul O. Zelinsky
What about books pleases babies?

I think babies may enjoy a very wide range of things, including books you might think are much too old for them. Little babies are so busy cataloging the world around them, so to speak, that they're not ready for the kind of understanding that story requires. The difference between a good story and a bad story probably escapes a baby; instead, it's all about things, and the qualities of things—the findable details, the sensual pleasure in color and texture, and so on. I don't think this means that a good story ruins a book for a baby, and it certainly helps out whoever is doing the reading.

I know that *The Wheels on the Bus* has been loved by large numbers of babies as well as older children. Little subplots in the pictures make it more interesting for older readers. Perhaps they also add to the number of subjects for a baby to look at and get involved in: a box of kittens; a lady on a motorcycle; a tiny girl in a window looking at you through binoculars.

What do you remember about reading to your two daughters?

Both of my daughters loved to have books read to them as babies, but they went about it in such different ways. Anna, the older one, would sit on a lap in rapt attention, even as a tiny infant, and soak up the experience. Rachel, in the same situation four years later, would have to reach out and grab the book, and then chew on it. At that point we started stocking up on more board books.

Anna had a favorite book for several long months that drove us up a wall. It was a board book with a clock on its cover, featuring movable hands. Inside, the book showed a boy and a girl telling a cursory story of their day—breakfast, lunch, visiting a favorite aunt—all at certain times on the clock, illustrated by photographs of cloth dolls in dollhouse settings.

The text was painfully, even ridiculously, dull, not to mention ungrammatical—it was a bad translation from what I suppose was at least correct Japanese. And Anna loved it. I assume she did because the pictures were sharp, close-up, intensely real images of cute dolls. She wasn't especially interested in the movable clock on the cover. After a while, of course, she knew it by heart, and would "read" it out loud, in all its grammatical oddness, as she paged through it, even though she might be holding it upside down, or turning pages from back to front.

Did you remember books from your own childhood?

Once I was reading Anna a Babar book borrowed from the library, and I was startled by a strange memory. Suddenly I saw the spread I was reading from, in a memory that I dimly recalled from a very young age. In memory, the picture looked the same and yet very different. It showed the monkey Zephir's hometown, a village made of tree houses all interlaced with rope ladders and bridges. The picture before my adult eyes was nice, slightly abstract, and a bit crudely drawn. The picture I remembered was a thousand times more detailed, realistic, and (I have to say it) more wonderful. For a while I felt as if I were looking at a double exposure, these two not-quite-matching versions of the same image. I thought about this for a long time afterward, how richly my young eyes interpreted that sparely presented scene. It was like looking at a semi-abstract painting and seeing a photograph. What's amazing is how much of my own imagination was involved in my perception of someone else's image. It makes me wish I could have a peek inside the brain of children looking at my picture books.

Pop-Ups to Love

Pop-up books can go out of print very quickly, so if your child falls in love with one, buy a couple of extra copies in case of mishap. Here are a few titles that have, so far, stood the test of time.

- *Cookie Count*, Robert Sabuda. A simple counting book by the master of pop-ups. His art in *Peter Pan* and *Alice in Wonderland* is probably too intricate for any but the most careful of two-year-olds, but this serves as a great introduction to his work.
- *Duckie's Splash*, Frances Barry. Duckie and friends enjoy a romp in their pond. With only one simple pop-out element at the end, this is a great first 3-D book experience.
- *Trucks Go Pop!*, Bob Staake. Vehicle lovers will swoon as trucks explode from the page in this visual experience with few words.
- *The Wide-Mouthed Frog: A Pop-Up Book*, Keith Faulkner, Jonathan Lambert (illus.). A wide-mouthed frog is curious about the eating habits of other animals, until he meets a critter that only dines on wide-mouthed frogs…

Someone Cut a Hole in the Page!

Among the many ways to add texture and dimension to a book page is to cut out a piece, so that a glimpse of the next page is revealed. Pages of increasing size may gradually reveal a whole picture, as Eric Carle does in *The Very Hungry Caterpillar*, where each increasingly larger page shows the caterpillar eating yet another thing. Or the cutouts may combine to create a wholly different picture than each page offers on its own. Ed Emberley uses this technique brilliantly on *Go Away, Big Green Monster*. The monster starts out as just a pair of eyes, then each successive page adds a new scary feature. After the monster is complete, the fangs, hair, etc., are removed, one by one. It's great for putting children in charge of their fear.

Cutout holes can also be used to emphasize shapes and colors, or to hint at the answer to a question. Many young children love these books because they also give them a new (and sometimes easier) way to turn the page—by reaching right into the hole. Mostly, though, like lift-the-flaps, they add an element of peekaboo to reading. These books, a little more complex, will probably last a little longer.

Holey Page-Turners, Batkid!

- *The Game of Finger Worms*, Hervé Tullet. Draw a face on your fingertip and slip it through the die-cut holes to animate French artist Tullet's delightfully silly scenes.
- *Lemons Are Not Red*, Laura Vaccaro Seeger. Cutouts give clues to the right color of lemons, carrots, and apples, with clever surprises tucked in, too. Seeger is the reigning master of the die-cut page, so look for her sophisticated *First the Egg*, *The Hidden Alphabet*, and *Green* as well.
- *Look! A Book!: A Zany Seek-and-Find Adventure*, Bob Staake. From airplanes to robots, Staake gives us tons of stylized details to spot and the die-cut holes help highlight just a few. The sequel is *Look! Another Book!*
- *Peek-a-Who?*, Nina Laden. Peekaboo holes hint at what's coming in a sturdy board book with a mirror ending for the final "Peek-a-You!" Give Laden's *Grow Up!* a try, too.

- *There Was an Old Lady Who Swallowed a Fly*, Simms Taback. Die-cut pages reveal all that the old lady swallows as the reader sings along. And don't miss Taback's Caldecott-winning *Joseph Had a Little Overcoat*.
- *Where Is Tippy Toes?*, Betsy Lewin. As we follow a cat's explorations in Lewin's vibrant watercolors, playful page turns and clever shaped pages lead up to a satisfying ending.
- *Who Do I See?*, Salina Yoon. Readers are invited to guess the animals by the patterns of their fur or shells peeking through pages.
- *Yawn*, Sally Symes, Nick Sharratt (illus.). Sean's yawn is contagious. As it passes from one animal to another, the die-cut circle representing each open mouth gets passed along, too.

Prepare for Repairs

The mechanics of these more complex activity books are part of the fun. At first, the flaps will be pulled off and the pop-ups torn through sheer enthusiasm. Later, it may be the urge to figure out why pulling the tab opens the door to the bus that leads to the page being torn open and the magic destroyed. Take a deep breath and dry the tears. It's only a book and it doesn't seem fair to punish a child for enjoying a book too much. Most damage can be repaired, and the wipers on the bus will live to "swish, swish, swish" another day. If it's possible, include your child in the repair process. Helping to fix the mistake helps her deal with her upset feelings. It will also reassure her that she hasn't ruined the book forever.

A supply of tape, plain and double-sided, can work wonders. If a moving piece has been pulled off, limit your taping to the piece itself and the fragment remaining—try to keep the tape off the page, and as thin as possible, especially if the piece needs to fit down into a pocket. Push- and pull-tabs can be reinforced with new cardboard. In many books, the engineering is hidden inside the page (two pages folded or glued together). You may have to perform open-page surgery to give your patient a new (probably temporary) lease on life.

The Toy-Book Continuum

When is a book a book, and when is a book a toy? Sometimes books come packaged with a toy, and sometimes the books are the toy. There are books with wheels, books with removable parts for making a doll or a train, books with movable parts attached by strings, and books that form a house for a removable paper mouse. Are those really books at all?

"My almost-three-year-old daughter had an animal / alphabet pop-up book, which she has recently rediscovered. It's not quite the book it once was, but she still likes it. Now we read it like this:

Samantha: H is for…what's that?

Me: It used to be a hippo.

Samantha: Oh. P is for…what's that?

Me: It used to be a parrot." —Jennifer

All books are invitations to enter a new place, even books hidden within toy purses and tractors. Books contain possibilities for fun and learning. Some small children use their books as toys even though they are "just books." They stack books and knock them down as part of their creative play. Think back to the real reason you want to read with your child—so that reading will be fun. If the wheels on the book have to go round and round, so be it.

Irresistible Authors: Matthew Van Fleet

From his first interactive touch-and-feel book *Fuzzy Yellow Ducklings*, Matthew Van Fleet's innovating books invite toddlers to touch, press, pull, lift, and even sniff. The books are sturdy enough to hold up to repeated rough readings. Fun, often funny (try *Moo*, *Cat*, or *Dog*), you can't go wrong. These are books you will find your child huddled over, turning the pages for herself, or that she will bring to you again and again. His latest, *Sniff!* and *Lick!*, are smaller versions with equally sturdy tabs and fun textures to explore.

Twenty-Six Especially Engaging, Incredible Interactive Books

Check the back of any pop-up or interactive book you purchase and make sure it is safe for any child under three. Since small pieces can come off and these books are *tons* of fun, make reading these books something you do with your child and choose other books for independent play.

For Babies and Up:

- *Animal Kisses*, Barney Saltzberg. A touch-and-feel book introducing words that name textures like scratchy cat kisses. Or do you prefer squeaky pig kisses? Or a velvety cow kiss? *Peekaboo Kisses* is equally fun.
- *Baby Animals*, SAMi (that's actually how you spell his name). These pages morph with a flip of the page into another animal. Graphically perfect for babies. Also *Baby Talk*.
- *In My Pond*, Sara Gillingham, Lorena Siminovich. A felt finger puppet goldfish is attached to the center and pokes through the entire book. Each turn of the page places the fish in different environs with the grown-up (or child) doing lots of puppeteering from the back. Also try *In My Den*, *On My Leaf*, and *In My Tree*.
- *Inside Freight Train*, Donald Crews. Slide the page open to see what's inside the railroad cars.
- *Munch, Munch! Who's There?*, Karen Jones. The rare interactive book that works for babies but goes beyond flaps and textures, this tiny board book has a hole for baby to put a finger in and slide up the answer to the titular question. Also *Bang, Bang! Who's There?*
- *One Yellow Lion*, Matthew Van Fleet. Opening the flaps shows each large number becoming part of the animals depicted, all frolicking on the page and ready for counting. A final accordion pull-out reveals all the animals together.

- *Peek-a-Baby: A Lift-the-Flap Book*, Karen Katz. With babies hiding under various flaps, this one will encourage a pre-bedtime game of peekaboo.
- *This Little Piggy: A Hand-Puppet Board Book*, Little Scholastic, Michelle Berg (illus.). This plush-covered board book literally fits you like a glove for interactive nursery rhyme sharing.

For Nimble Toddlers and Twos:

- *Boat Works: Giant Fold-Out Poster Book*, Tom Slaughter. Each quarter page folds out in succession to reveal big images of lots of different boats. Fun for the nautically-minded.
- *Brown Bear, Brown Bear, What Do You See?* (Slide and Find), Bill Martin Jr., Eric Carle (illus.). This interactive version of the classic Q&A book works for ones and twos. Move the slider to find out what each animal sees without having to turn the page. Also try *Polar Bear, Polar Bear, What Do You Hear?* (sound book) with buttons to press for the various animal noises.
- *Find My Feet*, Salina Yoon. Spin the dial at the bottom of the book to match up the correct feet with the corresponding animal. Give *Wings* a whirl, too.
- *Funny Tails*, Liesbet Slegers. With split pages, the reader is encouraged to give each critter a silly tail. Try *Funny Ears* and *Funny Feet*.
- *Gallop!: A Scanimation Picture Book*, Rufus Butler Seder. Not quite sure how "Scanimation" works, but the movement of the page animates (in black and white) each animal depicted. It's mesmerizing for adults, too. Try *Waddle!* for the same technique in color.
- *IBaby: Goodnight, Baby*, IKids, Ana Larrañaga (illus.) The reader tucks each baby, attached to the book by a colorful ribbon, into the right bed.
- *Have You Ever Tickled a Tiger?*, Betsy Snyder. Rhyming couplets

and textured illustrations encourage lots of interaction with wild animals.

- *Maisy's Big Flap Book*, Lucy Cousins. Maisy enjoys some of her favorite activities with various friends. If your child is flap-obsessed, then this is the book for you along with *Maisy's Seasons*.
- *Poke-a-Dot: Old MacDonald's Farm*, IKids. On top of each of MacDonald's animals, there are raised pop-up buttons that click when pushed. All this makes for a fun, multisensory counting experience.
- *Simms Taback's City Animals*, Simms Taback. Each page spread folds out one quarter at a time to reveal a verbal clue and another segment of animal for the guessing. Also check out *Dinosaurs*, *Farm Animals*, and *Safari Animals*.
- *Who am I?*, Begin Smart Books. To encourage peekaboo, this book opens wide to become an animal mask (complete with eye holes and handles) for the reader to wear.

For Careful Preschoolers—Age Three and Up (and Their Delighted Parents):

- *ABC3D*, Marion Bataille. Letters of the alphabet pop out, twist, reflect, and swirl to reveal themselves in one of the most creative pop-up or alphabet books ever. Look for the YouTube video of the book to see it in action.
- *Alice's Adventures in Wonderland*, Robert Sabuda. The classic story, somewhat abridged, with iconic illustrations brilliantly rendered as pop-up art. Many three-year-olds will be able to sit still for this one (maybe with a little additional abridgment by the reader) with such amazing creations to look at. Give *Peter Pan* in pop-up form a try, too.
- *Big Frog Can't Fit In: A Pop-Out Book*, Mo Willems. Big Frog will need a little help from her friends when the book she is appearing in can't even contain her.

- *Maisy Goes Swimming*, Lucy Cousins. Maisy changes out of her togs into her swimsuit for a plunge in the pool. Read the book backward to help her get dressed again and to get the book ready for a repeat read. Not recommended for children under three due to small pieces.
- *My Little Red Toolbox*, Stephen T. Johnson. This interactive favorite has pop-out cardboard tools that you can actually use to saw, screw, and hammer within the confines of the book. Not recommended for children under three years due to small pieces.
- *One Red Dot*, David A. Carter. Find the red dot hidden in each elaborate paper sculpture.
- *A Pop-Up Book of Nursery Rhymes*, Matthew Reinhart. Mother Goose characters spring into action through beautiful, animated pop-ups. Not recommended for children under three due to small pieces.

Chapter Seven
NURSERY RHYMES, POETRY, SONGS, AND FINGER PLAY

◆◆◆◆◆◆◆◆◆◆◆◆◆◆◆◆◆◆◆◆◆◆◆◆◆◆◆◆◆◆◆

Both babies and adults love music, rhyme, and rhythm. If you haven't already started singing whatever pops into your head and noticing how quickly your baby responds, you probably will soon. Many a grandmother, tucked in next to the baby's car seat, has made a long drive endurable with the repeated toe touches of "This Little Piggy Went to Market." (Of course, the ride may have felt longer to everyone else in the car, but we've never known a baby who didn't love Piggy even more the sixtieth time around.)

These categories overlap. Some nursery rhymes are songs. Some have finger or hand motions. Sometimes you're not entirely sure where that half-remembered couplet came from, but it doesn't matter. The charm, for both you and baby, lies in the irresistible rhythms, the catchy tunes, and the universal appeal. These little rhymes and games have their roots deep in our culture. Our mothers tickled our wee little piggies; their mothers tickled theirs. Now it's our turn to be the tickler. Time to pass it along.

Nursery Rhymes
Nursery rhymes are often at the center of a young child's cultural world. It doesn't matter if we learn at our mother's knee or from our preschool class

Spanish Words, English Rhymes

Most languages have their own rhyming songs for children, but some rhymes have transcended a single language:

Mary tenia un corderito (Mary had a little lamb)

Lluvia lluvia vete ya (Rain rain go away)

Estrellita donde estas (Twinkle Twinkle Little Star)

Te quiero yo y tu a mi (I love you, you love me)

Los pollitos dicen (The little chicks)

Arroz con leche (Rice pudding with milk)

or caregiver, Mother Goose stays with us forever. Because nursery rhymes are so compelling, they can be a wonderfully effective form of shared connection. The rhymes, and in some cases the tunes, make them easy to remember. Babies learn them quickly, and nothing delights a parent more than to see baby respond to a rhyme with the right word or gesture. Forgotten the exact words to an old favorite, or something your Jamaican grandmother used to recite that you've never heard since? That's what Google is for (although you may find that not everyone remembers the words the same way).

"My mother recites 'Manina Bella' in Italian to my children, just like my grandmother did for me when I was little:

Manina (Little hand)

Manina Bella (Pretty little hand)

Dovi sei andata (Where did you go)

Sei andata de la nonna (To grandma's house)

Cosi ti ha dato? (What did she give you?)

Pane e latte (Bread and milk)

NiNiNiNiNiNi (Tickle tickle tickle!)

She touches each finger, like touching the toes in 'This Little Piggy.' That, plus ravioli, is our Italian heritage right there." —KJ

TIP: Once your toddler can recite "Hey Diddle Diddle," get out the video camera or phone and press record. He may refuse to perform, but if you can capture his rendition, complete with pauses and explanations, you'll have a real treasure.

Knowing nursery rhymes is key to future connections and fun. He'll hear the same rhyme again at school, do the same hand motions with his caregivers, and even play the game on the playground, instantly accompanied by the equally well-educated kids around him. Nursery rhymes are one of the few reliable shared pieces of our culture. With a few nursery rhymes under his belt, your baby is prepared for all kinds of things. Once he's learned one, the rest come even more easily. He's expanding his memory and his horizons all at once.

Once Upon a History Lesson

Once upon a time, these nursery rhymes actually taught, or at least mocked, a little piece of history.

Humpty Dumpty sat on a wall.
Humpty Dumpty had a great fall.
All the king's horses and all the king's men
Couldn't put Humpty together again!

Humpty Dumpty was a powerful cannon during the English Civil War (1642–1649), mounted on top of a great church. While the Royalists were defending the city against siege in the summer of 1648, the church tower was hit by the enemy and the top of the tower was blown off, sending "Humpty" tumbling to the ground. Naturally the king's horses (cavalry) and men (infantry) tried to mend him, but in vain.

Ironically, the rhymes survive where often the history does not. Linguists still debate whether "Ring around the Rosy" refers back to the Bubonic plague (the consensus seems to be that it does not), but agree that "Old King Cole" probably had its roots in an early Celtic ruler. Apparently, the power of nursery rhymes to attract and enchant lasts well into graduate school.

"I have a daughter who was adopted from China at almost four. By then, we were, as a family, pretty much past the nursery rhyme stage. At six, she chose a book from the library—Pat-a-Cake—and, sitting in the backseat of the car, began carefully sounding out the words. She'd never heard them before. It was one of my most powerful reminders of what she missed, and that there are probably rhymes she knows that we don't share." —KJ

Growing Up with Mother Goose and Friends

Nursery rhymes work at every stage, from babies to toddlers to twos. Babies are learning the charm and power of repetition. They'll appreciate the growing familiarity of the rhymes, recited with or without a book and accompanying illustrations. If there are exhilarating or stimulating gestures that go along with a rhyme, like a bump up into the air or a sudden tickle, they will quickly learn to anticipate the joyous payoff.

Nursery rhymes are a child's first experience with poetry. Don't worry if some rhymes have nonsense words and ideas in them (hey diddle diddle?). Children are just learning the sounds. Also, nursery rhymes are great vocabulary builders. Like books, they often use words we don't use in our everyday speech (Jack be "nimble" and "fetch" a "pail" of water).

As they grow older, a familiar rhyme can give them a chance to show off new words and new skills. A talking toddler can fill in "Hey diddle diddle, the cat and the fiddle, the cow jumped over the…moon." He can raise his arms to show the sun coming out in "Eensy Weensy Spider" and pat-a-cake awkwardly along with the baker's man.

At two, they get the meaning and appreciate the joke (a cow jumping over the moon!). You can both play on an unexpected twist in the familiar (the more ridiculous, the better): when she got there, the cupboard was bare, and so the poor dog had…macaroni and cheese! The hand gestures will become more accurate, the tunes somewhat less wavering. Many kids will be able to recite a surprising number of rhymes with little prompting before their third birthday, and will recognize a new book with a familiar rhyme instantly. Even better, he can "read" a well-known rhyme from a brand-new book by following the illustrations.

Nursery Rhyme Collections to Love

Have you ever pored over a big book of nursery rhymes, studying the illustrations and reminding yourself of the lyrics (perhaps even saying or singing them under your breath)? Many famous illustrators have enjoyed putting their own unique stamp on these familiar treasures. Because of its longevity, we urge you to acquire a really good and perhaps expensive edition. The production value of many big nursery rhyme collections is well worth it. Just keep some tape handy to repair inevitable page tears. You can borrow other collections from the library. There are so many examples of excellent illustrated nursery rhymes that inevitably you and your baby will begin to enter the lit crit world of compare and contrast, enhancing the pleasure.

- *Animal Crackers: A Delectable Collection of Pictures, Poems, and Lullabies for the Very Young*, Jane Dyer (illus.). A short, easy-to-carry collection of popular rhymes that radiate with Ms. Dyer's artistic talents.
- *The Baby's Lap Book*, Kay Chorao (illus.). Chorao's lovely, soft drawings bring to life "Sing a Song of Sixpence," "Little Miss Muffet," "Willie Winkie," "Jack Be Nimble," and more.
- *Clare Beaton's Farmyard Rhymes*, Clare Beaton (illus.). Illustrating seven rhymes, Beaton's fabric art, using felt, yarn, and buttons, has a playful, homespun feel.
- *Favorite Nursery Rhymes from Mother Goose*, Scott Gustafson. With one rhyme per page, Gustafson's realistic and playful illustrations of the classic rhymes can really take flight.
- *Mary Englebreit's Mother Goose: One Hundred Best-Loved Verses*, Mary Englebreit. This collection is really charmingly illustrated, in a slightly

toned-down version of Englebreit's usual style that works well for kids. It's nearly all-inclusive, with popular favorites, obscure rhymes, and useful bits like "Thirty Days Has September."

- *Mother Goose*, Gyo Fujikawa. Many have profound memories of this book from childhood. Fujikawa's iconic children reenact Mother Goose's canon.

- *Mother Goose: A Collection of Classic Nursery Rhymes*, Michael Hague. With a useful index of first lines at the end of this volume, there are plenty of old-fashioned illustrations of familiar and a few less well-known nursery rhymes.

- *Mother Goose Numbers on the Loose*, Leo and Diane Dillon. Focusing on the rhymes that include some kind of numeric element (such as "Baa Baa, Black Sheep" and the three bags of wool), the Dillons have given us a fun, new way to think about Mother Goose.

- *My Very First Mother Goose*, Iona Archibald Opie (editor), Rosemary Wells (illus.). A mix of rhymes both popular and more obscure in an oversize format, perfect for poring over the details of Ms. Wells's instantly recognizable style. See the companion book, *Here Comes Mother Goose*.

- *The Neighborhood Mother Goose*, Nina Crews. This hip collection uses photography to capture real kids in genuine city parks, streets, and houses acting out the rhymes.

- *¡Pío Peep!: Traditional Spanish Nursery Rhymes*, Alma Flor Ada, F. Isabel Campoy, Alice Schertle (English adaptations), Viví Escrivá (illus.). So much music comes pouring forth from this well-known classic collection that even those of us who can't sing will feel the lilt of these Spanish poems. Aided by English renditions of the familiar Spanish works, we also have kid-friendly finger play rhymes to try. From the same creators, try *¡Muu, Moo!: Rimas de animals / Animal Nursery Rhymes*.

- *Real Mother Goose: My First Mother Goose*, Blanche Fisher Wright. Seven favorites, with old-fashioned illustrations that seem just right.

- *Richard Scarry's Best Mother Goose Ever*, Richard Scarry. A big book with fifty favorite rhymes (one per page) and Scarry's classic animal illustrations.

W. W. Denslow, An American Classic

Nursery rhymes themselves are relics of another, nearly forgotten age, with their cupboards and curds and carriages. A collection from the first American picture book illustrator W. W. Denslow is still available in *The Denslow's Picture Book Treasury*. (You may recognize his style from *The Wonderful Wizard of Oz* or his curious seahorse signature.) Denslow's illustrations give us the opportunity to see those durable, unchanging little doggerels in the context of another era. As his Old Mother Hubbard rushes about to provide for her pet, we still find it funny to see this shoeless dog with his feet up on a table, wearing a smoking jacket and powdered wig, reading the news. It's a little like watching Shakespeare's *Romeo and Juliet* morph into *West Side Story* and then into *Romeo + Juliet*. The pictures, the costumes, the accessories all give us a new insight into the original story. Times change. Rhymes don't.

Just One Rhyme

Is it worth it to buy a picture book that illustrates just one nursery rhyme? Yes, particularly for babies and toddlers. To save money, check out a stack from the library. A single rhyme spread over focused illustrations is perfect, in fact preferable to a more elaborate book.

- *1, 2, Buckle My Shoe*, Anna Grossnickle Hines. In detailed quilted illustrations that include buttons for counting, a little girl cavorts with the big fat hen.
- *Big Fat Hen*, Keith Baker. This time the big fat hen is accompanied by her chicks and her henhouse buddies. Baker's paintings shimmer with color and vitality.

- *Cat & Mouse*, Ian Schoenherr. A playful cat and a teasing mouse create a mash-up of three different rhymes, "Hickory, Dickory, Dock," "Eeny Meeny Miney Mo," and "I Love Little Pussy."
- *Five Little Pumpkins*, Dan Yaccarino. This Halloween counting rhyme, with droll pumpkins, is delightful enough to share any time of year.
- *Hey, Diddle, Diddle!*, Salley Mavor. Illustrated with photographs of carefully constructed, detailed felt and fabric creations.
- *Humpty Dumpty*, Salina Yoon. In a cute twist on the old standard, Easter egg Humpty Dumpty has his inevitable accident and gets a little help from some bunnies. See *Jack and Jill*, also by Yoon, for a Halloween take on this rhyme.
- *Old Mother Hubbard*, Jane Cabrera. Mother Hubbard's talented dog is at it again in this wonderful bit of rhyming silliness with lively illustrations from Cabrera.
- *Pat-A-Cake*, Tony Kenyon. Simple illustrations show the baker playing the familiar clapping game.
- *This Little Piggy*, Annie Kubler. A gaggle of babies use their digits to demonstrate the classic rhyme.
- *Three Little Kittens*, Paul Galdone. Galdone illustrates the complete rhyme about kittens, mittens, and pie and sets a high standard for nursery rhyme picture books in the process.

Beyond Mother Goose: Poetry for Babies and Up

Many books for babies rhyme, but not many authors are really writing poetry for this age group. There's a somewhat intangible difference between a book of rhyming descriptions of textured bugs, the fabulous doggerel narratives of Dr. Seuss, and the slightly wistful verse of Shel Silverstein. However, you will find poetry books on a wide range of topics (cats, teddy bears, families, and bath time) and from the world beyond (India, Russia, China, and Japan). Without lingering too long on what's *not* poetry, we'd like to suggest some books that are.

Poems That Stand Alone

- *All of Baby, Nose to Toes*, Victoria Adler, Hiroe Nakata (illus.). In buoyant verse, at least three generations of a family celebrate all the various parts of their bouncy baby girl on the edge of toddlerhood.
- *Barnyard Dance!*, Sandra Boynton. This energetic, insistent rhythm book for babies has lots of chickens and cows swinging and dancing.
- *Chicken Soup with Rice*, Maurice Sendak. Celebrates the months of the year with said soup in this bouncy, joyous romp of a verse. From Sendak's wonderful *Nutshell Library*, which Carole King delightfully put to music.
- *Flip, Flap, Fly!*, Phyllis Root, David Walker (illus.). In an inviting rhyme scheme with cozy illustrations, animal parents teach their babies to fly, swim, wiggle, and slide.
- *Haiku Baby*, Betsy Snyder. Haiku for babies? Yes, indeed! Snyder's simple collages of the natural world and her spare verses make this poetic form accessible to the very young. The tabbed pages of this board book make it easy to handle, too.
- *Itsy-Bitsy Babies*, Margaret Wild, Jan Ormerod (illus.). A variety of babies engage in very babylike behaviors. Wild's rhyming text and Ormerod's pastel cherubs are perfectly matched.
- *Jamberry*, Bruce Degen. A fun and rhythmic listing of real and fanciful berries.
- *Jazz Baby*, Lisa Wheeler, R. Gregory Christie (illus.). The youngest baby of this extended African American family brings everyone together to make music in this bouncy read-aloud rap.
- *Is Your Mama a Llama?*, Deborah Guarino, Steven Kellogg (illus.). Llama Lloyd asks lots of animal friends if their mamas are llamas.
- *My People*, Langston Hughes, Charles R. Smith Jr. (illus.). Langston Hughes's glorious poem is illustrated with luminescent photos of African Americans of various ages.

- *Oh, No!*, Candace Fleming, Eric Rohmann (illus.). With playful rhythms and refrains that encourage repetition, Fleming and Rohmann have created a rollicking romp set in the jungle.
- *Sheep in a Shop*, Nancy E. Shaw, Margot Apple (illus.). Each book in the series with lambs getting into humorous and peoplelike situations is delightful.
- *Snowmen at Night*, Caralyn Buehner, Mark Buehner (illus.). Ever wonder what snowmen do at night? The Buehners tell the inside scoop in entertaining verse. A great book for sharing among siblings because each illustration includes hidden pictures for an older child to find.

Poetry Collections for Babies and Up

Books of poetry written especially for children are typically too grown-up for our age group, created as they are for older ones who are more verbally competent. But the more you nurture very young babies on nursery rhymes, the more they will get poetry later on.

- *Here's a Little Poem: A Very First Book of Poetry*, Jane Yolen, Andrew Fusek Peters, Polly Dunbar (illus.). From well-known children's poets, such as Margaret Wise Brown and Jack Prelutsky, to famous adult authors, such as Langston Hughes and Gertrude Stein, these short verses are all very child-centric. Dunbar's multimedia pictures are spot on.
- *Las Nanas de Abuelita: Canciones de cuna, trabalenguas y adivinanzas de Suramérica / Grandmother's Nursery Rhymes: Lullabies, Tongue Twisters, and Riddles from South America*, Nelly Palacio Jaramillo (compiler), Elivia (illus.). "Mommy and Daddy I'd like a chance to marry a girl / Who knows how to dance…" is how it all starts, and shifts easily in and out of Spanish and English, with illustrations of a very lovable granny and kids.

- *Now We Are Six*, A. A. Milne, Ernest H. Shepard (illus.). This is a true classic book of poetry for and about childhood. "Half way up the stairs is a stair where I sit," and "James James Morrison Morrison Weatherby George Dupree / Took great care of his mother though he was only three." Can't get better than this.
- *Poetry Speaks to Children*, Elise Paschen (ed.), Judy Love, Wendy Rasmussen, Paula Zinngrabe Wendland (illus.). A brightly illustrated collection of kid-friendly work by poets from Shakespeare to Langston Hughes and modern artists as well. With so much variety (and a CD of poems, many read by the poets), this should serve your family well from infancy into the teen years. Give *Hip-Hop Speaks to Children* a try, too.
- *Read-Aloud Rhymes for the Very Young*, Jack Prelutsky (ed.), Marc Brown (illus.). This collection is probably for kids older than our under-threes, but since there are multiple images and poems per page, it's a good choice for reading with siblings.
- *Rhymes 'Round the World*, Kay Chorao. From Japan to Mozambique, Chorao presents us with English translations of over forty international nursery rhymes and folk poems.
- *Welcome, Baby! Baby Rhymes for Baby Times*, Stephanie Calmenson, Melissa Sweet (illus.). This book contributes simple poems and drawings about things babies and toddlers know well: "Diaper Song," "Silly Toe Song," and "Babies in a Stroller."
- *Where the Sidewalk Ends*, Shel Silverstein. Although the content of his poetry will appeal more to older children, babies will enjoy his rhythm and preschoolers his nonsense. Try his recipe for a hippo sandwich or dancing pants and for sure his "Ickle Me Pickle Me Tickle Me Too."

"Whenever my toddler Gus wants to talk to someone now, he goes up to them, pats them gently on the leg, and asks, 'Is your mama a llama?'" —Judith

Irresistible Author: Dr. Seuss, a Marvelous Poet

Dr. Seuss certainly qualifies as a writer of poetic verse for children. His work offers so much pleasure to so many readers and listeners. His stories are a cornerstone for a lifetime of reading, epic sagas written to be spoken aloud and very decidedly in poetic meter.

Dr. Seuss is for children of all ages. Some of his books are better understood and appreciated by older kids who can follow the funny stories, but *Hop on Pop*; *One Fish, Two Fish, Red Fish, Blue Fish*; and *The Foot Book* all ring the bell. His *Yertle the Turtle* collection of stories, with their heavily accented rhymes, is suitable for all ages, starting at eighteen months. The stories describing complicated human-like dynamics are easy to understand, the illustrations are typically memorable Seuss, and the rhymes are captivating. His drawings, rendered in blue, green, and black on a white background, help children focus on the details being read aloud by the adult reader.

Finger Play and Action Rhymes

Finger play is combined entertainment for both parents and kids. "Whoops Johnny" and "Where Is Thumbkin" delight again and again.

A great way to learn finger play is to go to library story times with your little one. Librarians can teach you the classics and you'll learn many you've never heard of. Some librarians will give you a printout with the words from that day's program. Can't remember the hand motions? Many librarians, teachers, parents, and kids are filming themselves performing rhymes and putting them on YouTube!

Do you remember "The Grand Old Duke of York"? Generations of kids have enjoyed this historical rendition of what sounds like a rather futile army exercise. Like most nursery rhymes, it has a historical provenance (it's said to refer to the Duke of York's disastrous decision to march his troops down from their hilltop stronghold and attack during England's fifteenth-century War of the Roses). It also lends itself to action. Fourteen-month-old Connor and his mother Amy showed us how the Grand Old Duke marched his men up (arms overhead) or down (arms down) and how the arms, like the Duke's men, flailed up and down when they were neither up nor down. Librarian Peggy had her Lapsit Program babies and caregivers play it a little differently. Sitting on the floor, babies held on outstretched legs, her group bounced gently when the Grand Old Duke and his men were marching. When they were up, so were the legs. When they were down, the legs were down, too. Lots of exercise for the grown-ups' legs, and much open-mouthed fun for the little ones as the Grand Old Duke marched again and again pleasurably.

From the "Itsy-Bitsy Spider" to "London Bridge," many nursery rhymes have tunes and actions suited to their words. The tunes help babies to remember the rhymes, and the whole-body actions give them a chance to perform and an excuse to move around. Finger play exercises a baby's fine- and gross-motor coordination. Good finger wiggling leads to page turning and eventually writing. And besides, it's irresistible.

Don't be surprised if your child just stares the first several times he hears and sees finger play. Little ones need to do a lot of watching before they can imitate. Also, most kids will do the hand gestures of finger play before they will sing the tune.

Books to Get Bodies Moving and Fingers Wiggling

Several books achieve the gold standard for finger play. Because of them, you need not worry about remembering or learning the gestures. They include easy diagrams for you and fun illustrations for baby.

- *Busy Fingers*, C. W. Bowie, Fred Willingham (illus.). Bowie's simple verses read like a classic finger play, and Willingham's warm pastels show children from a variety of backgrounds in the act. See also *Busy Toes*.
- *Diez deditos / Ten Little Fingers & Other Play Rhymes and Action Songs from Latin America*, José-Luis Orozco, Elisa Kleven (illus.). This

bilingual collection (with hand and body motion directions, English author's notes about each verse, and music notation) serves up over thirty songs and rhymes. The companion book is *De Colores and Other Latin-American Folk Songs for Children*.

- *Itsy Bitsy Spider (Sign & Singalong)*, Annie Kubler. Teaching sign language to babies is a popular trend, and this board book uses Kubler's exuberant cartoon babies to demonstrate each sign of this classic song. Also try *Teddy Bear, Teddy Bear*; *Twinkle, Twinkle Little Star*; and *Baa Baa, Black Sheep*.

- *My First Baby Games*, Jane Manning (illus.). This board book edition, with baby-friendly art, has great finger play activities and simple directions for parents performing them.

- *Piggies*, Audrey Wood, Don Wood (illus.). The Woods offer an all-new finger rhyme filled with fat, smart, long, silly, and wee little piggies all cleverly illustrated on a pair of baby hands.

- *This Little Piggy: Lap Songs, Finger plays, Clapping Games, and Pantomime Rhymes* (with CD), Jane Yolen, Adam Stemple, Will Hillenbrand (illus.). Full of fun by this famous writer mother and her musical son.

Growing Up with Finger Play

In the beginning, moms and dads need to help their babies move their arms up and down, or swing from side to side, to the lyrics of the nursery rhyme or song. These delightful and useful baby calisthenics prepare a baby for the feeling of moving to the rhythm and introduce repetitive motions. Two to three reps will do for now.

When the children are able to hold things in their hands and move around on their own, the finger and body actions can become more elaborate. Can they eensy-weensy their hands into a sunshine arc? Can they tip like a teapot? Can they jump with Jack over a make-believe candlestick? Can they wiggle a finger to recognize Tall Man or Thumbkin? Yes.

Soon the big kids will Hokey Pokey and dance with you. They will march with the Grand Old Duke of York, and boogie with a rhythm from a heavily accented poem or rhyme and certainly from the music you provide.

"Colin was in Temple at his cousin's Bat Mitzvah. While the cantor was singing, I noticed he was moving his hands. When I looked closer, I realized he was doing the gestures to two of his favorite finger plays, 'The Eensy-Weensy Spider' and 'Tommy Thumbs.' I guess he thought the cantor's songs needed something extra!" —Rachel

---

Start Every Day with a Song

Music is vitally important. We all prick up our ears at the sound of a voice singing a familiar tune, a hum, a whistle, or even the music of water rushing into the tub. We are born with an innate appreciation for sounds and music, beats and rhythm, and that appreciation reveals itself almost from birth. Besides the research about how Mozart and Bach help develop the brain and our capacities to do math and science, therapists report that music helps children experience a wider and deeper range of emotions.

> **TIP: Try using the same song to announce a familiar, repeated activity, like a diaper change, pulling a shirt over the head, or a bath. You'll quickly start seeing signs that your baby knows what's coming next!**

Why talk about music in a book about reading? Music is part of a culture, and a way of learning a language. Music appeals to us in a way other art forms don't (or can't). Fast, cheerful music takes our mood up; slower tunes bring us back down. Speech and writing have elements of music, as do illustrations that suggest rhythm and movement. Music resonates at a profound level for all of us. It nurtures something deep within. It gives us pleasure.

"One-year-old Eric calms down the minute we approach the CD player. As soon as he sees one of us fiddling with the buttons, he stops crying and settles down. Then when the music is on, he smiles and twirls his feet. Since we have pretty eclectic tastes, he does, too. He responds to everything from Elvis to Coldplay to Mozart." —Jennifer

Every "baby class," nursery, and preschool includes music and singing. To grab the attention of one or more babies or children, all a librarian or preschool teacher needs to do is sing. "Hello, hello, hello and how do you do?" Songs get everyone involved. As anyone who's found themselves humming "Baby Beluga" alone at the grocery store would attest, some songs are irresistible. That musical assist to memory makes it easier to learn things—like the alphabet. We'll bet there's a *Schoolhouse Rock* lesson lurking in your memory somewhere. "Conjunction Junction," anyone?

A song can help make the transition from one activity to another easier (a "clean-up" song is common at many baby and toddler activities). Repeating the same song at the same time of day is soothing for a little one, and hearing the songs from home in a new environment or with a new person can be comforting, too. Of course, most of us now have nearly instant access to any song we can think of, but why not stick with singing? It's fast, easy, and totally hands-free.

Songs are also satisfying because the verses set up expectations that are then fulfilled in the refrains. Rhythmic repetitions arouse anticipation and simultaneously soothe or answer it. A song or rhyme with a satisfying finish can be repeated over and over again (think "This Little Piggy" or "Old MacDonald"). Books, new and old, work in the same way. A story begins and our interest is captured. We wonder what is coming next. Songs and books both satisfy that urge for completion—for a beginning and an end and the opportunity to do it all over again.

TIP: Ask your older child to sing to your baby to distract him at a difficult moment or just help change his mood from fussy to interested. A song (freshly invented or an old favorite) is a great attention-getter, an older sibling even more so, and the two together can be golden.

Growing Up with Music Playing

Babies respond to all kinds of music. Whether the parents sing well or poorly; whether it's Bach, Mozart, and the classics or whether there's some Lena Horne or Adele in the mix, babies all respond in mood and gesture. Older babies love to move and groove to the rhythm of songs and music. You can dance with them in your arms or fly them around the room to just about any song. They'll also like watching you clap, shake a rattle, or bang a drum to the beat.

Toddlers will want their own rattle or drum. It's fun to practice making a noise REALLY LOUD and then soft again and to listen to songs that allow you to move along, like "The Hokey Pokey." A child in a "music class" may refuse to shake his rattle or dance along in class but perform willingly at home. It takes time to get comfortable with new skills, and many kids like to absorb what other children are doing before they join in.

When they grow to the sing-along stage, new fun can begin. Include silly songs like the rhyming name game (Mary Mary Bo Berry, Banana Fanna Fo Ferry, Fe Fi Fo Farry, Ma-ry). Make up your own. At first, your child may laugh or protest if you begin substituting silly words for those of a favorite song. Later, he'll add his own. The more kids feel comfortable with singing, the more exuberant they will be. They'll sing out with gusto.

Sing and Read, Read and Sing!
Books to Illustrate Favorite Songs and World Music

Picture Books and Board Books

- *A You're Adorable*, Martha Alexander (illus.), Buddy Kaye, Fred Wise, Sidney Lippman. This 1948 chestnut is accompanied by Alexander's illustrations of enchanting babies, toddlers, and preschoolers.
- *Down by the Bay (Raffi Songs to Read)*, Raffi, Nadine Bernard Westcott (illus.). The watermelons grow in profusion, and the children and lively characters are dancing all about, down by the bay. (You can't go wrong with any of Raffi's books. They are all playful songs and full of toddler fun.)
- *Down by the Station*, Will Hillenbrand. This train is a zoo train, picking up baby animals on the way to the children's zoo and leaving room for an adventure or two along the way. With extra verses for each animal and even animal sounds.
- *He's Got the Whole World in His Hands*, Kadir Nelson (illus.). Nelson's gorgeous oils make this spiritual accessible to young listeners and soon-to-be singers.
- *Hush Little Baby: A Folk Song with Pictures*, Marla Frazee (illus.). In this pitch-perfect rollick, an old-timey family does everything it can to calm the most boisterous baby ever with everything from a mockingbird to a horse and cart.
- *I Love You! A Bushel & a Peck*, Frank Loesser, Rosemary Wells (illus.). Delightful ducklings dance around the farm to this infectious Loesser song.
- *Lady with the Alligator Purse*, Nadine Bernard Westcott. This childhood favorite, as envisioned by Westcott and her lively cartoons,

is as silly and wonderful as ever. Westcott has also illustrated *Miss Mary Mack*, *The Eensy-Weensy Spider* (both adapted by Mary Ann Hoberman), *Skip to My Lou*, and *Peanut Butter and Jelly*.

- *Little Bunny Foo Foo: Told and Sung by the Good Fairy*, Paul Brett Johnson. Can a mischievous bunny get three magic wishes if he stops bopping small forest creatures on the head with mud pies? If you prefer the variation that implies a bop with a mallet or hammer, try *Little Rabbit Foo Foo*, Michael Rosen, Arthur Robins (illus.). Both are great fun and infinitely repeatable.

- *Los pollitos dicen: ¡Vamos a cantar en inglés y español! / The Baby Chicks are Singing: Sing Along in English and Spanish!*, Ashley Wolff. One of the most popular songs for children in Spanish is also a delight in English, especially with this loving mama hen and her brood of chicks. For more bilingual picture books that you can sing, check out Wolff's *Oh the Colors / De Colores* and *Ten Little Puppies / Diez perritos* (Alma Flor Ada, F. Isabel Campoy, Ulises Wensell [illus.]).

- *Row, Row, Row Your Boat*, Annie Kubler. All of Annie Kubler's series of songs are adorable and immediately accessible for toddlers. (The series includes *I'm a Little Teapot!*, *If You're Happy and You Know It*, *Ring Around a Rosie*, and *Head, Shoulder, Knees, and Toes*. Toddlers love them all. Some songs are available in Chinese, Spanish, Urdu, and more.)

- *Today Is Monday*, Eric Carle (illus.). This popular song celebrates a week's worth of eating and Carle's painted-paper collages, depicting animals enjoying the fare, help the book sing.

- *You Are My Sunshine*, Jimmie Davis, Caroline Jayne Church (illus.). From the shiny foil cover to children expressing their affection for their stuffed animal playmates on each page, never has this song been sunnier.

Song Anthologies

- *Arroz con leche: Popular Songs and Rhymes from Latin America*, Lulu Delacre. All of the poems and songs are written in both English and Spanish, with music at the end, and joyous, colorful pictures to illustrate the sights and sounds and families of Latin America.
- *Let It Shine: Three Favorite Spirituals*, Ashley Bryan (illus.). In cut-paper collage, Bryan's illustrations of "This Little Light of Mine," "Oh, When the Saints Go Marching In," and "He's Got the Whole World in His Hands" have never been more joyful. Give *All Things Bright and Beautiful* (lyrics by Cecil F. Alexander) a try, too.
- *The Peter Yarrow Songbook: Songs for Little Folks*, Peter Yarrow, Terry Widener (illus.). With twelve favorite songs (such as "The Green Grass Grew," "A-tisket, A-tasket," "Mary Had A Little Lamb," and "Row, Row, Row Your Boat") and a CD with the tunes sung by Yarrow and his daughter Bethany, this collection is a crowd-pleaser. Also in the series: *Let's Sing Together*, *Sleepytime Songs*, and *Folk Song Favorites*.
- *Songs from the Baobab: African Lullabies & Nursery Rhymes*, Chantal Grosléziat (compiler), Elodie Nouhen (illus.), Paul Mindy (music arrangements). This unique collection with accompanying CD includes twenty-nine songs from ten African countries (such as Rwanda, the Ivory Coast, and Senegal). The music here is haunting and lovely.

Why Can't He Just Listen to My Music?

Your first kids' CDs will probably arrive as gifts. Who is Raffi, and why would my toddler listen to an Australian boy band called the Wiggles? If you're one of the many parents who rule out specialty music because you're going to raise your kid on "real" music, you might want to think again. Rock-and-roll and opera have their places, and you'll want your child to

Featured Book

Philadelphia Chickens!
Sandra Boynton

The book has funny pictures, lyrics, and even musical notation, and the CD features every song in an "imaginary musical revue" starring artists like Meryl Streep and the Bacon Brothers. This book / CD combo is perfect for long car trips and sing-alongs. If you're looking for more, there's also *Blue Moo, Dog Train*, and *Rhinoceros Tap.*

enjoy, or at least listen to, your favorites—but there's something about kids' music that gets them moving and singing.

There are some wonderful artists working in the children's music field today, and you may find yourself enjoying a new version of "Polly Wolly Doodle" just as much as your baby. Just like celebrities and authors, when musicians have kids, they're often inspired to create something that's right for them. You'll find famous names like Dan Zanes (formerly of the Del Fuegos), Tom Paxton, and They Might Be Giants mixed in with great work by Laurie Berkner, Joe McDermott, and Daddy-A-Go-Go. Give them a try…and give Raffi and the Wiggles a chance.

"The Yo Gabba Gabba CDs have been lifesavers; we listen to those on long car rides, and it seems to remind her of the show and keep her occupied. When she was a baby, we surveyed friends to list their top ten songs most played from their iPods. You could tell the new parents, because their top-played tracks were all hour-long recordings of white noise!" —Kelly

Great Music to Enjoy with Your Child

- *Baby Beluga*, Raffi. Something about the name Raffi just puts off some parents. We imagine mind-numbing, new-age croonings that will leave us banging our heads against a wall. In reality, Raffi's popularity is well deserved; his songs are bright and clever, and while they may appeal more to your child than to you, that is, after all, what they're for. *Singable Songs for the Very Young* has some great tunes as well.
- *El Elephante*, Ben and Leo Sidran. "Popcorn's Got a Brand New Bag" and "Pushing and Shoving" suggests the breadth of the creative playful songs created by father-and-son jazz musicians.
- *For the Kids*, various artists. A compilation album created to benefit VH1's Save the Music Foundation, on a mission to restore music education in public schools across the country. Offers the priceless opportunity to hear Bare Naked Ladies singing "La La La La Lemon" and Sarah McLachlan's soulful rendition of "The Rainbow Connection," plus original songs by Bleu and Tom Waits.
- *Move Your Boots*, The Bramble Jam. It's a small New Hampshire band of parents with big sound: no lessons, no messages, just pure fun for everyone in the family.
- *Music Is Awesome*, Yo Gabba Gabba. Many parents swear by these compilations of music by various bands from the popular *Yo Gabba Gabba* show. Several volumes are available.
- *No!*, They Might Be Giants. There really are songs on this album you might willingly listen to when your kids aren't in the car. Fans of the band might not be surprised at the turn to kids' music, since much of their adult music had a fanciful, surreal twist that works perfectly when applied to "Fibber Island" (where they meet friends from Mars and sew buttons on their hats). The title track might be the only thing that could make the word "No" funny again. Try *Here Come the ABCs* and *Here Come the 123s*.

- *Ralph's World*, Ralph Covert. His infectious and melodic tunes have enough in them to cross generational lines. "Drivin' in My Car" is perfect road music and, be warned, "Freddy Bear, the Teddy Bear" will get stuck in your head.
- *Rocket Ship Beach*, Dan Zanes. It's no surprise that when the former front man for Del Fuego turns his attention to kids music, he'll come up with something that makes both the front and the back-seats happy. This album includes both hip versions of old standards like "Polly Wolly Doodle" and inventive new songs, as well as a reggae-rap "Father Goose" featuring dancehall rapper Rankin' Don. And there are lots more Zane albums to be had.
- *Victor Vito*, Laurie Berkner. Berkner's cheerful original songs will get the whole family moving. Look for *Whaddaya Think of That* and *Buzz Buzz* also.
- *World Playground*, Putumayo. If you want to introduce your child to world music, the Putumayo collections are the way to go. This album includes tunes by such luminaries as Buckwheat Zydeco and Cedella Marley Booker (Bob Marley's daughter). Winner of a Parents' Choice Award. There are several other collections to fit a variety of moods and interests.
- *You Are My Little Bird*, Elizabeth Mitchell. Gentle, lovely, clearly sung lyrics of children's folk tunes, with simple seeming, meaningful accompaniments. Enchanting.
- *You'll Sing a Song and I'll Sing a Song*, Ella Jenkins. There is a reason Ella Jenkins has been around for so long. She is unrivaled in getting kids and their grown-ups singing. With folk songs, call-and-response songs, and songs from various cultures, this is the album to get if you want to expand your own repertoire of songs to sing with your child.

Ages and Stages: Simple Suggestions

Newborn	Play music in the nursery. Babies don't need total silence! Sing or say whatever you remember of songs, poems, advertisements, and nursery rhymes. You'll get better at it, and the baby will always love your voice.
Heads Up	Move baby's arms or legs according to a rhyme or song you're singing. Invent a diaper changing song. (Or several. Or several hundred.) Play a game of Hokey Pokey, carrying the little one on your hip and putting your right hands in, then your left legs…then shake them all about.
Sitting	Bang on a pot festival! Open your kitchen cupboards and give the budding musician a wooden spoon. Do the "Chicken Soup with Rice" (Carole King [music] and Maurice Sendak [words and illustrations]) song and dance at mealtime when you've got the little one captive in his high chair.
Crawling / Creeping	Actions that go with nursery rhymes are starting to be copied, memorized, and lots of fun.
Cruising / Walking	Try some stand-up nursery rhymes or songs, with gestures for him to imitate.
Talking (a few words)	Stop reading the whole rhyming sentence and let your baby add the missing word. Simple Simon met a _____, or Jack be nimble, Jack be quick, Jack jump over the _____.

Talking More	He can probably remember his first full nursery rhyme, with some prompting. Sing made-up songs to accompany everything you do: bath time, kitchen cooking and cleanup, walking the dog. Act one out. You be Miss Muffett, and he can be the spider.
Running (but not talking much)	Marching in different styles: sideways steps, giant steps, scissors steps. (See *Jonathan and His Mommy*, Irene Smalls, Michael Hays [illus.], and Jonathan London's *Wiggle Waggle* [Michael Rex (illus.)], and *Carry Me!*, Rosemary Wells.) Play a rhyming game of identifying ordinary things that rhyme. Bring me something that sounds like hall? Ball. Like power? Flower. Like bat? Cat.
Talking ALL THE TIME!	Take notebooks into the park or the playground. Compose a poem about the place together. Play rhyming games. Remember the old "name game" song of old? Dust it off now for maximum fun. Mary Mary Bo Berry Banana Fanna Fo Ferry, Fee Fi Fo Fary…Ma-ry; Sam Sam Bo Bam, Banana Fanna Fo Fam, Mee My Mo Mam, Sa-am. Cut sandwiches with cookie cutters, making stars, gingerbread guys, candy canes, or children, then sing or tell stories featuring these characters. We call them peanut-butter persons. Then eat.

Chapter Eight
SCREEN TIME

◆◇◆◇◆◇◆◇◆◇◆◇◆◇◆◇◆◇◆◇◆◇◆◇◆◇◆◇◆◇◆◇◆◇◆

Apps, Ebooks, and Video

Screen time is a fact of life. Like the rest of their families, most babies, toddlers, and preschoolers in this country watch videos and play with computer games and apps—and they enjoy it. And many parents struggle with that fact. We agonize over the amount of screen time our kids get and fear its impact. We judge ourselves by the hours spent or unspent in front of the TV or computer, and we judge others.

In the first edition of this book, we encouraged parents to relax about screen time, and in some sense, we still do. Parents need breathers, and parents need showers, and a video can grant you a little time—no one, we said, is going to die if you "plop the kid down" in front of a video or the television once in a while.

But things have changed. You don't need to "plop a kid down" in front of a screen anymore. You can hand over the screen in your pocket or turn on the screen in your car. There is no longer a single moment in a child's life when she need fear being too far away from her favorite electronic media-dispensing object. Access is instantaneous. How many times a day does the average parent hand over a cell phone to a child in a stroller, in line at the grocery store, at a restaurant, or in the car seat? It's a research study waiting to happen.

Until then, the screens are here: big, little, and in between. The videos, apps, ebooks, and other kinds of storytellers are likely to be a part of your child's reading life. How can you use them best?

1. Use screens to enhance reading together, not to replace it. It's obvious that a video doesn't replace a bedtime book, but the app and ebook options are more tempting, and less clear. Reading together is sharing—but tapping the laundry basket icon to make a cat appear over and over again is more akin to singular play than reading books. If you've set out to read one on one with your child, then read.

2. Encourage sociability. No one would ever tell you to stop handing your child a board book in a restaurant—why are we suggesting that the Cat in the Hat app is any different? Consider this: anywhere your toddler expects to get that phone—whether it's serving as book, video player, or game—your preschooler, and then your child, will expect to be engaged by a gadget. If there are people around, let's talk.

3. Plan for a "Balanced Media Diet." Too many apps and not enough books isn't good for you, just like too many carbs and no protein isn't healthy either. While books are great, kids also need to play with blocks and play dough and run around outside. Even Cookie Monster has declared that a cookie is a "sometime thing." While Cookie Monster's evolution may border on sacrilegious, screens, too, are "sometime things."

4. Look for ways to make screens about reading. When the little screens are in their hands, or the big ones are calling for their attention, do look for ways to connect the world on-screen and the world of reading together. Favor ebooks over apps for reading together, and apps that develop literacy over those that don't (more on that in the app section). Choose videos that spring from books over those that don't.

TIP: Don't make a big deal out of choosing some "baby videos" when kids are sharing the TV. *Sesame Street* **is great for mixed ages, but plenty of "big kids" enjoy settling down with their old favorites—especially if no one makes them feel like a baby for doing it.**

Using Ebooks with Babies, Toddlers, and Twos

What makes an ebook different from an app? An ebook is a virtual book. It is read on an electronic reading device (which may also play apps and videos). But more importantly, an ebook is a book: the only action is to turn the pages by electronic means, usually with a swipe of a finger. An app (short for application) *does* things at the touch of the finger. Others may define apps vs. ebooks differently, but for our purposes, that's the distinction we will make.

So, is reading *Winnie-the-Pooh* from an ebook different from reading it on paper?

The answer, like so many things in parenting, appears to depend on you. Lisa Guernsey, author of *Screen Time: How Electronic Media—From Baby Videos to Educational Software—Affects Your Young Child*, watched videos of parents reading to young children from various electronic devices, and found that the parent-child interaction over the book was different. Instead of taking time from the text to ask "what do you think will happen next" or talk about what the child might be seeing or touching, parents focused their comments on the mechanics of the device, not the story. Careful! Don't push that! Touch here, not there!

In a study at Temple University, researchers found that children sitting with parents understood far less of a story read to them by a device than children whose parents read aloud. They attributed the difference in part to the questions and comments the parents typically asked while reading the book—Why would she do that? Ooh, I bet George will get in trouble! Parents busy coaching a child through technological intricacies aren't asking those simple questions, and without them, their children may not be follow-ing the action.

That's a problem that a savvy parent can fix, and ebooks are a great option in many situations—when traveling, when facing an unexpected wait. We still wouldn't advise sacrificing individual copies of picture and board books to your desire for an ecologically friendly, clutter-free home, or buying into a theory that somehow apps and ebooks are "smarter" than regular books.

You may ultimately read an interaction-free, exactly-like-the-book copy of *Goodnight, Goodnight, Construction Site* in the same way you'd read any book to your child, and point to and discuss the same illustrations—but your baby can't interact with the ebook the same way she would with a single paper edition. She can't crawl to it and pick it up, or bring it to you for an unexpected read, or decide to sleep with it or take it along on a stroller ride without your help, and probably not without your guidance. If most of your books are ebooks, you won't find your toddler sitting by the bookshelf turning pages (or using them to build a tower when she runs out of blocks). She can't turn to a certain page first, or read backward or safely teethe on the thick cardboard corner.

Older babies and toddlers can learn to turn ebook pages with a button or a swipe, but with ebooks and limited coordination, it's hard for them not to make the unexpected happen as often as not—which means those books are probably limited to the time you spend reading together. That's fine—but part of raising a child who reads is giving her the freedom to explore. (And older children "exploring" ebooks? They're all too likely to end up exploring the latest game apps instead.)

Ebooks for the E-Crowd

More and more children's books are available in several formats including ebook. Here are a few titles that are available from a variety of vendors (and maybe even from your public library) to download to various devices.

- *Baby's First Book*, Garth Williams. A lovely, old-fashioned look at all the objects familiar to a baby or toddler.
- *Best Little Word Book Ever*, Richard Scarry. With busy "pages" to pore over, Scarry introduces kids to all the people and things you can find in a house, downtown, at the airport, and in a harbor.
- *Bugs! Bugs! Bugs!*, Bob Barner. A hymn of praise to all things buggy with Barner's friendly art.
- *Curious George*, H. A. Rey. Yes, you can download George's first bit of monkey business and some of his subsequent adventures, too. Makes you wonder what George would do with a smartphone!
- *Dancing Feet*, Lindsay Craig, Marc Brown (illus.). A rollicking read-aloud that encourages the reader to guess which feet belong to which creature. See *Farmyard Beat* for more from the same duo.
- *Duck & Goose*, Tad Hills. Duck and Goose try to hatch a multicolored ball. Also try Hills's *Duck, Duck, Goose*.
- *Go, Dog. Go!*, P. D. Eastman. These dogs drive cars, wear hats, and get up to all kinds of silliness. A childhood favorite of many.
- *Goodnight, Goodnight, Construction Site*, Sherri Duskey Rinker, Tom Lichtenheld (illus.). All the hardworking construction vehicles get ready for bed.
- *Put Me in the Zoo*, Robert Lopshire. A leopard, who can do amazing things with his colorful spots, tries to find his place in the world.

Choosing and Using Apps

Apps for children, like apps for grown-ups, come in all varieties—and their quality is equally varied. There are book apps, learning apps, and game apps designed to appeal to babies and their siblings at all ages. Book apps represent the interactive book side of on-screen reading—think of them as pop-ups or flap books, and enjoy them accordingly. Some add a whole new dimension to an old or new tale, and some—well, it's always fun to poke,

Featured App: JibJab Jr.

JibJab Jr. is where ebooks, cameras, and apps meet. You can upload a picture of your child easily into any JibJab Jr. book (the first one is available for free, the others will cost you) and then read your child a clever rhyming story with his image in the leading role. Other than the initial uploading of the picture, JibJab Jr. books are (to date) close to pure ebook apps: the figure with your child's face will perform one action on each page, but otherwise there's nothing to distract from the stories, which are mostly well done, if not exactly great kid literature. A great kid-pleaser, although if you have more than one child, you'll be reading it more than once.

Great Resources for Great Apps

Common Sense Media (www.commonsensemedia.org)
GeekDad (www.wired.com/geekdad)
The iPhone Mom (www.theiphonemom.com)
Moms With Apps (www.momswithapps.com)

push, or prod and get a response. See what you think of Sandra Boynton's Moo Baa, La La La app or her Going to Bed Book app. A very young child can "turn" pages with a wiping gesture, choose a voice or character to read to her, touch a word to have it pronounced, and maneuver the characters at will.

Learning apps, though, present an entirely different question (and often the categories are not so distinct: learning apps based on books are abundant). Can a baby or young child learn from interacting with an app?

The tentative answer, based at this point on one study and a whole lot of extrapolation, is yes. Researchers at Georgetown University have done a series of studies involving demonstrating to young children the location of things in a room using a variety of teaching methods—video, video with a guide calling for a response, and face-to-face teaching. They found that children struggle to learn only from a video every time. Children learn better by interacting, even with a video guide (think of the way the best educational children's television calls on them to respond to questions).

It appears that computers—and presumably other devices—can provide that interaction. The researchers had two- and three-year-olds participate in a hide-and-seek retrieval game. Children were shown where three characters were hidden in one of three different ways: by watching an adult find the characters, by watching a video showing where they were hidden, and by playing an interactive computer game that required the child to press the space bar to see where the characters were hidden.

Even that simple interaction made a difference: researchers found that children who played the computer game or watched the adult were significantly more likely to be able to find the hidden characters when presented with a live version of the room they'd seen on screen or when allowed to enter the room where the adult had shown them the hidden characters.

More research is bound to come—there's a lot of money to be made in developing apps that successfully teach children. For now, it looks like interaction with a computer game or app may be able to teach children something—but what? It's safe to say nothing more than you can.

So when it comes to choosing educational apps for your child, we'd like to emphasize that you have a choice—and one choice is not to worry about it at all. If your only intent is to use your phone or tablet as an occasional distraction, then we suggest that it matters not one whit if the educational value is nil. There's an argument to be made for not fooling yourself into thinking that time prodding the screen is beneficial to your baby or toddler. Not every moment of your child's life needs to be invested in some productive activity. Download whatever she likes, and have done with it.

But if you'd prefer apps that offer some of the same value as crayons and paper, puzzles, or cause-and-effect toys, they're available in abundance (and they're pretty distracting, too). Know that for your child to get the most out them you'll probably need to sit down with her, at least in the beginning, to demonstrate. And know, of course, that your real goal (and hers) is to have fun.

How to Choose a Great Learning App— from Common Sense Media

Pay when appropriate. Many free apps have ads that are easy to click on by mistake—disrupting kids' experience and exposing them to consumerism. Sample free / lite versions, and upgrade later if you like what you see. Full versions are more complete and contain fewer ads.

Look for clarity. Apps should have clear audio, proper pronunciation, and a straightforward tutorial or instructions. Letters and numbers should be in a standard typeface, especially for alphabet and number apps. They should look close to the way kids learn to write them.

Seek specific feedback. Choose apps that give your kids feedback that will help them get better. Avoid apps with phrases such as "You're amazing!" Opt instead for prompts that will give them specific information about how to improve or what to do next.

Find apps that promote curiosity and fun. Fun and engaging apps aren't easy to find. Take it as a great sign if your kids are engrossed. Also look for apps that give them choices about what to do and where to go while still offering structure.

Use parental options. Some apps allow parents to easily tailor the experience. Parents might get to choose the range of numbers to cover for a number app, select capital or lowercase letters, control whether the app plays music, or turn off unwanted bells and whistles.

Reinforce off-screen learning. Find apps that can help your child draw connections to everyday situations. Use apps that have commonplace content you can expand on in lots of different situations—for example, apps that use animals and their sounds can generate conversations as you pass farms or visit a zoo.

Play it yourself. Once you install the app, play it yourself before playing it with your young child. Also, remember that some apps work better as a guided experience, while others are easy for kids to explore on their own once you've familiarized them with it.

Look for personalization features. Some apps allow you to personalize the photos or audio so kids can have practice identifying images and playing with concepts that contain familiar content. These can be great for helping kids connect with the content.

Read up. Search Common Sense Media's ratings for learning, age-appropriateness, and quality at www.commonsensemedia.org/app-reviews. Read developers' descriptions, user reviews, or view YouTube videos. You can also "test drive" many apps.

Tap the Bunny: Picture Book Apps

Picture book apps are like ebooks, but they have animation or special features that make them playfully interactive. While apps based on children's books or stories are the brave new world of children's publishing, we thought we would give a shout-out to some early adopters. You may have as much fun as your kids with these apps for smartphones, tablets, or both.

- *Dr. Seuss Collection # 1*, Dr. Seuss, Oceanhouse Media, Inc. This set of five lightly interactive Dr. Seuss classics includes *The Cat in the Hat*; *One Fish, Two Fish, Red Fish, Blue Fish*; *The Foot Book*; *Fox in Socks*; and *Mr. Brown Can Moo! Can You?* There are some fun sound effects here, and objects, people, and creatures identify themselves when tapped.
- *Freight Train*, Donald Crews, HarperCollins Publishers. Crews advised on the creation of this app with delightful train music, freight cars that open, and a train whistle you can blow with a tap.
- *Go Away Big Green Monster*, Ed Emberley, Night & Day Studios, Inc. You can read this story by yourself, sing the story to music, or read

along with Ed Emberley. The Green Monster slowly disappears with a swipe of the page and the monster wiggles and jiggles when touched.

- *Goodnight Moon*, Margaret Wise Brown, Clement Hurd, Loud Crow Interactive Inc. While much too stimulating for bedtime, this is a playful take on a beloved classic. Tapping almost everything in the great green room creates some special effect.

- *The Monster at the End of This Book*, Jon Stone, Michael Smollin (illus.), Sesame Street. In this animated app that is true to the original book, Grover struggles to keep the reader from turning (or swiping) the pages for fear of the inevitable monster encounter. Includes tips for parents.

- *Moo, Baa, La La La!*, Sandra Boynton, Loud Crow Interactive Inc. This is one of several apps based on Boynton's delightful board books. Here you can touch the animals to make their noises, change one page from day to night with a tap of the sun, and swipe the pigs to hear their harmonious "La La La!"

- *Pat the Bunny*, based on the book by Dorothy Kunhardt, Random House Digital, Inc. This is a whole new *Pat the Bunny* for the digital age, with some very clever features. The mirror uses the camera on the device to capture your child's image. There are bubbles to pop, butterflies to catch, and bunnies to find.

- *Planes*, Byron Barton, Oceanhouse Media, Inc. Barton's book is here in its entirety with some extra bells and whistles. You can move the planes, clouds, and the passengers around on the screen. *Boats* is available, too.

- *PopOut! The Tale of Peter Rabbit*, Beatrix Potter, Loud Crow Interactive Inc. This app does feel like Potter's classic, except now there are bunnies to tickle, blackberries to squish, and pop-up-like tabs to swipe. The music and narration fit the book perfectly.

- *The Three Little Pigs*, Nosy Crow. This app is an original work based on the ever popular tale. The animation here is delightful, and you can even help the wolf knock down houses by blowing into the microphone.

"Our granddaughter Sophia is only two years old and surrounded by books and screened devices. When she came to our house, she went up to the dark TV screen and made a swiping gesture, seeming to want to fire it up or move to a new page. I'm not a dinosaur or Luddite, but I wonder how this generation's 'reading' will develop." —Del

Television and Video

If screen time is a fact of life, video screen time must be even more so. But many parents beat themselves up even harder over television and video: passive screen time (be it on a television, a computer, or a small screen) is the worst screen time of all!

As a result, sometimes, when we're feeling pressure to come across as the super mom or the great dad, we…lie. We downplay the amount of time involved; we excuse the enthusiastic bellowing of the catchy *Bob the Builder* song as the result of too much time with a neighbor child. In fact, we deny the enthusiasm our children bring to this supposedly low-brow activity.

We think this embarrassment is silly. It's true—the American Academy of Pediatrics still recommends no screen time for children under two. That recommendation is largely based on old data and research done using flickering, stimulating, noisy adult television, unintelligible to a baby and incomprehensible for a toddler. But times have changed, and for toddlers, twos, and threes, there's some wonderful children's television out there. At its best, it's educational. Children who watch *Blue's Clues* regularly score higher on cognitive tests. At the very least, in moderation, it's harmless—and you may well decide that it's harmless for your baby, too. Let's acknowledge that some TV is often a part of the day, and declare that in a life otherwise filled with books and playtime and music, there's absolutely nothing wrong with that.

Why Talk about TV in a Book on Reading?

It may come as something of a surprise that in a book focused on reading we're not going to condemn screen time as inherently evil. Good video, like good computer games and apps, can combine sight and sound to create a unique learning experience. We're certainly not advocating for two-year-olds to slump in front of a screen for hours a day, eyes glazed and mind on autopilot, but there's a lot more to the story than that.

So, why talk about TV in a book about reading? Partly because it's impossible to avoid—so many books are based on TV shows and TV shows are based on books. Partly because there's a growing concern that TV and reading are mutually exclusive—that kids raised with the box will never crack open a book. That doesn't have to be the case. This chapter is designed to help you find ways to use TV to encourage and enrich reading and playtime instead of taking their place. Screens, big and little, aren't going away anytime soon. Now is a good time to begin figuring out what role these increasingly dominant media will play in your child's life.

> **TIP: TV and videos getting a little out of hand at your house? Use a vacation or having visitors to interrupt regular viewing habits. Then reintroduce TV time back in gradually at a level you're more comfortable with.**

Book-Friendly, Kid-Friendly TV and Videos

It's no exaggeration to say that TV is pop culture. It's a fact of life. A first-grader with absolutely no awareness of the kid's television and movie characters currently in vogue is going to be somewhat out of place in most American communities. At some point, kids are going to want to watch what's popular.

That's clearly not true of babies, and not for most toddlers or preschoolers, either. Even kids in day care or preschool aren't really aware that their friends may do or watch something different than they do at home. One child may know all the words to the *Bob the Builder* theme song and another may not, but three minutes of listening to a friend bellow it out will fix that. What's more, they don't see any distinction between "Can We Fix It?" and "Jingle Bells." They're just having fun.

So there's probably no pressure on you to let a young child watch anything in particular, or indeed, anything at all. You can pick and choose the programming that works for you and your child. And whatever you choose, you can ensure that it's part of a day filled with reading and other activities…because at this point, they can't work the remote!

Videos for Babies

What is there for a baby under three to watch? For newborns, nothing. Their eyes just aren't set up yet to take in anything on television, although they might enjoy the music. It isn't until five or six months that they begin to have the depth perception and focusing ability necessary to view an object on the screen.

There are plenty of videos designed for slightly older babies. Most present screen shots of simple objects and toys, rotating or rolling or doing whatever they do, with a background of classical music, children's music, or even identification of the object in several languages. Some wash the screen with a color, then say the color name, or offer and identify a shape. Some show puppets interacting with babies to identify, describe, and sort the objects. All are intentionally slow and free of confusing narrative or flash editing.

After complaints by the Center for a Commercial Free Childhood and an FTC investigation, the producers of these videos no longer make educational claims—and without an adult companion, babies and children are unlikely to learn anything from a video. Julie Clark, founder of the Baby Einstein Company (now owned by Disney), likened her products to "video board books," but the comparison's not particularly apt. There's nothing to chew, no pages to turn, and no underlying lesson about the joys of a book. The baby can't control it or interact with it.

But you can't read board books, or any books, to your baby all the time.

Nor can you play peekaboo, dance, and sing for all of baby's waking hours, and sometimes, even the nicest little ones just won't amuse themselves. So if a video helps you take a shower in peace, we say turn it on.

TIP: Try a homemade video. Who is baby's favorite video star? Baby! If you've got a video camera in your phone or tablet, you can easily create a slow, easy-to-watch video for your baby just by…recording your baby. Or yourself singing a song to baby. Or your baby lying next to another baby. No action, no flash cuts, just baby.

Slow-Moving Videos for Babies

- Baby Einstein: *Baby Mozart: Music Festival* and *Baby Bach: Musical Adventure*. There are many titles in this series, but these two originals, created by Julie Aigner-Clark before the sale to Disney, outshine the others for their simplicity: no bells and whistles, just toys, the occasional puppet, and music.
- Fisher Price: *Baby's Day, Musical Baby, Baby Moves, Nature Baby*. A trio of puppets, babies, and parents interact accompanied by fun music.
- Baby Nick Jr.: Curious Buddy Series. With titles like *Curious Buddies: Look and Listen at the Park* and *Exploring at the Beach*. (Incidentally, these were the videos used in the Georgetown University research regarding whether babies could learn from interacting with a computer.)
- Brainy Baby: *Left Brain, Right Brain*. These take the educational premise a bit far by introducing French, Spanish, and early math concepts, but there are plenty of baby faces and toys to engage your baby.
- PBS Kids: *Teletubbies*. People either love or hate this oddly mesmerizing show with its baby-talking life-size puppet creatures frolicking through their evergreen land and offering a very early introduction to concepts like color and shape and basic social lessons.

Toddler TV

Gone are the days when the only educational television came out of the Children's Television Workshop and most other viewing involved cartoons with falling anvils or hunting "wabbits." Thirty-odd years ago, Susan's four-year-old son Ben had memorized the video they'd made of a *Charlie Brown* special and could recite it, complete with character voice imitations. His younger sister Emma, conquering her fear of the Wicked Witch of the West, acted as "Dorfy," traveling regularly to her own imaginary Oz, stuffed dog Toto and basket in hand.

Today there are more programs than ever before, and even whole cable networks directed specifically at toddlers. Programs are simple and offer take-away lessons that you can use in a package your child will enjoy. These shows are not designed for you. If you watch too long, you may feel your brain leeching out of your eyeballs. There are no inside jokes and no clever references—nothing, in fact, to take the toddler away from the story. That's what makes them work so well for small children.

Of course, there's a catch. Kids have been watching television since it

What about the Commercials?

Here's the thing about commercials aimed at babies and toddlers—they work. Justine was changing channels, looking for a program for three-year-old Hailey, when she paused at a Dannon commercial. As the familiar logo filled the screen, Hailey turned to her mother and said, "I want yogurt."

So if you want your child to develop a pressing need for anything and everything that advertisers choose to put in front of her, then commercials are fine. If not, you might want to avoid them. Some networks offer commercial-free programs but allow sponsors for their shows to include a short, nonproduct-oriented message with their name and logo. In other words, if your child is familiar with McDonald's, it will make her think about McDonald's, and if not, it won't. Most videos or DVDs include commercials for other videos or even movies, but these are easily skipped as long as you're in charge of the machinery.

first flickered its way into our lives and living rooms, but a primary difference between the way we watched then and the way we watch now is that families used to all watch the same thing together. Twenty-five years ago *The Wizard of Oz* was an annual TV event, not a DVD, and kids enjoyed it curled up on the sofa between Mom and Dad. There may be more programming out there for toddlers, and toddlers may be able to get more out of it than ever before, but if you're going to refer back to the lessons learned in today's episode and help your baby connect with the material, you're going to have to watch, too.

We understand that you're not encouraging your child to watch TV because you have a pressing desire to see the animated version of *Maisy*. That's fine. Here's our suggestion—watch with her at least once. From there, if you're nearby, you can field questions, reinforce any lessons, and just generally know what's going on, and when you're not, you're not. As with books, your child learns better if you're with her, but she doesn't have to learn all the time—and eventually, she'll have the hang of the various call-and-response games all by herself.

Eleven Great Programs (Video, DVD, or Live) for Toddlers and Twos

1. *Blue's Clues*. This program (Blue the puppy leaves three clues to help viewers solve a simple riddle in each episode) genuinely teaches children useful reasoning skills and problem solving with every episode, and yet it's completely entertaining to them. They don't tune out or become suspicious when the learning starts, because it's all part and parcel of the whole. It takes the political correctness thing a little far by celebrating "Love Day" and "Thankfulness Day" instead of Valentine's Day and Thanksgiving, but it's tough to fault anyone for being too inclusive.

2. *Bob the Builder*. These talking construction vehicles entrance most children. Although clearly a sidekick, Wendy appears to be Bob's equal

in the construction business, a nice gender-neutral touch, and the townspeople come in all races, shapes, and sizes—rare in cartoons and claymation, which generally handle diversity by creating blue and green and purple people rather than using more prevalent skin tones. Bob and Wendy hammer home the moral a little too hard at times, but kids don't seem to notice.

3. *Caillou.* This is perhaps the most realistic children's program available, about a sometimes whiny four-year-old doing everyday four-year-old things, like getting sick, learning to ice skate, and struggling to deal with his younger sister. It's an idealized life but one with plenty of useful lessons and encouragement for kids having the same experiences.

4. *Clifford.* Clifford and friends teach those ubiquitous lessons about feelings and friendship but with a nice pro-reading message in every episode.

5. *Daniel Tiger's Neighborhood.* This is PBS's adaptation of *Mr. Roger's Neighborhood*, a simple, story-driven program focused on social lessons featuring animated versions of the puppets who starred with Fred Rogers long ago.

6. *Maisy.* The straightforward, matter-of-fact voice of the narrator actually addresses Maisy and her friends as they encounter common toddler problems, like forgetting to go to the bathroom, and fantasies, like driving a train or a plane.

7. *Oswald.* This surreal, colorful little program about an octopus and his friends, a penguin and a flower, holds younger children's attention just through the artwork and animation and offers funny stories and unusually presented lessons for older toddlers and up. ("Try new things" is conveyed by a day in which the more adventurous Oswald has all kinds of good things happen to him, while "just like always" Henry the penguin misses out.)

8. *Sesame Street / Elmo's World.* This is the classic, the one kids' program almost everyone is happy to see. Because it's something of a variety show and not very predictable (each season did different things in a different

order, and all seasons are rerun constantly, so that there's no consistent format), some toddlers won't be able to enjoy it until they're a little older. If yours doesn't want to stay tuned, save the whole program for later and try an Elmo video or DVD instead.

9. *Team Umizoomi*. A diverse computer-animated team of charming characters explores simple math concepts through teamwork and narrative.

10. *Word World*. Words come alive, interact, and save the day in this simple show dedicated to learning letters, letter sounds, and social skills.

11. *Yo Gabba Gabba*. A musical extravaganza dance party, with goofy costumed characters, famous guests, and brief segments encouraging kids to interact, dance, or solve puzzles.

Books Based on Television, and Television Based on Books

Sesame Street, *Blue's Clues*, and *Dora the Explorer* all have at least two things in common. They're clever, honestly educational programs created especially for toddlers and preschoolers. And they have toy and book and clothing tie-ins galore. Shows like *Maisy*, *Max and Ruby*, and *Clifford* come from the other side of the spectrum: they were books first, television second. Either way, if one of these programs becomes your child's favorite, you'll find plenty to delight her on the bookstore or library shelves.

Here's one area where the old-fashioned technology of a book is actually an improvement over the video: you can take it with you. It's a physical companion, a little bit of your child's video friend that can come along in the stroller or car seat. Unlike a phone or small video player, dropping it won't hurt it, it won't run out of batteries, and you can't accidentally press a button and end the whole thing. Your child can return to certain pages or moments in the story again and again without the help of an adult with a remote control.

Generally, books that were books first and television shows second read better than books that were created as TV tie-ins, but either way, they really work.

Books and toys encourage kids to take the characters they've already fallen in love with beyond the screen. If Blue can go for her checkup in the book, she can go for her checkup on your couch, too, and maybe Mommy and the rest of your toys can be patients as well. She doesn't always sound like the Blue on TV, and she doesn't always do things in the exact same order. It's liberating.

There's a great fear that watching videos (or television) of favorite characters will replace children's ability to imagine characters of their own. It may be that a child who's seen a moving, talking video character may be fascinated enough to add that character to her play repertoire, but for most kids, what they've seen isn't going to be enough. They're going to want to bring the character into their world.

Books That Started It All: Great Books That Became Good Television

- *Clifford the Big Red Dog*, Norman Bridwell
- *Bunny Cakes* (Max and Ruby), Rosemary Wells
- *I Will Never Not Ever Eat a Tomato* (Charlie and Lola), Lauren Child
- *Where's Maisy?*, Lucy Cousins
- *Miffy*, Dick Bruna
- *Winnie the Pooh*, A. A. Milne
- *Thomas the Tank Engine*, Wilbert Awdry, C. Reginald Dalby (illus.)
- *Little Bear*, Else Holmelund Minarik, Maurice Sendak (illus.)
- *Miss Spider's Tea Party*, David Kirk

For toddlers, the appeal of these books is also the extension of the familiar. These characters are proven through years of strong kid appeal (or heavily test-marketed and designed to appeal to your child)—which is why you'll find kids who've never watched a program gravitating toward the tie-in shelves. If the effect of all this market research spooks you, remember that the Sesame Street characters were designed in the same way. It's not necessarily done with wholly commercial intentions.

"Sam certainly watches some kids' television, but even the shows that bring some of his favorite characters to life don't seem to have affected the way he sees them. The Percy on the Thomas the Tank Engine videos may be a boy, but the Percy on his train table is a girl, and his Thomas can fly. Occasionally his Thomas acts out something from a video, but for the most part, he leads his own odd little life. The day I overheard Thomas learning to be a sushi chef, I stopped worrying about Sam's imagination for good." —KJ

Books associated with television programs or videos can also help ease your child's transition from board books to longer stories with more narrative. They can encourage a child to sit alone and turn the pages—another step on the road to reading. For older children, the increased familiarity with the characters and illustrations makes them prime learn-to-read material. There's something about being comfortable with the story structure and the pictures that makes it easier to take a risk like trying to read the words.

And most importantly, a book is a book, whether it evolved into television or was based on a television character. It's a subliminal reminder that entertainment is not confined to the screen. Reading may link your child to a program or video she knows and loves, but it engages her in a different way.

TIP: Looking for short videos based on children's books? Look no further than those created by Weston Woods (now distributed by Scholastic). Many libraries carry these gems in DVD. The array of books Weston Woods has faithfully adapted is staggering. Check out the video and the book and let your child enjoy two different experiences of a favorite story.

Talking to the Author: Norman Bridwell

What's it like to have your book turned into a TV show? Norman Bridwell, writer and creator of Clifford, knows.

I was really delighted because I knew it would be a quality product if Scholastic was producing it and PBS was going to show it. Somebody else was interested in doing a *Clifford* show years ago, and they wanted gangs of boys, they wanted conflict, they wanted evil villains. And that's just not Clifford. Clifford is a gentle, nurturing character, and I think PBS is the right spot for him. There aren't any disasters or car chases. It's a nice, gentle show. I've watched my six-year-old granddaughter sit absolutely glued to the set. She's a very active little girl, but during *Clifford* she sits. It's almost like Mr. Rogers with fur.

Is Educational TV Really Educational?

Do kids learn from TV? Absolutely. Researchers have found that babies as young as twelve months can take a cue from a video of a woman reacting negatively to an enticing object. When offered a choice between that object and another, babies avoid the item they've seen create the negative effect. Will an hour of *Sesame Street* "sponsored by the letter A" help a toddler recognize the letter A? Yes, especially (always the catch) if the lesson is reinforced by a living person.

> **TIP: Stick to age-appropriate programs for as long as you can. It's worth noting that *Blue's Clues* is intended for ages three to six, and often features reading or pre-reading activities, yet some parents consider their four- and five-year-olds to have "grown out of it." Be honest: which of you is really tired of *Sesame Street*?**

From age two on, high-quality programs can actually increase vocabulary, letter-sound knowledge, comprehension, and the ability to follow and relate to a narrative. It appears that kids can and do learn from programs like

Blue's Clues that are designed to teach and achieve educational goals in each episode. Colors and shapes appear and are described, words are written on the screen, snacks are measured and counted, and your child learns.

True literacy is reading, writing, speaking, and listening. For children three and under, the last two are primary. TV and videos provide content for them—fodder for their own conversations. Watching improves listening skills and gives them something to talk about. Of course, they may learn a few other things, too. The creators of kids' TV excel when it comes to teaching letters, colors, and other concepts. Things get a little fuzzier when it comes to behavior. There's no guarantee that your child will remember the moral of a story instead of imitating the bad behavior that led up to it. "Mean words hurt" may not cancel out the clarion call of "Stupid!"

The key, again, is to know what shows and videos your child is watching. This allows you to reinforce the positive lesson, especially if some of the less-desirable behaviors start showing up in your child. It also allows you to reinforce any new vocabulary as well as narrative skills by encouraging your child to tell you about what she watched. Sometimes, if you want TV to be specifically educational, you're going to have to dig in and create the education yourself.

"Joey loves every detail of the ever-popular Thomas videos, and he's definitely learning from them. "'Out of my way,' Gordon said as he rushed past,' he'll shout as he runs through the room. Only three, but his ability to write fictional dialogue already seems secure." —Laura

---

Audio Books for Babies and Toddlers (A Treat for Them, a Break for You!)

Many parents swear by audio books. Audio books can work for babies as a soothing pre-nap listen or background noise in the car. A pleasant voice and rhythmic words please almost any baby, and the more familiar a particular song or story becomes, the happier it will make her. Toddlers can hold a book themselves and learn to turn the pages at the "ding" sound—another great activity for the back of the car or rest time.

New mom Amanda, on leave from her job in publishing, remembers being stunned by the amount of time she spent sidelined, nursing her newborn. She couldn't juggle a book, daytime TV left her cold, and she was desperate for some distraction. Her office sent over audio books of all the Newberry award winners (some of the best books for older children). Her baby boy seemed to find them just as soothing as she did.

Longer audio books, without an accompanying picture book, might please toddlers in the car as well, and they definitely work for an older child with a toddler sibling. Most bookstores carry audio / picture book sets, and libraries have a large selection to borrow. For longer audio books, you may have to check online bookstores, catalogs (Chinaberry usually has a nice selection), or order from your local bookstore. Many are also available for download at www.audible.com.

Ten Great Listens

Some children's audio books come packaged as a book and CD set, and others are just the audio either for download or in CD format. Most audio books can be listened to in snippets online. It's a great help to all of us. And don't forget www.audible.com if you use any kind of MP3 player. In addition, many public libraries have downloadable audio available for check-out via their websites.

1. *Abiyoyo*, Pete Seeger (author and performer), Michael Hayes (illus.). Book and CD set. This is Seeger's famous "story song" with the folk artist singing and telling it himself. A wonderful story to hear repeatedly.

2. *Alexander and the Terrible, Horrible, No Good, Very Bad Day, and Other Stories and Poems*, Judith Viorst, Blythe Danner (narrator). Alexander's rotten day is the perfect lead-off for this humorous collection of Judith Viorst's stories and poems about the ups and downs of childhood, read by Blythe Danner. Also included are *Alexander, Who Used to Be Rich Last Sunday* and *The Tenth Good Thing about Barney*.

3. *The Cat in the Hat and Other Dr. Seuss Favorites* and *Green Eggs and Ham and Other Servings of Dr. Seuss*, Dr. Seuss. Each collection contains nine complete stories, read by luminaries like Jason Alexander, Kelsey Grammer, Dustin Hoffman, David Hyde Pierce, and John Cleese.

4. *Corduroy*, Don Freeman, Allyson Johnson (narrator). This little girl and her chosen bear remain enchanting and endearing. (Also *Corduroy Lost and Found*.)

5. *Don't Let the Pigeon Stay Up Late*, Mo Willems (author and reader). Willems himself narrates this tale of the pigeon begging to stay up past his bedtime despite his obvious fatigue. An ALA Notable Children's Recording for 2012.

6. *Joseph Had a Little Overcoat*, Simms Taback (author and reader). In today's throwaway world, Joseph's old-fashioned frugality is a welcome change. Based on a Yiddish song from Simms Taback's youth, the book / CD package is filled with delightful rhythms (provided by The Klezmatics music troupe) and arresting colors.

7. *Mama Don't Allow*, Thacher Hurd, Tom Chapin (narrator). Wonderful for its jazzy music and bayou feel, this is a story of a band playing their hearts out at the alligator ball…until they discover that they're on the menu for the final feast.

8. *Mouse Tales Audio Collection*, Arnold Lobel (author and reader). "Papa, please tell us a tale." When Papa's seven little mouse boys ask for a bedtime story, Papa does even better than that—he tells seven stories, one for each boy! *Mouse Soup* finds Mouse in a jam—soon he'll be weasel soup! Just in time, he thinks up a clever and entertaining way to distract

weasel from serving up mouse soup for supper. Other Arnold Lobel titles are also available in audio.

9. *Snowy Day*, Ezra Jack Keats, Linda Terheyden (narrator). A favorite story of a child's first snowfall read aloud.

10. *Stone Soup*, Jon Muth, B. D. Wong (narrator), This fine version of the classic folktale has received accolades from the American Library Association and the Audies (the "Oscars" of audiobooks).

Love Trucks, Trains, or Turtles? Video Coming Up!

Toddlers and preschoolers often develop an all-consuming interest in a particular subject. They can be surprisingly sophisticated about the information that interests them—if it involves their beloved trucks, snakes, or planets, they'll remember it.

Fortunately, you can find videos designed for young children on a variety of nonfiction subjects, as well as videos that work for all ages. These can also be a nice way for a child to share an interest with an adult. Like Sam, KJ's father loves trains, and the two are happy to watch videos on the Age of Steam together. There are videos about trucks, airplanes and airports, space travel, bugs, and every kind of animal you can imagine. Even older babies are often intrigued by animal programming.

YouTube offers free, simple, usually user-created video of just about any obsession a toddler could have, including garbage trucks and penguins (we think sympathetic grandparents must be uploading the former). User comments will usually tell you if there's anything to be wary of in a given clip.

> **TIP: Put together a few packages that combine a new book, a video or DVD, and a small toy or treat (like stickers or small plastic animals) on something that interests your child to pull out on a rainy day.**

Learning More from Book and Video Teams

- *National Geographic—Really Wild Animals: Deep Sea Dive* (National Geographic Video) with *My Visit to the Aquarium*, Aliki, and *Fish* (DK Eyewitness) by Steve Parker
- *Real Wheels: Mega Truck Adventures* (Warner Home Video) with *I Stink*, Kate McMullan, Jim McMullan (illus.), and *The Little Fire Engine*, Lois Lenski
- *The Alphabet Train* (Railway Productions) with *All Aboard!: A True Train Story*, Susan Kuklin

When Matt's daughter Hailey was two, he was searching for something to interest her on a hotel TV and came across what looked like a nature program about snakes. He drew her attention to it—just as the man holding the snake popped the snake into his mouth and bit its head off. Matt finally calmed Hailey down, but over a year later, he's never been able to explain why to her satisfaction.

Watching Adult TV in a Toddler's House

Parents of toddlers might fear that the "addictive" quality of TV will mean their child will "zone out" and watch anything. Instead, it turns out that those elements that make adult television compelling for us are exactly the same elements that turn off a toddler. We get hooked by a developing plot and stay tuned when characters are excited and all talk at once. We can tolerate some confusion; in fact, we're intrigued by it.

Toddlers can't do this. Most toddlers are ready to tune out when the television show is clearly not for them. But nothing creates conflict like an adult who wants to watch something on TV and a child who wants the adult to watch, well, her. As anyone who has ever watched an NBA final basketball game with an articulate two-year-old can testify, it just doesn't work. "What that?" "Where it go?" "Why you say 'Oh!'?" "Why he do that?" "Why you say 'No!'?" "Why?" "Why?" "WHY?" They go quickly from trying to join you, to trying to get you to join them, to the kinds of crashes and "accidents" that always command your attention. It's not a happy picture.

> **TIP: Don't put a TV or video player in your child's room. If you'd like her to be able to watch her TV while you watch yours, try a portable DVD player or tablet instead. They're increasingly inexpensive, versatile, and far easier to control.**

Should you turn it off, or save it for later? Your choice. You are the adult, and you deserve the kind of break in your day that a favorite show or sporting event represents. Understanding that the baby feels she is competing for your attention may help, if it's a problem. You could offer a special snack or set out special toys for her during your TV time. You might want to encourage her to play nearby, although not right in front of the TV. Eventually she'll understand that you'll return your attention to her soon and enjoy the time for solo play.

"I remember watching the Wimbledon tennis tournament on TV when Ben was about twenty months old. The TV was on a shelf above his head, and he stood squarely in front of it, looking up, and declaring, 'I HATE Wimbledon!'" —Susan

Babies, Toddlers, and Computers

Televisions are no longer the only fascinating big box in the house. Your baby or toddler sees you using your computer every day, and they're likely to want to join you. Plenty of toymakers, marketers, and even publishing companies are ready to help them jump on the bandwagon by offering computer games and even special "laptops" for small children.

"Our kids love the computer. We like boohbah.com. Both my two- and three-year-old (and thirty-two-year-old me!) get such a kick out of this fun, wordless site, and both kids are great at using the mouse (in our case touch pad) because of it. It has games, art / color pages, and music pages. I do try to stop while we're still having fun. It's easy to get frustrated or fight over who gets to do what. Once that starts, we stop. We also use the computer to practice recognizing letters. They love touching the buttons so we play Touch the A. I call the letters and they find them and strike them and they go up on the screen in lowercase. I make the font extra big and the kids really love it." —Jane

Special computer keyboards and software can allow your child to sit down, press a red key, and watch a red circle appear on the screen. It's fun, and it does convey the connection between the keyboard and the screen. Other than that, computer software generally offers the same "lessons" in colors, shapes, and letter recognition that are available in board books, and for a child under three, most of it requires special hardware. It's expensive, and there's no evidence that starting your child off on the computer before three is going to increase her abilities later, although for children three and over, computer time seems to increase school readiness.

The interactivity of the computer is both its appeal and its downfall for children under three. Even with a special keyboard, they're likely to need your help and not just to get them set up. A missed mouse move sends them off to the parents' instructions or freezes the action. A bump to a child's keyboard placed over a regular keyboard moves it and changes the meaning of every key hit. When you're just developing fine motor control, just pushing the button you meant to push can be a challenge, and a keyboard is a ready source of frustration.

Many popular kids' websites have activities that kids under three can enjoy with an adult, no additional hardware needed. Some have short video stories with a "button" to push to reach the next "page" or a game that allows her to dress a favorite character. You may have to do the keyboard and mouse manipulation, but your child can make the decisions. These games can be a nice treat for a child who's played at your side while you pay the bills or email friends, and can gradually encourage a child to try a little mouse-work herself.

TIP: Put a bright green sticker (green = go) on the left-click button of your mouse to help a young child learn where to press.

Websites That Work for Babies, Toddlers, and Twos

Keep in mind that most sites are geared towards a wide age range. Each site identified here has several activities that work for very young children, but you'll want to take a quick look and choose something you think your child can manage and enjoy before logging on with her.

- **Funwithspot.com**. Simple games and printable activity pages with Eric Hill's popular little dog.
- **HITEntertainment.com**. Activities from favorite videos like *Bob the Builder* and *Thomas the Tank Engine*.
- **Jacksonpollock.org**. With the tap or flick of the mouse, you can create dribble and splash color on the screen in the style of the famed painter. It's addictively fun for adults, too.
- **Nickjr.com**. Lots of games for Nick-created shows like *Yo Gabba Gabba*, *Max and Ruby*, and *Dora*, plus "stories" that are read aloud using an arrow click to turn the page.
- **PBSKids.org**. Games, activities, and printout coloring pages from PBS favorites like *Daniel Tiger's Neighborhood*, *Teletubbies*, and *Caillou*. Try "Dress Caillou" and "Find Gilbert" (Caillou's cat).
- **Sesameworkshop.org**. Simple, non-flashy site with lots of games. Not surprisingly, those featuring Elmo work well for toddlers and twos, but check out other favorites as well.

Ages and Stages: Making the Big Boxes Interactive

We know, you're not always watching with her. But when you are, make it fun! And here are a few simple computer activities to try.

Newborn	Best TV strategy for the teeny-tiny? None. You and the other faces in your house are better than anything else. If you have digital cable, try using the digital music option to provide soothing classical background music. Moms might be able to email with one hand while nursing on the other. A happy, connected mother makes for a happier baby!
Heads Up	If you have any baby videos, watch together, and briefly. Try to gauge whether she's able to see the things on the screen. Giving her a disconnected mouse to hold might let you pay just one more bill with her on your lap.
Sitting	If you're watching a baby video, gather a few things in the house that appear on the screen. Give her a ball when the ball bounces by.
Crawling / Creeping	Let the baby video be background if she chooses. Make sure she has other things to amuse her when one is on (including books!). Give her an old, disconnected keyboard to crawl to and bang.
Cruising / Walking	Help her "dance" to a video with music and dancing, since she's unlikely to be able to sit still and watch anything. With her in your lap, set a word processing program to a really large font. Let her hit the keyboard and watch the letters appear.

Talking (a few words)	Start watching some programs with narrative together. Choose one and watch it over and over, then move on to another episode. Find books with a similar theme. Find (or draw) an image that supports one of her words. Show her the picture on the screen, then print it for her.
Talking More	Encourage her to make up stories of her own about favorite characters. Cut Elmo, or whoever, off a video or cereal box and tape a straw to his back to make a puppet. Take him along on an adventure. Check out (on your own) a website with games featuring favorite characters. Choose one you can do together and let her tell you how to move the mouse or what to click.
Running (but not talking much)	More dancing to videos, this time with less help from you. Look for characters appearing in books, but moving and doing more active things she can join in. Check out (on your own) a website with games featuring favorite characters. Choose one that allows her to point to things in answer to your questions.
Talking ALL THE TIME!	Ask her to tell you the story of the video she just watched. Encourage her to make up her own story about the characters. Help her to write a letter to a favorite character. Start to support the lessons in the programs. If A is the letter of the day, carry it forward. If Blue makes an alphabet train, make a few letter cars yourself. Can she begin to learn to use the mouse? Find a simple game on a kids' website and sit with her while she moves and clicks.

Chapter Nine
SEPARATION, FEAR, LOVE

◆◇◆◇◆◇◆◇◆◇◆◇◆◇◆◇◆◇◆◇◆◇◆◇◆◇◆◇◆◇◆◇◆◇◆◇◆◇◆

*Books to Help Babies
Understand What They Feel*

Babies are born fully equipped with the capacity to feel. From the very beginning, they are able to interact with their new world. Every new experience brings a rush of new and intense emotions. As they grow, they learn to identify and handle their feelings—and they learn it from you.

Some babies may start with a proclivity toward being calm or active, sensitive or sturdy, needy or competent, but all operate on a constantly fluctuating emotional continuum. Every experience, whether it's a diaper change, a first taste of banana, a sniff from the family dog, or visiting Grandma, is charged with a variety of feelings.

New parents are also experiencing a rush of new and intense emotions, interrupted sleep, new anxieties, and the sudden onset of enormous responsibility. As a new parent, you must constantly consider your baby's needs and work his existence into yours, all while trying to maintain your normal sense of self. Even the most empathetic parent can use a little help.

The Emotional World of Picture Books
Picture books offer both entertainment and comfort. Nearly every picture book has an emotional element, but many spotlight the emotions that babies and toddlers feel so intensely. When "Again! Again!" becomes a constant

Featured Book

How Are You Peeling? Food with Moods
Saxton Freymann and Joost Elffers

These two author-artists have identified personalities and feelings in peppers and oranges. They invest fruits and vegetables with a delightful humanity by the deft insertion of black-eyed peas and specifically articulated eyebrow carvings. We see and understand what the lemon is feeling. Beyond its surefire entertainment value, the point of this creative and humorous book is to help us all talk about feelings that can emerge when we are in or out of groups, loved or shunned, afraid or adored. A *New York Times* Best Illustrated Children's Book.

refrain, you have a rare opportunity to understand something of the child's mind at work. There could be a reason behind the request. It could be pure enjoyment, or it could be that the child himself is trying to master what is happening in the book. Like Susan's Ben, who loved Ferdinand's mother's willingness to just let him be, and KJ's Sam, who used Supercat to ask for a night-light, some children use books as a way to talk about something important.

No two-year-old is mature enough to say, "Mama, I feel that you are infringing on my developing personality. Please let me be who I am." Or even, "I've slept in the dark for two years but all of a sudden it's bothering me. Could I have a night-light please?" A book raises the issue in a way the child can't. What is your child asking you to read again and again?

Feelings enliven our lives. Without love, anger, fear, joy, and excitement, what is there? Life is full of frustrations, jealousies, and disappointments, feelings of anger and sadness about loss. No child grows up without them. Books help us all look at, think about, and talk about feelings.

What Is a Feeling?

- *Don't Worry Bear*, Greg Foley. Bear worries about his friend, a caterpillar, when his friend wraps himself in a cocoon. Simple, direct, and clear. Try *Thank You Bear*, too.
- *Feelings*, Aliki. All kinds of facial expressions suggest the feelings of the children.
- *Grumpy Bird*, Jeremy Tankard. When Bird wakes up feeling grumpy, a walk with his friends does the trick. Bird's grumpy face is priceless. Try *Boo Hoo Bird* for more of Bird's emotional life.
- *A Kiss Means I Love You*, Kathryn Madeline Allen, Eric Futran (photos). Through simple rhyming text and up-close photos, this volume explains body language and its meanings and feelings like no other.
- *Lots of Feelings*, Shelley Rotner. A multicultural group of preschoolers demonstrate their emotional range in expressive photos.
- *Mouse Was Mad*, Linda Urban, Henry Cole (illus.). Despite advice from other animals, Mouse learns his own way to deal with anger. A delightful lesson in anger management for those closer to three years.
- *Mrs. Biddlebox*, Linda Smith, Marla Frazee (illus.). A grown-up lady gets up on the wrong side of the bed and deals with it creatively by cooking away a very bad day. Whirling artwork supports this lady's can-do attitude.
- *My Many Colored Days*, Dr. Seuss, Steve Johnson and Lou Fancher (illus.). So many feelings and moods in such a small volume. Brilliant.
- *The Pigeon Has Feelings, Too*, Mo Willems. Willems' sparsely drawn pigeon reacts with characteristic testiness when the bus driver tries to command a happy face in this original board book.
- *Sometimes I Like to Curl Up in a Ball*, Vicki Churchill and Charles Fuge. A young wombat chronicles a day in his life and expresses himself quite well.
- *Sometimes I'm Bombaloo*, Rachel Vail, Yumi Heo (illus.). A really good big sister gets really angry when her baby brother messes with her things.

What's Going On in There?

All feelings are legitimate. Some emotions are just bigger, scarier, and tougher to deal with than others. Children feel these feelings, too. They come up at major times in our lives—the birth of a sibling, the death of a pet or grandparent. Filtering those emotions through the characters and story line of a book can help both of you learn to cope.

The big bad wolf can huff and puff, but the baby can tolerate the danger because he is cuddled up with you. Perhaps the big bad wolf symbolizes fear of the scary unknown, from the dark night sky to baby's own poorly understood destructive impulses. By sharing the book, you are educating him about his feelings. As he empathizes with the characters, he is expanding and understanding his emotional repertoire. He learns that small creatures overcome scary situations and triumph. It's right there, in his hands, in his book.

I Love You, I Hate You: Ambivalent Feelings

Ambivalence defines life with a baby and toddler. A parent may never have loved anyone quite so intensely as her new baby, nor felt such impotent, incoherent fury after weeks of sleepless nights or hours of colicky screaming. A baby or a toddler loves nothing more than his parents. He's totally, utterly dependent on them for physical and emotional nurturing. But sometimes they don't do exactly what he wants! Maybe some of those screams come from the shock of being angry at the ones he loves most.

Feelings are often complex. When he's frightened he may also be excited or sad. Anger begets confusion and sadness, as well as, perhaps, a feeling of power.

Sometimes it's easiest to look at emotions in the context of the issues that create them. Books that help describe the most common issues, like separation, may also apply to other feelings and emotions. For a specific concern or issue like divorce, adoption, or illness, you can consult your local librarian for guidance.

Separations: Planning Together for Being Apart

From the moment the umbilical cord is cut, separation from Mother and from family is inevitable and constant. From naptime to child care, from bedtime to the death of Grandma, from the big kids going to school to the whole family moving houses, separations are going to happen to your child. Some are family-specific: a family member or parent may deploy with the military, or a much older sibling or aunt go to college—while some, like going to preschool, or having a babysitter, happen to everyone. Either way, separations are intense.

Reading Together about Being Apart

- *Don't Want to Go!*, Shirley Hughes. Hughes expertly uses a classic childhood scenario in her tale. Lily does not want to be dropped at a neighbor's house when her mom is sick, but when Dad comes to pick her up at the end of a fun day, she doesn't want to go home.
- *The Kissing Hand*, Audrey Penn, Ruth E. Harper, and Nancy M. Leak (illus.). Putting a kiss into the palm of your brave young child before he goes to school is a good coping strategy for separations.
- *Little Owl Lost*, Chris Haughton. When Little Owl falls out of the nest, he receives help from the other forest dwellers to find his way back home.
- *A New Year's Reunion*, Li Qiong Yu, Zhu Cheng Liang (illus.). Maybe this book is a little mature for our target audience, but it deals with an important topic—a parent's extended absence. Because of his work, Maomao's father comes home only once a year to celebrate the Chinese New Year. A *New York Times* Best Illustrated Children's Book.
- *Oh My Baby, Little One*, Kathi Appelt, Jane Dyer (illus.). A book almost as much for you as for the baby, about how Mama Bird misses Baby when they're apart.

- *Owl Babies*, Martin Waddell, Patrick Benson (illus.). Perhaps the ultimate book on separation anxiety, three owl siblings deal with their mother's surprising absence in the night.
- *Pouch!*, David Ezra Stein. A joey experiments with independence as he plays outside of his kangaroo mother's pouch, but he quickly hops back to his home base when things get a little scary. Little ones will recognize themselves here.
- *The Runaway Bunny*, Margaret Wise Brown, Clement Hurd (illus.). This toddler version of a romantic, chivalric poem affirms a mother's love: My love is so deep that if you go away, I'll follow right behind. (In Spanish, *El conejito andarín*.)
- *When I Miss You*, Cornelia Maude Spelman, Kathy Parkinson (illus.). A little guinea pig narrates what it is like to be separated from Mom and Dad and explores some coping strategies.
- *You Go Away*, Dorothy Corey, Diane Paterson (illus.). The simple, repeated text of "You go away. You come back…" and the recognizable scenes of toddlerhood in watercolor have made this the go-to book on separation anxiety for years. The board book edition has illustrations by Lisa Fox.

"My two-year-old godson Malcolm was visiting from New Hampshire. His parents left me in charge of him for the evening, one of the first times he had been left with a sitter. Malcolm was fussy that night and cried and seemed to miss his parents. I pulled out Go Away, Big Green Monster, *and we read it over and over and over again. He would shout 'G'Way!' at the top of his lungs at the appropriate moments. I think we read it twenty times that night. It was the only thing that distracted him. That book helped him get through his separation anxiety. A couple of months later, I gave him the book for Christmas. After he ripped off the wrapping paper and saw the cover, his face lit up. He ran over to me immediately, and we read it together. We made a strong personal connection through that book." —Rachel*

The feelings connected to these separations can trigger a sense of loss, or even of abandonment. These are profound feelings. They may influence the reunions, too. Has your baby ignored you when you pick him up from the babysitter, or screamed when you came home from work or shopping? Or like the smallest owlet in *Owl Babies*, did he appear happy to have you return?

Parents have feelings about separation, too. Of course a mother wants a child to move on and go to day care, elementary school, and college. But we also want them to stay right here in our arms. Similarly, even the most loving child sometimes wants nothing more than to move away from his parents and have more grown-up experiences and adventures without a mother hovering behind. But the very idea can be terrifying. Children's books like *Alice in Wonderland*; *Peter Pan*; *Charlotte's Web*; *Stuart Little*; *Babar*; *Bambi*; *The Lion, the Witch, and the Wardrobe*; *The Wizard of Oz*; *The Secret Garden*; and the Harry Potter books are safe ways of trying it out.

The good news is that these books exist for younger children as well, with richly imagined characters who have real feelings and grow to know more about their needs and capacities. Seeing a fictional character endure and triumph fortifies a child for separations of his own.

Charlotte's Top Ten

"These days when Charlotte (eighteen months) can't sleep, instead of asking for milk or Mama, she plaintively cries for 'booky,' hoping against hope that we'll turn on the light and read. Often we do because it's the only thing that calms her down. Even in less stressful moments, Charlotte loves to read. She sits and looks at books on her own, pointing out things she recognizes, and she'll sit and be read to for longer than she'll do just about anything else. Charlotte is pretty fickle about books; she'll love a particular book for a few weeks and then, like that, drop it for something new. Some books she's rejected since the moment I've brought them home. If I pick up a book she doesn't want, she says *NO* adamantly and pushes it away. She asks for books by name, and I better produce them immediately or watch out. These days she seems to prefer bigger books with a simple story rather than board books, but as I said, her tastes change pretty radically every few weeks. Here are the current favorites." —Jane

1. *Maisy Goes Shopping* (and all of the other paperback Maisy books), Lucy Cousins
2. *There's a Wocket in My Pocket*, Dr. Seuss
3. *I Can Do It Too!*, Karen Baicker, Ken Wilson-Max (illus.)
4. *Please, Baby, Please*, Spike Lee, Tonya Lewis Lee, Kadir Nelson (illus.)
5. *The Monster at the End of This Book*, Jon Stone, Michael Smollin (illus.)
6. *Eat Up, Dudley!*, David Wojtowycz (out of print)
7. *Five Little Monkeys with Nothing to Do*, Eileen Christelow
8. *Miss Spider's Tea Party* and *Miss Spider's New Car*, David Kirk (though she's always hated Little Miss Spider)
9. *Green Eggs and Ham*, Dr. Seuss
10. *Baby's Bedtime* and *Baby's Mealtime*, Fiona Watt, Racheal Wells (illus.) (out of print)

"We have been singing the same bedtime song, 'This Pretty Planet,' to Colin since he was a baby. Now, at age two, when he hears us sing it, he gets up and walks himself to his crib. Not sure how long this is going to last, but it is nice now! For nap we sing 'You Are My Sunshine' so Colin knows it is a different time of day." —Rachel

The Bedtime Parting

For babies, bedtime is another form of separation. Toddlers may understand that morning will come, but even two-year-olds have some trouble with why they have to go to sleep without you! A baby quickly develops myriad techniques for keeping the parent with him, from the marvelous litanies of "good nights" in the venerable *Goodnight Moon* to the demand "I want to hear one book more" in *How Do Dinosaurs Say Goodnight?* Best to start now with getting bedtime techniques down pat since you've got plenty of bedtimes to come.

Twelve Books for Bedtime

1. *Baby BeeBee Bird*, Diane Redfield Massie, Steven Kellogg (illus.). Silence settles over the noisy zoo, until BEEBEEBOBBIBOBBIBEE-BEEBOBBIBOBBI! The animals will have to teach the Baby BeeBee Bird what night is for before anyone will sleep. Especially great for families with a new baby who's not exactly sleeping on schedule.

2. *Back to Bed, Ed!*, Sebastien Braun. Ed, a young mouse, does not want to sleep alone, but soon, with patient help from his parents, he discovers a comforting way to rest easy in his own bed.

3. *Bedtime for Mommy*, Amy Krouse Rosenthal, Le Uyen Pham (illus.). This little girl pulls Mommy away from a highly recognizable messy computer desk for a tub, a book (*Anna Karenina*, and there's no time for just one more), and—after a last glass of water—bed.

4. *The Bunny's Night-Light: A Glow-in-the-Dark Search*, Geoffrey Hayes. Bunny and his parents search for the perfect night-light. Hayes's art is endearing, and the glow-in-the-dark features are fun.

5. *Chicken Bedtime Is Really Early*, Erica S. Perl, George Bates (illus.). Bright farm backgrounds get dimmer as it gets later, and more and more of the animals are off to bed. Chicken bedtime is early. Hamster's is late, but everyone's up at dawn when the rooster crows.

6. *Good Night, Harry*, Kim Lewis. A stuffed elephant has trouble falling asleep, unlike his two companions.

7. *It's Bedtime, Wibbly Pig!*, Mick Inkpen. But let us count the ways Wibbly Pig delays the inevitable!

8. *Jibberwillies at Night*, Rachel Vail, Yumi Heo (illus.). Katie and her mother come up with a creative solution when the "Jibberwillies" bother Katie at bedtime.

9. *Joshua's Night Whispers*, Angela Johnson, Rhonda Mitchell (illus.). What's a little boy to do when afraid of noises in the night? Dad is reassuringly available.

10. *Llama, Llama, Red Pajama*, Anna Dewdney. Mama's read a story and turned out the light, and where is she? When he calls and she doesn't immediately return, baby llama begins to wail in this little drama every parent will recognize. The big, bold pictures and the way baby llama's stuffed llama echoes his every expression are charming. For a simplified board book depiction of the nighttime routine also from Dewdney, try *Llama Llama Nighty-Night*.

11. *No Go Sleep*, Kate Feiffer, Jules Feiffer (illus.). The frogs promise to croak soothingly, the moon promises to shine, but baby says, "No Go Sleep!"

12. *Es hora de dormir / Time for Bed*, Mem Fox, Jane Dyer (illus.). This lovely good-night poem with soothing watercolors shows baby animals (and one token human) getting ready for bed. This one has that rare *Goodnight Moon* magic to help lull a child to sleep. In Spanish and English, but an English only edition is available. For Denise Fleming's beautiful take on a similar theme, try *Sleepy, Oh So Sleepy*.

Death and Dying, the Ultimate Separation

Death, of course, is the most permanent loss, but it's also part of life. Although you might have an instinct to shield young children from this reality, if your family is dealing with a death—of a pet, a friend, or a relative—it's better to address it than to have him coming up with his own ideas, which are bound to include the idea that this is not a safe subject to talk about. Once again, a good book can help to create a framework for talking and for understanding.

Six Books to Help Discuss Death

1. *Frog and the Birdsong*, Max Velthuijs. Out-of-print but worth searching out, this is a very simple and accepting description of death, prompted by the discovery of a dead bird. From an award-winning Dutch artist.

2. *Good-Bye, Sheepie*, Robert Burleigh, Peter Catalanotto (illus). This is a direct story of a boy losing and burying his beloved dog. With some abridgement, this could be accessible for twos.

3. *Missy Mommy: A Book About Bereavement*, Rebecca Cobb. An honest look at a difficult time in a young boys life, but he finds comfort in his family's love and support.

4. *Nana Upstairs & Nana Downstairs*, Tomie dePaola. This is a gentle but clear story about losing a grandmother.

5. *The Old Dog*, Charlotte Zolotow, James Ransome (illus.). The inevitable tears and sadness at the death of a pet are treated as appropriate and expected. While the resolution may be a bit quick, it is a very honest, sympathetic, and artfully painted picture book.

6. *When a Pet Dies*, Fred Rogers, Jim Judkis (illus.). Mr. Rogers offers a comforting way of talking and thinking about this huge permanent loss in a child's (and parent's) life.

"We have a sweet (but a little heartbreaking) story about Hondo & Fabian. The book is about a dog named Hondo and a cat named Fabian. I had been reading it to Jack almost from birth. The cover has this great drawing of Hondo and Fabian on it. When our dog Goose passed away, Jackson was about fourteen months old. He missed his friend and he used to crawl to the bookcase, pull this book off the shelf, tap on the picture of Hondo the dog, and point to where Goose used to sleep. It was so nice to know that he understood his friend was gone and that he missed him. Since he was not verbal yet, his only way to communicate this to us was through the book." —Brian

Growing, Changing Families

For all the angst surrounding separation from family, there is a fair bit of struggle involved in being a part of a family as well. Who are these people? What do they do with the baby? What happens if another baby comes along?

The family is a young child's universe: his academy for learning, his laboratory for experimenting, and the mirror in which he sees himself. Books abound that describe and celebrate baby's growing awareness of himself in relation to his family, helping him learn their names and the names of other things and places in his life.

Books and Traumatic Events

The stories of natural disasters and violence can hit families very close to home. Parents often search for a book to explain it all to children in times like these. Young children respond to these events differently than adults and may find explanations and books intended for older kids on such topics confusing and overwhelming. At these times, it is important for young children to know they are loved and the adults around them will do everything in their power to keep them safe. Sharing a familiar, well-loved book can be healing when scary things happen, like an old friend telling a comforting story.

Mom! The Center of Baby's Universe

In many books, mothers represent the ideal of a supportive presence, always there, always reassuring, a bulwark of love. But sometimes mothers aren't quite so perfect (gasp!), and babies and toddlers need to see this represented in books, too. In books and in life, mothers (and children) can be frustrating and loving at the same time.

Moms, Perfect and Not-So!

- *Harriet, You'll Drive Me Wild!*, Mem Fox, Marla Frazee (illus.). When Harriet gets into mishap after mishap, her usually patient mom loses her temper. A realistic depiction with lots of heart in the resolution.
- *Mamá and Me*, Arthur Dorros, Rudy Gutierrez (illus.). In his text sprinkled with Spanish, Dorros celebrates the mother-daughter bond, and Gutierrez's colorful and energetic illustrations glow. *Papá and Me* is the award-winning counterpart by the same team.
- *Mama, Do You Love Me?*, Barbara Joosse. The mom's answer for her Inuit daughter is always yes, even though the child is a handful. The companion book, *Papa, Do You Love Me?*, features a father and son of the Masai.
- *Mama Mama / Papa Papa*, Jean Marzollo, Laura Regan (illus.). This double-sided board book is a love poem to the mothers of the animal kingdom. Animal fathers get equal time on the flip side.
- *My Mom*, Anthony Browne. Here's a big-faced appreciation of one mom. Fathers get their say in *My Dad*.
- *Olivia*, Ian Falconer. Olivia's mother heaves what is clearly a sigh at the end of a long day and tells Olivia, "You know, you really wear me out. But I love you anyway." And Olivia gives her a kiss back and says, "I love you anyway, too."

Daddy

More Daddy books are appearing every day. Dads dance and sing, play and cook, and generally have fun with their children.

Daddy: The Modern Version

- *Baby Dance*, Ann Taylor, Marjorie van Heerden (illus.). Daddy and baby dance around while Mama naps. The drawings make it really joyous.
- *Daddy Makes the Best Spaghetti*, Anna Grossnickle Hines. This is a very engaged and fun-loving daddy with his preschooler. He not only shops and cooks, he's Bathman.
- *Faster! Faster!*, Leslie Patricelli. A little girl imagines her daddy is a variety of animals as he gives her a piggyback ride. As delightful as *Higher! Higher!*, which was mentioned previously, and also celebrates Dad's superhuman qualities.
- *The Fathers Are Coming Home*, Margaret Wise Brown, Stephen Savage (illus.). Animal fathers return home to their babies, and a sailor dad is reunited with his son. Savage's graphic linocut illustrations are comforting.
- *My Daddy*, Guido van Genechten. This is a delightfully exuberant depiction of a father / son relationship with everything from swinging from Dad's arms to listening to Dad's quiet bedtime stories.
- *Vroomaloom Zoom*, John Coy. In a twist on the usual daddy-putting-baby-to-bed theme, this daddy zooms around adventurously in his yellow car with an I-can't-sleep daughter Carmela. It's noisy and fun, and one suspects that Mommy might do things differently.
- *What Dads Can't Do*, Douglas Wood, Doug Cushman (illus.). The things dads can't do somehow correlate to those things dads have to do: dads can't cross the street without holding hands, or sleep late, or hold on to their money. Wry illustrations reveal both sides of the story. Moms get their due in *What Moms Can't Do*.

- *When Dads Don't Grow Up*, Marjorie Blain Parker, R. W. Alley (illus.).
  You can tell dads that don't grow up; they know grocery carts are for
  racing, and they'd always rather hang out and eat in the back of the
  truck. A lovely variety of dads and kids romp through this funny book.

Families Come in All Varieties and Languages

Families come in all colors, sizes, and shapes, and no matter who's a part of
yours, you'll find a book to mirror it back to your baby. Also many families speak more than one language. Besides your local bookstores, ask your
local public library for excellent bilingual choices. For languages other than
the usual, the International Children's Library online is helpful: http://en
.childrenslibrary.org/ (see appendix D for more information).

Books for Families of All Sizes and Stripes

We have tried to include books with families from diverse backgrounds
and a variety of configurations and circumstances throughout all our lists;
however, children's literature, like most media, does not yet adequately reflect
our multicultural and multidimensional world. There are many authors,
illustrators, editors, and publishers working hard to change this. Here are a
few books that deserve a shout-out:

- *Black Is Brown Is Tan*, Arnold Adoff, Emily Arnold McCully (illus.).
  This interracial family has all these shades and celebrates them all.
- *Everywhere Babies*, Susan Meyers, Marla Frazee (illus.). We've ment-
  ioned this wonderful book before, but its illustrations, depicting every
  imaginable kind of family, make it worth including here, too.
- *The Hello, Goodbye Window*, Norton Juster, Chris Raschka (illus.).
  An interracial pair of grandparents enjoy inside and outside play with
  their granddaughter through the kitchen window.

- *I Love Saturdays y domingos*, Alma Flor Ada, Elivia Savadier (illus.). A bilingual girl has twice the fun visiting her two sets of grandparents. It's a colorful celebration of lives and cultures.
- *Little Mister*, Randy Duburke. This high-spirited toddler, who just happens to be biracial, gets into *everything*! The cover of "Little Mister" wearing a colander for a hat and playing with pots and pans says it all.
- *Louie's Search*, Ezra Jack Keats. A boy's dream of having a father is wonderfully rewarded. The drawings are Keats's usual collage style that amounts to more than the pieces.
- *Mommy, Mama, and Me* and *Daddy, Papa, and Me*, Lesléa Newman, Carol Thompson (illus.). In these two board books, Newman and Thompson depict the everydayness of two kids who have two moms or two dads with simple verse and warm colors. No politics, no exposition, just life.
- *Monday Is One Day*, Arthur A. Levine, Julian Hector (illus.). A variety of families work their way through each busy day of the week to find time to be together as a family. With single parent, same-sex parent, grandparent-headed, rural, and urban households, kids will find their lives reflected here.
- *Two Homes*, Claire Masurel, MacDonald Denton (illus.). A younger describes what it is like to have two places to live, sometimes with Mom and sometimes with Dad.
- *Who's in My Family?: A Book About All Our Families*, Robie Harris, Nadine Bernard Westcott (illus.). Through prose, speech bubble dialog, and accessible cartoons, every variety of family enjoys an outing to the zoo.

Reading with Children with Disabilities

All children grow at their own pace, but if you have any concerns about your child's development, the earlier you seek help, the better. Contact your local early intervention program (www.nichcy.org/babies) for more information. The program is confidential, and no one will know of your family's participation without your consent. It won't hurt your child's chances of future academic success; in fact, it can only help it. We know one little boy with a speech delay who loves it when his special teachers (a speech therapist and a special instructor) come to the house. They always bring a big bag of toys and books. Therapy, play, and fun happen all at the same time.

If your child has been diagnosed with a disability, it can leave you reeling. While you are navigating a brave new world, don't forget to share books together. Here are some things to think about when reading with children with disabilities (and really all children):

- **Share books with your child with images of people like her.** If your child uses a wheelchair, check out *Susan Laughs*. If your baby has Down syndrome, share *My Face Book*. Can't find books about your child's experience? Make your own using your own photos. We all want to see ourselves reflected in the literature we enjoy, and we all should see images of our diverse world.
- **Books can help us communicate and deal with our experiences.** This is particularly true for children with disabilities. Children who have difficulty speaking can learn to use pictures to communicate. Children with autism find "social stories" or books about an upcoming experience comforting and helpful. If you can't find books in print that work in your situation, make your own or see if someone has self-published or shared something online.
- **Read and speak to your child in the language with which you are most comfortable.** This is true for all children, but it is crucial for children with disabilities. They need a strong foundation in their home language, which will support all their future learning.
- **Reading comes in all formats.** Your child's path to reading and enjoying books may not look like a child who is developing typically.

Listening to a book or having a tactile experience with a Braille book is reading. Technology may be the way into reading for some. Just because your child can't or won't sit on your lap and cuddle up with a printed book does not mean that books, stories, and literature won't be a part of your child's life. Ask your local librarian for suggestions and resources.

- **Most children can learn to read.** We've heard stories of educators and doctors telling parents their children will never learn how to read. The road to reading for some children may be difficult. Some children with autism may learn to read *before* they learn to speak, but research shows that most children can learn to read. Reading with your child is the first step.

Books Featuring Children and Parents with Disabilities

- *Brothers and Sisters*, Laura Dwight. Big, colorful photos of kids with special needs and their siblings who are typically developing or also have disabilities. The text is a little long for most little ones, but there is plenty to enjoy and discuss in the pictures.
- *I Can, Can You?*, Marjorie W. Pitzer. Babies and toddlers with Down syndrome play patty-cake, play ball, and look at books (sometimes with their siblings) in simple caption-bearing photos. Also try *My Up & Down & All Around Book*.
- *Mama Zooms*, Jane Cowen-Fletcher. A toddler loves to ride with his mom in her "zooming machine"—her wheelchair. Cowen-Fletcher's soft drawings capture the playful scenes beautifully.
- *My Brother Charlie*, Holly Robinson Peete, Ryan Elizabeth Peete, Shane Evans (illus.). Actress Peete and her daughter depict the emotional ups and downs of life with a sibling with autism. While it is written for an older audience, this one resonates.

- *My Face Book*, Star Bright Books. An incredible array of babies demonstrate a baby's emotional range, including a baby with Down syndrome. Available in several languages, including Arabic, Chinese, Hebrew, Somali, and Spanish.
- *Some Kids Are Deaf*, Lola M. Schaefer. While this title in the Understanding Differences series is written for beginning readers, it will work for the very young as well. It is particularly useful in explaining the disability to those who don't have it, such as classmates and relatives. Other books include *Some Kids Are Blind*, *Some Kids Have Autism*, *Some Kids Use Wheelchairs*, and *Some Kids Wear Leg Braces*.
- *Susan Laughs*, Jeanne Willis, Tony Ross (illus.). Simple spreads with one line of text per page and playfully sketchy illustrations show the ups and downs of a girl with her family. On the last page, we see she uses a wheelchair.
- *We'll Paint the Octopus Red*, Stephanie Stuve-Bodeen, Pam DeVito (illus.). A six-year-old girl imagines what things will be like once her brother, who has Down syndrome, is born.

And Baby Makes...Change, Trouble, Fun?

Anticipation and arrival of a new baby brings major changes to the family as a whole. Before baby's arrival, most younger children are excited about the change. Books can help them to have realistic expectations (many expect a much older, more active baby than the one they actually get). After the baby arrives, the worries start, and there's a whole subset of books illustrating the jealousy, irritation, and fear of being pushed aside that might help.

"When I was expecting Lily, I went a little overboard and brought home a stack of 'new baby' books. After a day or two of this, when I sat down with Sam and suggested we read, he took one look at the baby book in my lap and shook his head. 'I want a real *book.'" —KJ*

Waiting for Baby

- *The BIG Baby Book*, Guido van Genechten. This lovely, simple book describes what human and animal babies are like once they come into the world.
- *I'm a Big Brother* and *I'm a Big Sister*, Joanna Cole, Rosalinda Kightley (illus.). What can the big brother or big sister do with the new baby? Lots of wonderful family activities.
- *I'm Your Peanut Butter Big Brother*, Selina Alko. A big brother-to-be, a member of an interracial family, uses food metaphors to imagine what his new sibling will look like.
- *It's Quacking Time*, Martin Waddell, Jill Barton (illus.). It's mostly a quiet book about waiting for *that* big blue egg in Mama's nest to crack. It's ducks and eggs, yes, and it's wonderful. In Spanish, it's *¡Cuac, cuac!*
- *Waiting for Baby*, Rachel Fuller. One edition of this board book has words and another does not, but either way, this is a simple depiction of a young child's experiences while Mom is pregnant.

But I Thought I'd Like the Baby!

- *Julius, the Baby of the World*, Kevin Henkes. Big sister Lilly's disgust ends only when a visitor criticizes her baby. Then Lilly takes possession of the Baby of the World, befitting her own royal status.
- *Look at Me*, *My New Baby*, and *You and Me*, Rachel Fuller. These three titles, the companion books to *Waiting for Baby* (mentioned previously), show toddlers helping, playing, and learning to live with their new sibling.
- *Mail Harry to the Moon*, Robie H. Harris, Michael Emberley (illus.). A preschool boy expresses his very real anger at the new baby and suggests they mail Harry to the moon or flush him down the toilet

(which is what real kids have been known to say). When he thinks Harry might truly be missing, he stages a playful rescue of his own.

- *Now We Have a Baby*, Lois Rock, Jane Massey (illus.). Learning to cope with the new baby, with patience and interest, some quiet and love.
- *On Mother's Lap*, Ann Herbert Scott, Glo Coalson (illus.). Despite the older child's insistence on bringing everything he values onto Mother's lap, there's still room for him and the baby.
- *Peter's Chair*, Ezra Jack Keats. Peter has to give up his crib for the new baby, and he has clear feelings about, against, and then for it.
- *Tenemos un bebé / We Have a Baby*, Cathryn Falwell. These parents offer wonderful role modeling for helping a toddler-aged sibling feel loved in the presence of a new baby. In Spanish and English.
- *What Shall We Do with the Boo Hoo Baby?*, Cressida Cowell, Ingrid Godon (illus.). Every cow, cat, and duck offer suggestions for soothing this wide-mouthed wailer. The ultimate suggestion may come from pure exhaustion all around.
- *Za-Za's Baby Brother*, Lucy Cousins. A big sib zebra deals with feeling neglected because of a new baby's arrival.

TIP: Try to read some books that give a realistic view of life with a new baby. We all have a tendency to talk about how much fun it will be to have a new sibling, and you may find your child is expecting a much older baby and has big—and unrealistic—plans.

Adoption

In 1997, the Evan B. Donaldson Adoption Institute survey found that six in ten Americans have had personal experience with adoption, meaning that they themselves, a family member, or a close friend was adopted, had adopted a child, or had placed a child for adoption. Families are full of kinship and stepkids, interracial and international kids. There are few picture books for our targeted age group, but we hope these please you.

- *Happy Adoption Day!*, John McCutcheon, Julie Paschkis (illus.). This story celebrates diversity and how families are made by joining together loving parents and children.
- *Happy Halloween, Biscuit*, Alyssa Satin Capucilli, Pat Schories (illus.). Biscuit's family includes his blond owner and her Asian cousin, whether by adoption or for some other reason isn't clear—but what's nice about it is exactly that: it's never mentioned. It can be whatever your children perceive it to be, and what they'll perceive it to be is normal.
- *I Love You Like Crazy Cakes*, Rose Lewis, Jane Dyer (illus.). One mother's story of her travels to China to adopt a baby girl is like a love letter to her daughter. The artwork is gorgeous, although it too might be for older children. *Te quiero, niña bonita* is the Spanish edition.
- *I'm Adopted!*, Shelley Rotner, Sheila M. Kelly. The photos depict a diverse assortment of faces from a variety of backgrounds and situations. Although probably more suitable for older children, it's nice to be able to identify visually with one or more children.
- *A Mother for Choco*, Keiko Kasza. The lonely yellow bird's quest for a mother isn't directly "about" adoption, and yet of course it is.
- *My Family Is Forever*, Nancy Carlson. Nancy Carlson's thoughtful, straightforward text and cheerful illustrations combine to create a reassuring look at how one little girl came into her parents' world— and made them a family forever.
- *Over the Moon: An Adoption Tale*, Karen Katz. The swirling, colorful artwork communicates the dream come true for a family's international adoption.
- *Ten Days and Nine Nights: An Adoption Story*, Yumi Heo. A loving family counts down the days until their Korean-born baby girl arrives.

Brothers and Sisters: Can't Live With or Without Them

Siblings constitute another enormous category. Being a sister or brother brings with it rich rewards and many battles. There's getting a brother or a sister, and then there's actually being one, which is a whole different ball game. Books generally handle the crisis in a benign way; the frustrations give way to some good fun and playtime.

Books for Brothers and Sisters (Twins, Too!)

- *Baby Bear's Chairs*, Jane Yolen, Melissa Sweet (illus.). Being the youngest has some clear advantages, like Dad's lap and parental attention after the others get put to bed. Nice reworking of the three bears and chairs trope.
- *Best-ever Big Brother*, Karen Katz. Big brother shows off all the things he can do, going to the potty and getting dressed, that his little brother can't. Also *Best-ever Big Sister*.
- *Big Sister, Little Sister*, LeUyen Pham. Little sister envies the many things her big sister can do, but she realizes she has some talents of her own.
- *Chloe*, Peter McCarty. Chloe, the middle child of twenty siblings in her rabbit family, teaches the whole brood how to have fun with nothing but a big cardboard box and some bubble wrap.
- *Con mi hermano / With My Brother*, Eileen Roe, Robert Casilla (illus.). A little boy's lovely tribute to his older brother. In Spanish and English.
- *Do Like Kyla*, Angela Johnson, James E. Ransome (illus.). A big sister deals with her little sister's copycat ways.
- *Do You Know What I'll Do?*, Charlotte Zolotow, Javaka Steptoe (illus.). A sister's affection for her baby brother emerges charmingly as she dreams about doing things for his pleasure.
- *Hello Twins*, Charlotte Voake. These twins, a brother and sister pair, may not look or do things alike, but "they like each other just the way they are."
- *Lola Reads to Leo*, Anna McQuinn, Rosalind Beardshaw (illus.). Big sister Lola reads to baby Leo, but Mom and Dad still have time for one-on-one reading with Lola.

- *Max's Bedtime*, Rosemary Wells. Max can't go to sleep without his red rubber elephant, and Ruby tries to help in her know-it-all way. Ruby and Max's relationship is realistic and priceless. For a longer story, try *Bunny Cakes*.
- *The Twins' Blanket*, Hyewon Yum. Identical twin girls, with some help from Mom, must figure out how to share the baby blanket from their one crib in their two twin beds.
- *You Can Do It Too!*, Karen Baicker, Ken Wilson-Max (illus.). A big sister shows her little toddler brother the ways of the world, or, at least, how to make a ruckus with pots and pans. The companion book to *I Can Do it Too!*

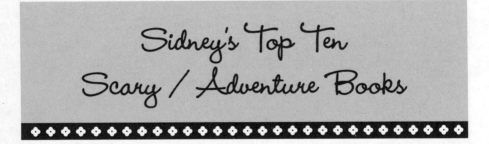

Sidney's Top Ten
Scary / Adventure Books

"We do bedtime stories separately for our two girls (ages two-and-a-half and five). It is a special time that they each get to be alone with one parent, and they each get to choose three stories. It has been so much fun watching them progress through different phases of literary interests. Lately Sidney, our younger one, is really into adventure stories and scary books. Anything with monsters or growling bears or kids who save the day is a hit with her. Last night, for the first time, I read her *Abiyoyo* by Pete Seeger, about a giant who is outsmarted by a small boy and his ukelele. What joy! After I tucked her in and left the room, I heard her singing to herself, 'Abiyoyo, Abiyoyo,' over and over." —Sadie

1. *Abiyoyo*, Pete Seeger, Michael Hays (illus.)
2. *The Judge: An Untrue Tale*, Harve and Margot Zemach (out of print)
3. *Outside Over There*, Maurice Sendak
4. *Snip Snap! What's That?*, Mara Bergman, Nick Maland (illus.)
5. *Bear Snores On*, Karma Wilson, Jane Chapman (illus.)
6. *King Bidgood's in the Bathtub*, Don and Audrey Wood
7. *In the Night Kitchen*, Maurice Sendak
8. *We're Going on a Bear Hunt*, Michael Rosen, Helen Oxenbury (illus.)
9. *The Day the Babies Crawled Away*, Peggy Rathman
10. *George Shrinks*, William Joyce

"With three older siblings, one eight-year-old and two five-year-olds, my nine-month-old baby has quickly adapted to the whole family piling on the bed at night and reading books together. We still read classic board books like Goodnight Moon *and* Is Your Mama a Llama?*, but we also read lots of nonfiction books about animals and American history. The baby loves it. He focuses for brief moments, looks at the pictures, crawls around between us, and, quite often, grabs a book page and gobbles it up. He's so hungry for words." —Bruce*

Frustration, Anger, and Tantrums

Frustrations are a big part of life for a baby and toddler. Obstacles abound as they try to achieve the simplest of goals: asking for a bottle, pouring milk on cereal, and grabbing that tempting coffee cup off the dinner table. Their lack of language and skill thwarts them; you thwart them. The question becomes what to do with that frustrated, thwarted feeling. The answer isn't always pretty, and tantrums are a part of life with a small child. There is likely to be at least one meltdown for your children from birth to three. And perhaps for you.

Teaching appropriate ways to experience and express anger is one of many tasks of being a parent. Talking to your infant, guessing at what might be bothering him, can help. Telling yourself to count to ten, and teaching your child to do so as well, may be one of the healthiest and most helpful things you can do, but meanwhile, a tantrum has to be dealt with.

Seven Screaming, Tantrummy, Let-It-All-Out Books

1. *The Day Leo Said I Hate You!*, Robie H. Harris, Molly Bang (illus.). While preschool-age kids tend to act like Leo more than their younger peers, twos will relate to Leo's anger and appreciate the mother-and-son resolution.

2. *Finn Throws a Fit!*, David Elliott, Timothy Basil Ering (illus.). A cranky toddler has a tantrum so explosive it causes an earthquake, a hurricane, and a blizzard.

3. *If I Were a Lion*, Sarah Weeks, Heather M. Solomon (illus.). Here's the inner life of the angry kid in the time-out chair. We always wondered what she was thinking.

4. *Llama Llama Mad at Mama*, Anna Dewdney. Llama Llama has a full-blown tantrum in a store.

5. *Mean Soup*, Betsy Everitt. Horace is having a very bad day, so his mother cooks up a soup to soothe his frustrations. Once again the artwork helps describe the emotional stew.

6. *When Sophie Gets Angry—Really, Really Angry…*, Molly Bang. When Sophie gets angry, her rage is gloriously, colorfully, and even violently illustrated, and the art calms down with her mood after she gets herself away from the sister who's made her so crazy. A Caldecott Honor book.

7. *Where the Wild Things Are*, Maurice Sendak. Max goes wild at dinnertime. Banished to his room, he takes an imaginative journey to the island of wild things, where he realizes he'd rather be home and loved and fed

than be wild. This offers the clearest representation of a temper tantrum we know. (In a 2006 interview in the *New Yorker*, the author explains that Max is punished for disturbing, wild behavior during those difficult 5:00–8:00 p.m. hours. "His mother is in emotional disorder, and he's pushing her to the limit.")

Tantrums can be as scary and upsetting for a child as they are for the adult. Regardless of the reason for the tantrum, you will have to handle it. Ensuring your child's physical safety is paramount. How you cope will depend on the child and the circumstances. Sticking with him through this terrible moment in his life communicates your support and sends a message about coping. You're still there. That says he can be angry and still be loved. You're trying to help. That says problems are things that can be solved. You're trying to soothe. That says that problems are better solved when the huge surge of anger has passed. Whatever you say, and however you cope with the tantrum at the time, eventually it will pass. He'll collapse, exhausted and spent, into your arms, and you'll move on.

> **TIP: Get out a tantrum book after a tantrum, and use it to talk about how reasonable it is to be angry and to suggest different ways of dealing with it that wouldn't have been so hurtful or destructive. It may not seem like your words mean much to so young a child, but you may achieve more than you know.**

Friends: Real, Stuffed, and All

Babies branch out from their families and start making friends in many ways. Some start with a "transitional object": the binky, the blankie, the filthy remnants of a loved stuffed dog. Those are treasured possessions, and (with the exception of the binky) usually stick around when real friends start to appear.

Binkies, Blankies, and Stuffies:
Books about First Friends

- *Ben Loves Bear*, David McPhail. An enchanting story of a boy and his teddy bear. The companion book is *Bella Loves Bunny*.
- *Binky* and *Blankie*, Leslie Patricelli. These two separate board books feature a diapered toddler's life with his beloved transitional objects.
- *The Flyaway Blanket*, Allan Peterkin, Emmeline Pidgen (illus.). When a young boy's blanket flutters off the clothesline, it has an eventful journey which, thankfully, is a round-trip.
- *I Lost My Bear*, Jules Feiffer. There is no better illustration of a perfect SCREAM than Feiffer's drawing of the girl when she realizes her bear is missing!
- *Knuffle Bunny: A Cautionary Tale*, Mo Willems. This is an excellent (and funny) depiction of the gulf in understanding between the baby and her daddy about the importance of a stuffed animal that's disappeared. This baby means business! The other Knuffle Bunny books are also a delight.
- *No More Pacifier for Piggy!*, Bernette Ford, Sam Williams (illus.). Piggy discovers that his pacifier gets in the way of a game of peek-a-boo. Also try *No More Bottles for Bunny!* and *No More Blanket for Lambkin!*
- *Owen*, Kevin Henkes. Owen's clever mother invents a way to preserve her young mouse's personal need for his oversize blanket when he goes to school by creating small pocket-size ones to carry discreetly. Winner of a Caldecott Honor Award.

As your baby grows into a toddler and preschooler, his neighbors or companions from the playground, day care, or the mommy-baby group will become playmates. They may start by staring at one another. Soon they'll be grabbing for one another's noses, hands, feet, and toys. Toddlers begin by playing next to one another (called parallel play) and progress from there. Those first actual conversations between the new friends are an odd experience—your little baby, talking and relating in a way that doesn't involve you.

These new relationships offer opportunities to learn about relating to another person outside of the immediate family, and it's not always clear sailing. Sharing and being together is tough. There may be bites, sulks, screams, and squabbles over nothing, but it could still be the beginning of a genuine long-term friendship.

"My daughter Alice, three, has an older friend Anya, five, and Alice ADORES Anya. Sometimes Anya can get bossy or mean and makes Alice feel bad that she is smaller and can't write her name or hang upside-down on the monkey bars. It makes Alice feel sad and she gets angry and will act out against Anya. 'The Dream,' a story in Arnold Lobel's Frog and Toad Together, *really helped Alice understand her own feelings toward Anya, and it built a vocabulary for us to use as a family to discuss these kinds of situations. (Toad dreams that he is the greatest and most exceptional person, pianist, and aerialist. But as he becomes greater, his friend Frog shrinks into insignificance. As the crushed Frog starts to leave, Toad realizes how much he needs his friend Frog and is relieved to wake up.) Now if someone is really overwhelming Alice, I whisper in her ear, 'Do you feel like you're shrinking?' She'll say yes, then I'll smile and tell her, 'Remember, it's only a dream.' This reminds her of the story and she is able to have a moment of perspective about her situation." —Jane*

Some Favorites about Friends!

- *Best Friends for Frances*, Russell Hoban, Lillian Hoban (illus.). This beloved badger Frances offers clever maneuverings when dealing with friends.
- *Buster*, Denise Fleming. Can a dog have a cat friend? Of course the answer is yes, although this pointy-nosed scaredy-dog has to overcome his original fears of the fluffy white kitten who purrs at him.
- *Dog and Bear: Two Friends, Three Stories*, Laura Vaccaro Seeger.

Frisky Dog and shy Bear have an enchantingly real friendship in this beginning reader picture book that works for the younger set, too. Winner of a *Boston Globe / Horn Book* Award.

- *Frog and Toad Are Friends*, Arnold Lobel. This is one of several volumes of rich stories about two good friends. A classic and a Caldecott Honor winner.
- *I Will Surprise My Friend!* (An Elephant & Piggie Book), Mo Willems. Gerald, an elephant, and his friend Piggie have some mishaps trying to surprise each other. These two buddies appear in many more delightful beginning reader books, most of which are simple enough for twos to enjoy as well.
- *Leon and Bob*, Simon James. While Leon's dad is away serving in the army, Leon does everything with his imaginary friend, that is, until a new boy moves in next door. A simple yet sophisticated story your child will grow into.
- *Let's Be Enemies*, Janice May Udry, Maurice Sendak (illus.). Not surprisingly, being friends is better—but the journey there is cute and classic.
- *Maggie's Ball*, Lindsay Barrett George. With her bright yellow ball, Maggie the dog's quest for a friend is endearingly accessible.
- *Mine's the Best*, Crosby Bonsall. Two boys meet carrying identical balloons…and argue over whose is better.
- *My Friend Rabbit*, Eric Rohmann. There's gentle trouble when friends Mouse and Rabbit play with a favorite airplane toy. A Caldecott Award winner.
- *Owen & Mzee: Best Friends*, Isabella Hatkoff, Craig Hatkoff, Dr. Paula Kahumbu, Peter Greste (photos). This board book version tells the true story of two unlikely best friends, an orphaned hippo and a 130-year-old giant tortoise.
- *What About Bear?*, Suzanne Bloom. Can Fox, Bear, and Goose figure out a way to play together? Try *A Splendid Friend, Indeed* and *Treasure* for more about Bear and Goose.

- *Where Are Maisy's Friends?*, Lucy Cousins. Maisy's supporting cast members, her gaggle of friends, are featured in this lift-the-flap game of hide-and-seek.
- *Will I Have a Friend?*, Miriam Cohen, Ronald Himler (illus.). Little Jim innocently asks his dad this question on their way to his first day of school. Little ones who worry about having friends will find solace in this gentle, reassuring book that's been around for years. An out-of-print edition features art by Lillian Hoban.

He Did What?! Helpful Behavior Books

When children start acting out, biting, kicking, pushing, and taking toys from playmates, many parents do not know what to do. Good modeling, patience, and a calm attitude can help. Sharing a good book together can break through lots of tension. Here are a few titles that are fun and model appropriate behavior in the process:

- *Banana!*, Ed Vere. Told through simple cartoons of monkeys with expressive faces and only a couple of words, this is a playful lesson in learning to use the "magic word."
- *I Can Help*, David Hyde Costello. In this chain of good karma, animals help each other out of minor difficulties. The helped always politely thanks the helper.
- *Lively Elizabeth!: What Happens When You Push*, Mara Bergman and Cassia Thomas (illus.). When one push creates a domino effect of toppled playmates, Elizabeth offers a sincere apology. Playful verse and art make this one work.
- *Mine!*, Shutta Crum, Patrice Barton (illus.). One baby, one toddler, one dog, lots of toys, and only one word in the text—"Mine!" Barton's digitally augmented sketches capture all the action.
- *No More Biting for Billy Goat!*, Bernette Ford, Sam Williams (illus.).

Billy Goat gets so frustrated that he bites his friends, but Ducky teaches him a gentler way to make his needs known. Also in the series: *No More Hitting for Little Hamster!*

- *Nobunny's Perfect*, Anna Dewdney. Bunnies, drawn by Dewdney of *Llama Llama Red Pajama* fame, demonstrate inappropriate behaviors, such as kicking, biting, and throwing, but also model appropriate actions in counterpoint.
- *Sheila Rae's Peppermint Stick*, Kevin Henkes. A sibling tussle, told using Henkes's popular mouse characters, results in some unintentional sharing.
- *Will Sheila Share?*, Elivia Savadier. Toddlers and their parents will recognize Sheila, who isn't particularly inclined to share. With some gentle coaxing from Nana, Sheila's sharing goes to the other extreme.
- *Yummy Ice Cream: A Book about Sharing*, Emma Quay, Anna Walker (illus.). A panda and a sheep decide to share their ice cream cones with their buddy owl. Mo Willems also tackles this one in *Should I Share My Ice Cream?* We know how most toddlers would answer this question.

That's Funny!

Babies and parents all need a good giggle. Life is full of funny things, and laughter helps all of us to relax and even to enjoy some of the more boring or difficult parts of caring for (or being) small children. Sharing a laugh is a welcome and gorgeous feeling. Babies actually laugh as early as two or three months. Rachel's nephew Luk laughed at three months. He thought the "oot oot" sound in the song "Apples and Bananas" was funny. Also, Colin rolled on the floor laughing at seven months while Rachel shook a bag of "Snap Pea Crisps." She caught a video of this, and it went viral among her family and friends. So what makes them laugh? What is funny to a baby and toddler? Let us know.

Very young babies laugh at stimulating motion, tickling, or bouncing on the knee. As they get bigger, both babies and toddlers tend to like silly sounds, goofy faces, and slapstick. A raspberry on the tummy, a big donkey "hee-haw," crossing your eyes, or balancing a slice of bread on your nose might all bring on the giggles. Babies make jokes, too. Once the baby laughs, you will find yourself laughing, too. Then, because you are laughing, your baby will laugh some more. Laughter is infectious.

A cat that barks is very funny, if you know that a cat really says meow. Toddlers who are just learning who says what will be delighted when the world of "Old MacDonald" is turned upside down. Kids learn fast and may actually crack themselves up with language jokes, some of which are on the order of the cat saying bowwow, or the cow saying oink, or endlessly repeating a word, product, or place.

Building an expectation that then gets upended is funny. Culmination stories or pileups offer a crescendo of tension and a welcome relief. Every page has basically the same information, but by the end something's gotta give.

> ## Irresistible Authors: Sandra Boynton
>
> Almost every mom we talked to listed one of Boynton's colorful, hippo-filled books as a funny favorite. *Red Hat, Green Hat* is wonderful for all the getting-dressed jokes it creates (the squirmy toddler who won't let you put a shirt over his head will dissolve in giggles if you try to put the shirt on his feet instead), *Barnyard Dance* has wonderful dancing farm animals, and *Hippos Go Berserk!* features clever counting and a riotous party. Early forays into ebook and app-land include her excellent *Moo Baa La La La!* (Spanish version: *Muu. Beee. ¡Así Fue!*) and *The Going To Bed Book*.

Laura's son Joey, at two, developed an unaccountable affection for the words "Taco Bell." He'd never been to a Taco Bell, never even eaten a taco, but something about the phrase charmed him. Soon his mirth infected all of his friends, until there was a whole pack of two-year-olds running in circles, all shrieking "Taco Bell! Taco Bell!" To this day, nearly two years later, any of them will dissolve in giggles if you say those two words.

Being contrary is really funny too, starting with babies as young as nine months. In real life it might express a certain inclination toward mischievousness, independence, or even defiance. But stubborn refusal in a picture book is just plain funny. Furthermore it's very funny to hear the adult reader acting out such a traditionally kid role.

The works of Nancy Shaw and Rosemary Wells offer good visual and verbal silliness for most families. These gifted children's book author-illustrators don't seem to write or talk down to any of us, but rather describe immediately identifiable human quirks and experiences that provide us with the gentle humor of recognition.

Given that humor is often personal and unpredictable, it is a difficult task to find books to recommend for everyone. But really humorous books are often funny for young and old. Since young children tend to laugh if an adult is laughing first, and vice versa, we don't need to analyze too closely. Just find a book that tickles your fancy.

Well, WE Think These Are Funny

- *Baby Danced the Polka*, Karen Beaumont, Jennifer Plecas (illus.). It's nap time on the farm, but one un-sleepy baby has a different plan.
- *The Cow That Went OINK*, Bernard Most. This funny book is all about what happens when a cow oinks. In Spanish, it's *La vaca que decía OINK*.
- *The Doghouse*, Jan Thomas. When each one of Mouse's friends goes into the doghouse to fetch a wayward ball, Mouse assumes the worst when Dog says he is having them for dinner. Little ones may not get the word play, but they will certainly get all the feelings and enjoy Thomas's bold cartoons. Try *Rhyming Dust Bunnies* and *A Birthday for Cow!* also by Thomas.
- *Froggy Gets Dressed*, Jonathan London, Frank Remkiewicz (illus.). Frogs may be supposed to sleep all winter, but when this one sees snow, he wants to play in it—but he keeps forgetting key pieces of

clothing and having to go in, undress, and do it all over again. When he finally realizes he's forgotten his underwear, he gives up and goes back to bed. There are many more Froggy adventures available.

- *Hippos Go Berserk!*, Sandra Boynton. Look out! The hippos are having a party in another of Boynton's comic gems.

- *Leonardo, the Terrible Monster*, Mo Willems. Leonardo is hilariously terrible at being a monster but pretty good at being a friend, and funny to look at on top of it all.

- *Maybe A Bear Ate It!*, Robie H. Harris, Michael Emberley. When an endearing little monster can't find a favorite book, there are a lot funny shenanigans.

- *Me Hungry!*, Jeremy Tankard. When a hungry cave boy decides to hunt for food, he ends up making friends with a cuddly wooly mammoth instead. The text, written in caveman speak, is a hoot to read aloud.

- *The Monster at the End of This Book*, Jon Stone, Michael Smollin (illus.). Grover's heard there's a monster at the end of this book, and he's determined to keep the reader from turning the pages. Lovely suspense, as both Grover and the first-time reader forget that Grover is a monster himself. Classic Muppet illustrations. And now there's an app for it.

- *My Little Sister Ate One Hare*, Bill Grossman, Kevin Hawkes (illus.). The sister is capable of eating all manner of gross things, except for healthy peas. The over-the-top humor is not for the weak of stomach.

- *The Seals on the Bus*, Lenny Hort, G. Brian Karas (illus.). In this version of the favorite song, there is a noisy zoo along for the bus ride. This is a fun read-aloud / sing-aloud that works for a wide age range.

- *Snip Snap! What's That?*, Mara Bergman, Nick Maland (illus.). An alligator stalks a group of terrified children with comic results. Maland's art makes the action seem silly and not scary at all.

- *To Market, To Market*, Anne Miranda, Janet Stevens (illus.). Based on a traditional nursery rhyme, a lady does the shopping for ever larger animals at the supermarket. Everything is oversize, including the humor.

Ages and Stages: Emotional Milestones

This chart is a little bit different from those in other chapters. The information here describes a significant issue for each stage of emotional development and what parents can do to facilitate its successful accomplishment, with or without books.

Newborn	**Issue:** The newborn's basic issue is trust. **Parent Response:** The more you nurture your infant with love, holding, and caregiving, the more you communicate your reliability and trustworthiness to him. Paying attention with books, looks, words, and songs—it's all good.
Sitting	**Issue:** Sitters begin to engage more with the world around them. This includes socializing, and a developing sense of being a separate person and not totally a part of Mommy and Daddy. **Parent Response:** Using books, mirrors, and conversations, you can tell your child who he is and how much you love him. **Issue:** Stranger anxiety (fear of strangers) begins because the baby knows that you are his mommy, his daddy. That stranger isn't you. **Parent Response:** Once this begins, parents need to spend more time smoothing the transition to the new babysitter or babysitting arrangement. Providing a special transitional object from home helps. And of course playing lots of peekaboo—you will leave *and* you will come back.

Crawling / Creeping	**Issue:** Age of Exploration. This age brings with it wonderful discoveries as the physical capacities of babies grow and develop. As they practice going away from you, they also return to the security of "home base." Like real explorers, when they find something, they give it a name. Baby's first words in his language might include family members, pets, or favorite objects in their world. **Parent Response:** Trust your baby to explore everything by tasting, feeling, manipulating, and exploring objects. Also trust that although he begins to move away from you, he will come back. You can appreciate what he is learning and talk about it with him.
Cruising / Walking	**Issue:** Advanced Age of Exploration. Babies develop an increasing sense of being like grown-ups along with an interest in people outside the family. **Parent Response:** Create a safe environment for them to explore and practice moving around (make the baby safe from furniture, and vice versa) and seek opportunities to be around others.
Talking (a few words)	**Issue:** "No" signals the beginning of clear independence, when he does things his own way as opposed to his parent's way. "No" becomes a significant new word to go with his new status. **Parent Response:** Take a deep breath. Create choices as opposed to confrontations: instead of insisting on your book, offer the baby a choice of two. Defiance is actually a social milestone.

Talking More	**Issue:** Personal pleasure. With the growth of his powers to do and be in control of his own self, his own choices, the baby becomes pleased and proud. He will gain in personal competence in many spheres and express his accompanying feelings of joy. **Parent Response:** Give opportunities to succeed and credit his accomplishments. Share your child's glorious pride. **Issue:** Anxieties about the power to destroy. Baby may worry that he has broken or wrecked things that cannot be repaired, which may include your love. **Parent Response:** Help him tape up the torn page in the book, or pick up the mess he's caused due to his immature reflexes, dexterity, or speed.
Running (but not talking much)	**Issue:** The Age of Possessiveness: It's MINE! Once the baby knows something is his, it's very hard to share it with someone else. Do you know the Toddler's Creed? If I want it, it's mine. If I give it to you and change my mind later, it's mine. If I can take it away from you, it's mine. If I had it a little while ago, it's mine. If it's mine, it will never belong to anybody else, no matter what. If we are building something together, all the pieces are mine. If it looks just like mine, it is mine.

Running (but not talking much) (cont'd)	**Parent Response:** Talk about frustrations, and praise the good things the baby accomplishes. Putting words onto feelings and difficult situations increases the baby's awareness of how to cope. Modeling sharing behavior will help. Take turns, and say you are taking turns, with him, and with your spouse. Praise others for sharing.
Talking ALL THE TIME!	**Issue:** Further developing sense of being separate and competent, and trusting parents' abiding love. They begin to understand that something out of sight is still in the mind. **Parent Response:** To reassure the child of his competence and your presence even though separated, try these ideas: 1) A penny in the pocket like Dumbo's feather as a reminder that he can do it *and* that you are with him; 2) For extended separations provide a little a calendar on which to check off the days and offer a token gift for each day. **Issue:** Creative and imaginative play grows exponentially as he learns to express himself through the manipulation of toys, and giving his dolls and cars things to say. Through various dress-up games, he can pretend to be other people. **Parent Response:** Provide materials for him to use in play (empty cardboard boxes, paper and crayons, glue, and old clothes or costumes).

Chapter Ten

BOOKS TO THE RESCUE

❖❖❖❖❖❖❖❖❖❖❖❖❖❖❖❖❖❖❖❖❖❖❖❖❖❖❖❖❖❖❖❖

Potty Training, Food, Big Kid Beds, and More

Even as she's learning to handle her emotions, a baby or toddler is busily trying to master the rest of our complex world. She's without any cultural context for events ranging from "birthday party" to "doctor's appointment," and she's constantly learning our expectations. Why eat with a spoon? Why *not* drop the food on the floor? And, oh boy, why do I have to poop in *there*?

Once again, books can help. A few dozen readings about Little Critter's dentist visit or Caillou's first plane ride can help a baby or toddler prepare for the unknown. *Everyone Poops* and *My Big Boy Bed* may smooth those transitions, or at least offer a nonconfrontational place to talk about them.

There are books out there for nearly every milestone or challenge you and your baby might face. There are even whole series dedicated to some of the many firsts ahead like *First Experiences from Fred Rogers* (of *Mr. Rogers' Neighborhood*), the stylish *First Experiences* books published by Usborne, and even *What to Expect Kids*, from the people who brought us *What to Expect When You're Expecting*.

What follows are the best books we could find for going beyond the easy chair: books for the kitchen and bathroom, books for being sick and being well, books that travel on planes, trains, and roller coasters. Don't keep your books cooped up on the shelf. Use them to help both of you solve problems at home and maneuver out in the world.

Once Upon a Potty and Other Bathroom Classics

There will be moments ahead when you believe potty training is going to be a lifelong activity. Fortunately, that's probably an exaggeration—it's only going to feel like a lifetime. For some kids, it's easy; for others, it's a struggle; but all seem to be fascinated by the process (and, when they're a little bit older, all the opportunities for humor that go along with it).

> **TIP: It's tough for a toddler or preschooler to sit still on that potty. Put a basket of books (on any subject) where she can reach them while she's waiting for action.**

Most kids potty train somewhere between two and four, and even younger kids are usually interested (and may want to try it out). You'll probably start a book or two on the subject before you actually start making the effort. (If you're potty training a boy, you may want to consider whether you'll be having him pee sitting down or standing up, and check the illustrations accordingly.) As with many milestone books, like moving out of a crib or starting school, you can probably find a potty training book starring one of your child's favorite video friends like Elmo or Grover from *Sesame Street*. You might even find a video or DVD. It never hurts to put a familiar face on a new experience, particularly if it turns out to be something of a struggle for your child. We say, if it makes it easier (or faster), it's worth it!

A Little Potty Reading

- *Everyone Poops*, Taro Gomi. A great place to start, since it's more about the poop itself than exactly where you're supposed to put it.
- *My Big Boy Potty* and *My Big Girl Potty*, Joanna Cole, Maxie Chambliss (illus.). A boy and girl demonstrate some of the best practices in potty training. There are helpful tips for parents at the end.

- *My Big Boy Undies* and *My Big Girl Undies*, Karen Katz. In each of these board books, a boy or a girl celebrates their graduation from diapers to underwear.
- *No More Diapers for Ducky!*, Bernette Ford, Sam Williams (illus.). Ducky decides to give the potty a try after she sees her friend Piggy using one.
- *No Potty!, Yes, Potty!* and *Go, Girl! Go Potty!*, Emily Bolam (illus.). Simple lift-the-flap fare that answers the question, "Whose potty is it anyway?" The first title stars Max, and the second features Sara.
- *Once Upon a Potty*, Alona Frankel. Truly the genre classic and available, like most potty books, for boys and girls—which, much as we may resist the whole pink / blue dichotomy, is important when it comes to illustrations. Some editions even include buttons to push for sound effects.
- *Potty*, Leslie Patricelli. A very simple and direct potty book with Patricelli's delightful cartoon baby.
- *A Potty for Me!*, Karen Katz. A joyous lift-the-flap instruction manual.
- *Time to Pee!*, Mo Willems. Complete with a sticker chart, this is stylish and fun.
- *Uh Oh! Gotta Go!*, Bob McGrath, Shelley Dieterichs (illus.). Twenty toddlers experience the potty in different ways (standing up, flushing).
- *You Can Go to the Potty*, William Sears, Martha Sears, Christie Watts Kelly, Renee Andriani (illus.).

Rub a Dub Dub, a Book in the Tub

The potty's not the only thing in the bathroom. You might see the bathtub as a place for getting clean, but your child sees it as place for playtime, bubble time, or pirate time. Sometimes there's a conflict there, but it's usually quickly resolved by a fast scrub-down and ample opportunity to play.

Books for Tub Time

- *Bubble Bath Pirates*, Jarrett J. Krosoczka. A mother playfully gets her two young kids to have great imaginative fun as pirates in the bath.
- *To the Tub*, Peggy Perry Anderson. A father-son bath-time book full of tolerance for the stalling techniques of the little frog child.
- *The Treasure Bath*, Dan Andreasen. In this wordless bath-time fantasy, a little boy discovers the world beneath the bubbles.
- *The Tub People*, Pam Conrad, Richard Egielski (illus.). Addresses that childhood fear of going down the drain as the seven members of a wooden tub family go to the rescue when the tub child slips away.
- *Tubby*, Leslie Patricelli. This baby demonstrates how much fun the bath can be.
- *Way Down Deep in the Deep Blue Sea*, Jan Peck, Valeria Petrone (illus.). Diving for tub toys turns into quite an imaginary adventure in rhythm.

Mia's Top Ten

"Although Mia (twenty-five months) enjoys the typical books-to-bed story time of most children, she also asks for books when she first wakes up in the morning. Both of us have a great amount of energy and appreciate a good snuggle to start the day. Books are also used as an incentive for toothbrushing. Sometimes Mia will say something familiar that I can't quite place, like 'You're suspicious of peas,' and I'll realize she's reciting text from a book we haven't read in days (*Little Pookie*). If the reader pauses at the end of a rhyming line of text, Mia proudly provides the next word." —Beth

1. *Little Pookie*, Sandra Boynton
2. *The Day the Babies Crawled Away*, Peggy Rathmann
3. *Each Peach, Pear, Plum*, Janet and Allan Ahlberg
4. *Harry the Dirty Dog*, Gene Zion, Margaret Bloy Graham (illus.)
5. *Swimmy*, Leo Lionni
6. *Knuffle Bunny*, Mo Willems
7. *If You Give a Mouse a Cookie*, Laura Joffe Numeroff, Felicia Bond (illus.)
8. *Llama Llama Misses Mama*, Anna Dewdney
9. *Ella Sarah Gets Dressed*, Margaret Chodos-Irvine
10. *Gossie & Gertie*, Olivier Dunrea

A Kitchen Full of Books

If reading is nourishment for the mind as food is for the body, then reading about food must be especially enriching (and reading about food while eating food is almost too much of a good thing). Food is a favorite subject for many children, and many children's authors. There are books about cooking it, eating it, growing it, and playing with it. All would be perfect for a little light high-chair reading.

Eating, Learning, and Playing in the Warmest Room in the House

- *Bee-Bim Bop!*, Linda Sue Park, Ho Baek Lee (illus.). A little girl and her mother make a mouth-watering Korean dish.
- *Bread, Bread, Bread*, Ann Morris, Ken Heyman (illus.). Photographs of various breads from around the world show how differently we are the same.
- *Eating the Alphabet*, Lois Ehlert. The fruits and vegetables are appetizingly described in colorful words and pictures. A modern classic.
- *First Book of Sushi*, Amy Wilson Sanger. Fun and funky collage

illustrations introduce new foods and make egg tamago, tortillas, and guacamole feel as familiar as pancakes and apples in the World Snacks series. (Also *Chaat and Sweets*, *¡Hola! jalepeño*, *Let's Nosh!*, *A Little Bit of Soul Food*, *Mangia! Mangia!*, and *Yum Yum Dim Sum*.)

- *I Will Never Not Ever Eat a Tomato*, Lauren Child. Big brother Charlie encourages Lola to eat her mashed potato "clouds" and mermaid sticks from the supermarket under the sea.
- *Little Pea*, Amy Krouse Rosenthal, Jen Corace (illus.). Little Pea's parents make him count and eat his candy before he's allowed to enjoy his vegetable dessert.
- *Now I Eat My ABC's*, Pam Abrams, Bruce Wolf (illus.). The alphabet letter is created out of photographed foods to eat and enjoy. Well done.
- *Pots and Pans*, Patricia Hubbell, Diane deGroat (illus.). A rhythmic chant about what happens when baby's in the kitchen with the pots and pans that ends with a very messy kitchen and a very frazzled daddy.
- *Rah, Rah, Radishes!: A Vegetable Chant*, April Pulley Sayre. A song (or chant) of praise to all things vegetable, accompanied by delectable photos. Also, *Go, Go Grapes*.
- *Soup Day*, Melissa Iwai. A little girl and her mother shop for and prepare vegetable soup on a cold winter's day. Recipe included.
- *Two Eggs, Please*, Sarah Weeks, Betsy Lewin. Every animal patron at the diner orders two eggs, but cooked in every possible different way.
- *What Pete Ate From A–Z (Really!)*, Maira Kalman. Pete, a dog, eats indiscriminately—including an accordion, egg beater, and underpants.
- *Yuck!*, Mick Manning, Brita Granström. What birds and other creatures eat isn't for our baby!

Mealtime with a baby is face-to-face time, and a great time for talking. Food is a great teaching tool, both in the pages of a book and on the plate. For baby, naming foods and talking about their color, shape, and texture is fun. Books that show babies eating messily might make her giggle. Older babies and toddlers will enjoy hungry animals, books about kitchen play, and reading books about a variety of foods, from sushi to tortillas to pancakes.

Toddlers and twos also like counting food, and there's no better way to start subtraction than with cookies. There are a bunch of commercialized brand-name counting books out there that feature various snacks. Whether they are a harmless gimmick or an early introduction to the pervasiveness of brand names and marketing depends entirely on your perspective. We think you'll be counting pastas and crackers and other foods with or without these books.

Someone's in the Kitchen with Mommy

There is no more enthusiastic cooking partner than a toddler or preschooler. This can be great when you need someone to shell peas and not so great if you're trying to put dinner together in a crunch (thus the box of toys and books on the floor!).

For those days when you have time, cooking together is a great activity. It's just messy enough to be fun and there's nothing like the pride that comes with making something other people will enjoy eating. Plus, kids are more likely to try something new if they've had a hand in making it, even if it was just to push the buttons on the food processor.

Most recipes can allow for some toddler participation: pouring in the olive oil or scooping the sugar. As your child gets bigger, she'll be able to do more. If you're interested in recipes that are kid-friendly in the kitchen and at the table, these books should help:

- *Pretend Soup and Other Real Recipes: A Cookbook for Preschoolers and Up*, Mollie Katzen, Ann Henderson.
- *Salad People and More Real Recipes: A New Cookbook for Preschoolers and Up*, Mollie Katzen.
- *Cooking Art: Easy Edible Art for Young Children*, MaryAnn F. Kohl, Jean Potter, Ronni Roseman-Hall (illus). There is also *Snacktivities: 50 Edible Activities for Parents and Children* with some of the same activities but for half the price.
- *Fanny at Chez Panisse: A Child's Restaurant Adventures with 46 Recipes*, Alice L. Waters, Bob Carrau, Patricia Curtan, Ann Arnold (illus.).

How Does Your Garden Grow?

Toddlers and two-year-olds are fascinated by the growing process. How can a tiny seed become food? If you have any earth at all, or even just a pot, watching that process happen is a thrill for a child. Sugar snap peas, pumpkins, and carrots are easy to grow from seed. Even growing just a few is exciting. Because the whole thing is such a mystery—even after you see it happen, it's still hard to believe—children usually love even the simplest books about young gardens and gardeners.

Great Books for Little Gardeners

- *And Then It's Spring*, Julie Fogliano, Erin E. Stead (illus.). The lovely poetic text and soft illustrations capture a young gardener's anticipation for the sprouts of spring.
- *Flower Garden*, Eve Bunting, Kathryn Hewitt (illus.). This flower garden comes in a box and comes home by bus—an urban gardener's story.
- *Jack's Garden*, Henry Cole. This is the garden that Jack built, from planting to sprouting to budding to bloom.
- *Lenny in the Garden*, Ken Wilson-Max. A toddler explores the outside while his mother gardens. Try *Lenny Has Lunch* to see Lenny and his dad in action.
- *Muncha! Muncha! Muncha!*, Candace Fleming, G. Brian Karas (illus.). Can you outsmart three hungry rabbits who think you planted a garden of vegetables just for them? For more rabbit fun, try *Tippy-Tippy-Tippy, Hide!*
- *One Bean*, Anne Rockwell, Megan Halsey (illus.). A young narrator describes what happens when you plant one bean.
- *Planting a Rainbow*, Lois Ehlert. Mom and her child plant a garden of bulbs and seeds that emerge in glorious half pages with all the flowers labeled. Vegetables star in *Growing Vegetable Soup*.
- *The Ugly Vegetables*, Grace Lin. A young girl is disappointed that

her mother has decided to grow ugly Chinese vegetables instead of the flowers their neighbors grow. When the ugly vegetables become delicious soup, all the neighbors want to try it and grow their own.

- *Whose Garden Is It?*, Mary Ann Hoberman, Jane Dyer (illus.). It's perfect, but does it belong to the bees, the worms, the rabbit, the rain? This garden needs them all to grow.

Clothes! No Clothes!

Getting dressed can be a minefield. Babies don't want to lie on that changing table for one more minute, toddlers are more interested in figuring out how to get their clothes off than letting you put them on, and twos, both boys and girls, often suddenly develop startlingly firm opinions about what they want to wear when. You'll have to pick your battles. There may be some wiggle room about the red shirt with the bicycle on it that she's worn for the last three days, but for much of the year there's no question that she's going to have to wear something. Books about clothes are a great source of inside jokes, and a few good jokes can make a tight shirt go over a little head much more easily.

Get Me Dressed!

- *Blue Hat, Green Hat*, Sandra Boynton. A bear, an elephant, a moose, and a very silly turkey demonstrate how to wear (and not wear) various items of clothing. In Spanish, it's *Azul el sombrero, verde el sombrero*.
- *Ella Sarah Gets Dressed*, Margaret Chodos Irvine. A little girl sticks firmly to her own inimitable style.
- *Get Dressed!*, Seymour Chwast. One of the most inventive lift-the-flap books for encouraging creative dressing for kids. An amazing gift from a well-respected artist.
- *The Jacket I Wear in the Snow*, Shirley Neitzel, Nancy Winslow

Parker (illus.). A cumulative dress-up-for-winter-time tale, starting with the jacket.

- *Jesse Bear, What Will You Wear?*, Nancy Carlstrom, Bruce Degen (illus.). A day's wardrobe for the bear, from pants to shirts to a tight high chair to PJs.
- *Little Mouse Gets Ready*, Jeff Smith. In this picture book constructed like a comic strip, a little mouse goes through all the stages of getting dressed, including Velcro and snaps.
- *Maisy's Clothes / La ropa de Maisy: A Maisy Dual Language Book*, Lucy Cousins. A bilingual (English and Spanish) exploration of Maisy's wardrobe.
- *Shoes*, Elizabeth Winthrop, William Joyce (illus.). This is a joyous book about what little kids do in all kinds of shoes.
- *Will You Wear a Blue Hat?*, Ken Karp (Rookie Toddler series). Simple text (which you could easily sing to your own tune) and bright photos show a young boy dressing for winter weather.

The Mess in the House

Kids' rooms are their kingdoms, the one place in the house that's uniquely theirs (and even shared rooms are kid territory). It's easier to leave a little mess on the ground in a room you don't have to walk through on the way to the kitchen, but a room that's been the center of a day of playing and reading is eventually going to need to be cleaned. Babies and toddlers often like helping—any activity that involves putting things into a box works for them—but twos may be more resistant. It only takes a few missing toy pieces and stumbles over the mess on the way to the bathroom in the middle of the night for them to begin to understand why this is important, but they still may not like actually doing it. Books, which usually take both the mess and the cleaning to wild extremes, illustrate both the problem and the many ways that cleaning up can be fun.

What a Mess!

- *Broom, Zoom!*, Caron Lee Cohen, Sergio Ruzzier (illus.). A pint-size witch and a diaper-wearing monster fight over a broom and then use it to clean up a spill and take a moonlit ride.
- *Brownie & Pearl Make Good*, Cynthia Rylant, Brian Biggs (illus.). When Brownie and her pet cat Pearl have a mishap, they do some cleaning up to make amends. The other Brownie & Pearl books are equally as accessible.
- *Clean Your Room, Harvey Moon!*, Pat Cummings. This very funny rhymed story is a rendering of the wish to push it all under the carpet. The volume of stuff that Harvey has collected is amazing. Why isn't a literal cover-up good enough to outsmart Mom?
- *How Do Dinosaurs Clean Their Rooms?*, Jane Yolen, Mark Teague (illus.). A number of toddler dinosaurs make attempts to put toys and messes away just like human kids. The major differences have to do with size and names, because the exasperated parents look very human indeed.
- *Little Oink*, Amy Krouse Rosenthal, Jen Corace (illus.). In another of Rosenthal and Corace's role reversal books, a little pig wants to be neat, which is not appreciated in his pigsty world.
- *Max Cleans Up*, Rosemary Wells. Big sister Ruby helps Max clean, but Max reminds her of the importance of leaving a place for his treasures, even if they aren't exactly to her taste.
- *Pigsty*, Mark Teague. When his mom said a boy's room is turning into a pigsty, she might have been joking. However, there are genuinely pigs who inhabit his room, and cleaning it up is both frustrating and grounds for a new friendship.
- *Tidy Titch*, Pat Hutchins. When young Titch's siblings clean out their old toys, he takes their cast-offs, and suddenly his room is the messy one.

My Very Own Bed in My Very Own Room

Some kids are thrilled at the idea of moving into a big kid bed. Others are determined to hang on to their crib forever (a problem if there's a new tenant waiting in the wings). And when it comes time to actually sleep in that new place in the dark, even little ones who originally embraced the idea can be nervous. Moving in to one's own room is another huge transition. Toddlers who've been sharing a room with Mom and Dad, a baby, or an older sibling and are about to move can be overwhelmed by the idea of a room of their own. Either is a big transition, and it takes time, patience, and a few nights (or weeks) of interrupted sleep before things settle down. Hearing that he's not the only small person who ever felt this way can help.

Books for Bedtime in a New Bed

- *Big Enough for a Bed*, Apple Jordan, John E. Barrett (illus.). A very short, very simple book. *Sesame Street*'s Elmo leaves his crib, chooses new sheets for his new bed, and gathers all the things he needs to snuggle up for the night. Good for making the crib-bed transition with a less verbal child.
- *The BIG Sleep Book*, Guido van Genechten. This board book shows how various animals sleep, from sleeping underwater to hanging from a tree. The last page shows a little boy dozing in his big bed.
- *My Big Boy Bed*, Eve Bunting, Maggie Smith (illus.). He's got a baby sib in the crib, so he's exploring all the advantages of his new big boy bed. As parents with children who face this change will note quickly, one of the advantages from the boy's point of view is the ease of getting in and out independently.
- *Rosa's Room*, Barbara Bottner, Beth Spiegel (illus.). Rosa has moved to a new house, and she's turning an empty space into her own cozy room.
- *Your Own Big Bed*, Rita M. Bergstein, Susan Kathleen Hartung (illus.). Just as all animals have their own special place to sleep, a little boy learns to sleep in his own big bed.

Books in Sickness and in Health

It's sometimes hard to tell what constitutes a new adventure for a child and what makes them anxious. A doctor or dentist visit could do both. Your presence is the ultimate reassurance, but a book can help turn the dentist's chair into a more familiar place before you've even left the house.

> **TIP: Buy your child a doctor's kit to go with a doctor's appointment book. A little role-playing makes appointments easier, and you'll be playing the patient and bandaging stuffed animals for years to come.**

Doctor and dentist visits will eventually become part of the routine, but a hospital stay, no matter how serious, is hard for a baby or a child at any age—not to mention his parents. It's overly facile to say that books will help if it feels like nothing can, but books can give both of you something else to occupy yourselves. For a toddler or two-year-old, books on topic are good some of the time, and books that take both of you away to a different place may be even better. A baby will be soothed just by the sound of your voice.

Bumps and Boo-Boos, Tummy- and Toothaches (and the People Who Make Them All Better)

- *Boo Hoo Bird*, Jeremy Tankard. When Bird gets knocked on the noggin, his friends chime in with ideas of things he can do to feel better. The companion book to *Grumpy Bird*.
- *Corduroy Goes to the Doctor*, Don Freeman, Lisa McCue (illus.). Corduroy's checkup might reassure and prepare your own little one.
- *Doctor Maisy*, Lucy Cousins. Maisy wears a white coat to help her ailing friend Panda.
- *Froggy Goes to the Doctor*, Jonathan London, Frank Remkiewicz (illus.). Regular checkups involve waiting, worries, and some funny exams.

Books about illness might be scary for young children, even if they have a happy ending. It's okay—in fact, it's good—to have a book that introduces some new ideas. And you're right there with her to talk about it. The combination of you and the book offer a reminder that she can manage or find ways to work around something she finds scary. She can manage being sick and getting better. If your child has a specific medical issue, a web search or a talk with your librarian is likely to turn up books that might help her to understand what's happening.

Get Well Soon Books

- *Bear Feels Sick*, Karma Wilson, Jane Chapman (illus.). When Bear is sick in his cave, his animal friends bring him soup, tea, and companionship to help him feel better.
- *Curious George Goes to the Hospital*, Margret and H. A. Rey. George the monkey, who swallows a piece of a puzzle, never loses his curiosity amidst all the hospital equipment and staff. There are few dated medical references here, but it is still a classic.
- *Don't You Feel Well, Sam?*, Amy Hest, Anita Jeram (illus.). Cough medicine for this coughing bear, along with extra closeness from his mommy, see him back to health.
- *Guess Who, Baby Duck!*, Amy Hest, Jill Barton (illus.). To help Baby Duck recover her usual healthy spunk, Grandpa and Baby Duck review happier times as they look at a family photo album.
- *Madeline*, Ludwig Bemelmans. The first Madeline book in which the irrepressible little Parisian girl has her appendix out.
- *Through My Window*, Tony Bradman, Eileen Browne (illus.). Jo is sick and has to stay home with her dad, but her mom promises to bring her a surprise at the end of the day.

And I Will Read It on a Train and I Will Read It on a Plane

Libraries and bookstores are full of books about planes, trains, and automobiles. In fact, many authors, like Byron Barton (*Planes, Trains, My Car*) and Lois Lenski (*The Little Airplane*), have written all three. For many kids, it would be tough to find a bad book on any kind of moving machine whether it's planes, trucks, spaceships, or bulldozers. Both boys and girls are fascinated. There must be dozens of books on each of these in every library, and you can always thrill a plane lover, or a train lover, by consulting with the librarian and coming home with a stack of fun books.

> **TIP: Big and little kids traveling together can share the *I Spy* board books. Both can look for the missing objects, and beginning readers may be able to manage the rhymes.**

Planes, Trains, and Automobiles

For more vehicle books, see the "What to Read When Your Toddler is Obsessed with…" list (see page 50).

- *Airport*, Byron Barton. A simple walk-through of a trip to the airport and onto a plane, done with typical Barton simple directness.
- *Amazing Airplanes*, Tony Mitton, Ant Parker. A whole airplane voyage for animals, and lots of information for readers about pilots, intercom, snacks, seat belts, and the bump of the wheels on landing. (The authors' other books in the Amazing Machines series are also very satisfying such as *Cool Cars* and *Terrific Trains*.)
- *Beep, Beep*, Petr Horáček. A simple board book with easy-to-turn shaped pages about a family's car trip to see Grandma.
- *Bus Stops*, Taro Gomi. Take a ride on a bus and see where it stops along the way.

- *Down in the Subway*, Miriam Cohen, Melanie Hope Greenberg (illus.). Oh how we'd like to be on *this* car, where a magical Jamaican lady transforms a simple ride into an island fiesta. Caribbean rhythms and pictures to match.
- *Everything Goes: 1 2 3 Beep Beep Beep!: A Counting Book* and *Everything Goes: Stop! Go! A Book of Opposites*, Brian Biggs. Cars, trucks, bikes, and more in Biggs's wonderfully goofy cartoons.
- *Lisa's Airplane Trip*, Anne Gutman, Georg Hallensleben (illus.). Lisa tells all about her airplane trip from Paris to New York.
- *Miles to Go*, Jamie Harper. Miles enjoys his daily commute to preschool in his ride-on car. Through the endpapers, which are maps of his route coming and going, we learn that preschool is across the street!
- *My Car*, Byron Barton. Sam has a car. He shows and tells us quite a lot about it.
- *On the Road*, Susan Steggall. Two kids in the backseat of Mama's car really do see a lot as they travel along the city streets into the country roads and to the sea. See also *The Life of a Car*.
- *The Rain Train*, Elena de Roo, Brian Lovelock (illus.). Through poetic text with great sound effects and enchanting watercolors, de Roo and Lovelock take us on a magical, nighttime train voyage.
- *Rattletrap Car*, Phyllis Root, Jill Barton (illus.). When an old jalopy breaks down several times on the way to the beach, the whole family, including the baby, comes up with crazy ideas to get it going again. A delightful fantasy.
- *Subway*, Anastasia Suen, Karen Katz (illus.). A little girl and her mom enjoy a ride on the NYC subway.
- *Trains*, Byron Barton. Wonderfully simplified with journeys and riders and routes.
- *Trainstop*, Barbara Lehmann. A wordless book about a girl's mysterious and magical train ride.
- *Two Little Trains*, Margaret Wise Brown, Leo and Diane Dillon

(illus.). A perfect new rendering of parallel play, as the small train inside replicates the big one's journey in the great outdoors. For more trains at play, see *My Little Train* by Satomi Ichikawa.

- *Trucks, Trucks, Trucks*, Peter Sís. Lots of different trucks and the jobs they do, some with foldout pages. Satisfying colors of yellow and white. (Also *Fire Truck*.)

TIP: Richard Scarry books are perfect for travel, because there's so much going on in each one. Try *Cars and Trucks and Things That Go* or *A Day at the Airport*. There's a story on every page, a continuing story, and recurring characters to search for throughout.

Everyday Outings: To the Grocery Store and Beyond!

Books can take us to exotic places, but sometimes the books that just stick close to home are equally appealing. Books can put a thrill in an everyday outing and remind kids to stay close and keep a good grip on a favorite toy while out in the world.

Little Trips into the Big World

- *Bebé Goes Shopping*, Susan Middleton Elya, Steven Salerno (illus.). Mamá and her bebé take a trip to the grocery store. It's written in English with smatterings of Spanish throughout.
- *Dim Sum for Everyone!*, Grace Lin. A family enjoys eating all sorts of little dishes at a Chinatown restaurant.
- *Every Friday*, Dan Yaccarino. Every Friday a boy and his dad enjoy breakfast at the local diner. Yaccarino's retro art warmly depicts this relationship.
- *Feast for 10*, Cathryn Falwell. In this counting book, a family shops for and then prepares a delicious meal. In Spanish, it's *Fiesta para 10*.

- *Harry and the Bucketful of Dinosaurs*, Ian Whybrow, Adrian Reynolds (illus.). Harry loses his friends, but finds that they come when he calls. Currently only available as an ebook.
- *Max's Dragon Shirt*, Rosemary Wells. Max gets lost looking for Ruby in a bunny department store. This book contains some of Ms. Wells's funniest illustrations.
- *A Pocket for Corduroy*, Don Freeman. Corduroy gets lost on a trip with Lisa and her mother to the Laundromat, all because he has no pocket on his overalls. Lisa is once again a model of compassion.
- *What Can You Do with a Paleta? / ¿Qué puedes hacer con una paleta?*, Carmen Tafolla, Magaly Morales (illus.). A young girl ventures out into her *barrio* for a *paleta*, a Mexican Popsicle, on a hot summer day. In Spanish and English.

Get Outside

Books help you to experience winter when the sun is shining or take a trip to the beach while a cold rain falls. Lots of outside activities can be a little intimidating for toddlers. The big kids jump into that water enthusiastically, but lots of little ones are more hesitant. Reading a book about characters learning to ice skate, swim in the ocean, and even go barefoot in the sand can make babies feel braver. Books about hikes, picnics, and parks create a point of reference and make a child's own outside fun even more enjoyable.

Books for the Great Outdoors

- *Baby Bear Sees Blue*, Ashley Wolff. Baby Bear explores the colors around him, from brown trout to red strawberries.
- *Blueberries for Sal*, Robert McCloskey. Sal is a little girl who gets lost alongside a baby bear who gets found on an old-fashioned blueberrying

expedition. This delightful book captures the sights and sounds of picking blueberries perfectly.

- *First Snow*, Bernette Ford, Sebastien Braun (illus.). We see a new season through the eyes of a bunny and his siblings. For another first snow experience, try *A Kitten Tale* by Eric Rohmann.
- *Sally Goes to the Mountains*, Stephen Huneck. Sally is a black Lab dog who eagerly explores the sights, smells, and animals on an outing to the mountains with her human. Sally investigates and enjoys the beach and the farm in other picture books.
- *The Snowy Day*, Jack Ezra Keats. Said to be the first picture book with an African American child protagonist when first published in the 1960s, *The Snowy Day* has achieved its classic, irreplaceable status for all young families because of its simplicity, elegance, and shared delight in watching a small boy explore a snowy day.
- *Spot Goes to the Beach*, Eric Hill. Seeing Spot surrounded by his spotty duck inner tube, carrying his sand pail, and wearing his jaunty hat is a suitable start for another adorable, fun, lift-the-flap toddler treat.
- *Summer Days and Nights*, Wong Herbert Yee. A little girl enjoys splashing in the wading pool, a picnic, an evening's walk, and more with her family in the good old summertime. See also *Tracks in the Snow* and *Who Likes the Rain?*
- *Ten Little Caterpillars*, Bill Martin Jr., Lois Ehlert (illus.). This is a playful counting book featuring a variety of caterpillars, which also doubles as a butterfly / caterpillar field guide.

As you read even the most ordinary-seeming book to your baby, try to think about how it relates to her day and her world. If she grows used to seeing herself, and her life, reflected and expanded on in books, she'll seek out that experience again and again as she grows up. Books take us out into the world, and they bring the world in to us.

Chapter Eleven
READING HAPPILY EVER AFTER

◆ ◇ ◆ ◇ ◆ ◇ ◆ ◇ ◆ ◇ ◆ ◇ ◆ ◇ ◆ ◇ ◆ ◇ ◆ ◇ ◆ ◇ ◆ ◇ ◆ ◇ ◆ ◇ ◆ ◇ ◆ ◇ ◆ ◇ ◆

You know reading to your child, as a baby, a toddler, or a two-year-old, can enhance your relationship. If you've been reading together, you've seen how valuable books are: how they calm both of you in times of fatigue and stress, how they add entertainment and conversation to your life together. As you continue to grow and read together, remember to leave special baby favorites on the bookshelf and on any e-reader. It's surprising how long they continue to have an important place in your child's life.

As your baby becomes a preschooler, reading only gets better. New picture books will get longer, more elaborate, and extend the range of your children's knowledge into science and nature, fables and fairy tales, humor and jokes. You'll probably want to make even more use of the library, since the phrase "Again! Again!" becomes less frequent and finding new favorites becomes more fun.

Depending on your child, sometime during the third or fourth year you may be able to introduce short chapter books. The earliest ones maintain plenty of artwork, but with expanded text comes a drop in illustrations. Your child's imagination will create its own. New and difficult concepts are absorbed as your child learns to follow the important parts of the story. As he gets even older, you will find beloved authors and illustrators and watch for their new books to be published together.

Parents of preschoolers worry unnecessarily about when their child will begin to read on his own. Some pointing and sounding out words in books is fine. Soon enough she'll be asking you for that kind of help. But our advice is to keep reading. Too much instruction, too much pressure (and your child will notice what you're doing, guaranteed), and reading isn't fun anymore.

Picture Books for Preschoolers and Up

A 2010 article in the *New York Times* commented that some parents stop reading picture books with their children as early as four years old. While it is great to bring chapter books, poetry, and nonfiction into the mix, don't stop enjoying picture books together even as your child enters the elementary years (we know high school teachers who use them with their students). Picture books can be quite sophisticated. The best are like great poems or short stories, deceptively simple and beautifully constructed. With so many talented artists illustrating them, don't underestimate their power to teach visual literacy skills.

- *The Adventures of Sparrowboy*, Brian Pinkney. A young boy collides with a sparrow and develops the ability to fly. A fun picture book for the superhero-obsessed.
- *Alice the Fairy*, David Shannon. Alice is a pretend fairy, not a real fairy, because it's hard to be a real fairy. Rough-and-tumble gap-toothed Alice figures she'll probably be a temporary fairy forever, because although she can turn her dad into a "horse" (for a horsey ride) and a plate of cookies into "mine," she's not ready for all the tests that come with advanced fairy school, and she's happy the way she is.
- *Alphabet Adventure*, Audrey Wood, Bruce Wood (illus.). This alphabet's been in training, and they're all ready for school—but little i's dot is missing, and everyone joins in the search. Readers can spot the hiding

dot in the glossy illustrations and help straighten out the letters as they line up for school once the dot is found.

- *Ananse and the Lizard: A West African Tale*, Pat Cummings. As he tries to win the hand of the chief's daughter, Ananse, the spider trickster, is outsmarted by a lizard.

- *The Best Pet of All*, David LaRochelle, Hanako Wakiyama (illus.). "No dog," says Mom, but she agrees to a pet dragon, little dreaming that the boy would manage to find one and bring him home. It turns out that dragons, even in a neat, graphic, and colorful world that evokes a nostalgic vision of the fifties, aren't very good pets. How to get rid of this one? Well, it turns out they don't like dogs.

- *Big Red Lollipop*, Rukhsana Khan, Sophie Blackall (illus.). Rubina, an Arab American girl, must take her little sister to the first birthday party she is ever invited to. The tables are turned when this little sister gets invited to a party of her own and she must take the baby sister of the family. A lovely family story and the art made it onto a *New York Times* Best Illustrated list.

- *Cloudy with a Chance of Meatballs*, Judi Barrett, Ron Barrett (illus.). Food falls from the sky in the land of Chewandswallow until the weather takes a turn for the worse in this silly tall tale with plenty of detailed illustrations for poring over.

- *Diary of a Worm*, Doreen Cronin, Harry Bliss (illus.). A worm's diary entries describe his life underground and why he likes being a worm. Harry Bliss, a cartoonist from *The New Yorker*, makes an already funny text even funnier with his clever drawings.

- *The Giant Jam Sandwich*, John Vernon Lord, Janet Burroway (illus.). How to catch a thousand wasps? Capture them in the world's biggest jam sandwich, of course. But it will take helicopters and giant machinery and a really big loaf of bread…all right there on the page to enjoy.

- *How I Became a Pirate*, Melinda Long, David Shannon (illus.). Pirates recruit a young sand-castle builder to join them and dig a hole for their buried treasure, promising to get him back for soccer practice. No vegetables and no manners are great, but this young pirate misses having someone to tuck him in at night. Shannon's characteristically rugged illustrations capture the boy and the pirate band. The sequel is *Pirates Don't Change Diapers*.

- *Jingle Dancer*, Cynthia Leitich Smith, Cornelius Van Wright (illus.), Ying-Hwa Hu (illus.). Jenna is a contemporary, suburban girl and a member of the Muscogee (Creek) Nation. She gathers jingles from the dresses of several friends and relatives so she can perform the jingle dance at an upcoming powwow.

- *Just a Minute!: A Trickster Tale and Counting Book*, Yuyi Morales. In this delightful bilingual (Spanish and English) counting book, Grandma Beetle cleverly delays her journey with Señor Calvera. Try *Just in Case* for an alphabet book with the same characters.

- *Raising Dragons*, Jerdine Nolen, Elise Primavera (illus.). The narrator was, she says, born to raise dragons, and when she finds an egg, she does, against a darkly colorful painted backdrop of Pa farming and Ma keeping up the farmhouse. Her dragon proves very useful, and even though he outgrows the farm, he sees to it that she has more dragons to raise before he goes. Try *Harvey Potter's Balloon Farm* also by Nolen and illustrated by Mark Buehner.

- *The Relatives Came*, Cynthia Rylant, Stephen Gammell (illus.). They came, and they stayed all summer, or so it seemed. All the inconveniences are forgotten in the fun of being a big family squashed together, perfectly captured by hazy, glowing pastel illustrations.

- *Pierre: A Cautionary Tale in Five Chapters and a Prologue*, Maurice Sendak. Pierre, who doesn't care, learns a thing or two when a lion comes calling. One of the books in Sendak's Nutshell Library—a must-have collection.

- *Sylvester and the Magic Pebble*, William Steig. In this tale of separation anxiety for the older crowd, Sylvester finds a magic, wish-granting pebble and inadvertently turns himself into a rock. The family reunion as depicted in Steig's Caldecott-winning art is priceless.

- *Zen Shorts*, Jon J. Muth. The serene watercolor illustrations come in two styles, Western for the children interacting with their new panda neighbor and more Eastern for the stories he tells—stories that link to the children's everyday problems and provide both a new way of looking at things and, for those who are interested, a brief introduction to Zen philosophy. Whether it's a jumping point for discussion or just a picture book, *Zen Shorts* is both engrossing and visually stunning.

Keep reading. And keep reading FUN! It's a great habit. A ritual of a chapter a night, a chapter after dinner, or a long book to read aloud in the evening could carry you and your child through elementary school and beyond. As you read, you'll always have a point of connection, a shared experience that lies outside of your relationship as parent and child. Books will become, and remain, a beloved common ground.

"Just a few weeks ago I caught one of my former toddlers (from library story time) who is now in fifth grade forming a reading circle and reading to several smaller children (holding up the book, modeling my behavior). Mom and I had a good laugh and I took a photo. It is amazing what they remember." —Lynn

First Chapter Books to Share

- *Alvin Ho: Allergic to Camping, Hiking, and Other Natural Disasters*, Lenore Look, LeUyen Pham (illus.). Alvin, a first-class worrywart and nature-phobe, must endure a camping trip planned by his father. Funny and warm, and Pham's spot art throughout is an energetic joy. For a girl's take on things, try Look's *Ruby Lu, Empress of Everything* (Anne Wilsdorf [illus.]).

- *Betsy-Tacy*, Maud Hart Lovelace, Lois Lenski (illus.). The first book in the series about two little girls in turn-of-the-century Wisconsin follows Betsy and Tacy through kindergarten, with familiar-feeling illustrations from Lenski. Holds the attention of boys and girls alike.
- *Catwings*, Ursula K. LeGuin, S. D. Schindler (illus.). A group of winged kittens fly out of the busy city streets in search of "hands" that will show them kindness. There are several other short volumes available in this enchanting fantasy series.
- *Charlie and the Chocolate Factory*, Roald Dahl, Quentin Blake (illus.). Charlie is just enough lighter and funnier than much of Dahl's work to be read to a fairly young child, and the entrancing word descriptions of the candy factory will fire up any imagination.
- *Clementine*, Sara Pennypacker, Marla Frazee (illus.). Like Ramona, Pippi, Madeline, or Olivia, Clementine is one of those heroines who (almost) can't be contained on the page. In the first of the series, Clementine has run-ins with her fourth-grade neighbor, her pesky brother, and the peskier pigeons of her apartment building. Frazee's black-and-white sketches throughout add to the fun.
- *Flat Stanley*, Jeff Brown, Scott Nash (illus.). With only four simple chapters and plenty of illustrations, Flat Stanley makes a nice first chapter book, and its mixture of the routine and the extraordinary is timelessly appealing. His adventures have inspired a whole curriculum unit for the elementary years.
- *Just So Stories*, Rudyard Kipling. These are simply wonderful for reading aloud, oh best beloved. When your preschooler hits the "why" stage, there's nothing better than the story of how the overly curious baby elephant got his trunk.
- *Little House in the Big Woods*, Laura Ingalls Wilder, Garth Williams (illus.). You probably remember this fairly gentle (but not without excitement) first book in the series, a look at a year in the life of young Laura and her family in pioneer Wisconsin. There's some bullet

making and animal killing among the stories of Christmas stockings and sugaring, all of which may lead to some questions. You can answer or edit the text as you choose.

- *Mr. Popper's Penguins*, Richard Atwater, Florence Atwater (illus.). Generations of kids have loved the tale of how Mr. Popper, a housepainter who dreams of exploring the South Pole, acquires a troop of trained penguins.

- *Mrs. Piggle-Wiggle's Farm*, Betty MacDonald, Maurice Sendak (illus.). If you read these as a child, you probably remember the magnificent silliness of Mrs. Piggle-Wiggle's cures for childhood ailments like talking back and tattling, and that's what will capture your child's imagination. The adult conversations can be lengthy, didactic, and remarkably sexist, but they'll wash right over your child's head as she waits to get to the good part.

- *My Father's Dragon*, Ruth Stiles Gannett, Ruth Chrisman Gannett (illus.). In the first book of a trilogy, a boy rescues a young dragon from enslavement and rides him home. A nice starter adventure story with nothing scary about it and a good introduction to many of the familiar elements of fantasy.

- *Pippi Longstocking*, Astrid Lindgren. Pippi is nine, red-haired, strong as an ox, and lives all alone in her house with a horse and her monkey and nobody to tell her what to do. What child wouldn't want to hear more about that?

- *Ramona the Pest*, Beverly Cleary. Ramona's adjustment to kindergarten and her struggle to understand the confusing world will ring true for many preschoolers. There are several more Ramona books your child can grow up with, and Cleary's *The Mouse and the Motorcycle* is also a delight.

- *The Stories Julian Tells*, Ann Cameron, Ann Strugnell (illus.). These playful and poetic short stories describe the life and times of tall-tale-telling Julian, his brother Huey, and their very clever father. There are other Julian and Huey books if your child clamors for more.

- *Winnie-the-Pooh*, A. A. Milne, Ernest H. Shepard (illus.). While Pooh has been repackaged and marketed more than any other bear, these tales from the Hundred Acre Wood are not to be missed in their original form with the perfect Shepard illustrations. If you can, hold off on introducing your child to other versions until after you can savor this one together. *The House at Pooh Corner* follows.

"This morning I heard the now four-year-old Sam playing on the floor of the kitchen, fully engaged in some sort of flying toy. When I tuned in, I heard him declare, 'My elevator is the fastest ever! We'll go all the way to the Space Hotel!' Evidently Charlie and the Great Glass Elevator, *even with sparse illustrations, confusing scenes with the president, and scary man-eating Knids, is making inroads on his imagination." —KJ*

Appendix A
AWARD WINNERS

The Caldecott and More

The Caldecott Medal

The Caldecott Medal was named in honor of nineteenth-century English illustrator Randolph Caldecott. It is awarded annually by the Association for Library Service to Children, a division of the American Library Association, to the artist of the most distinguished American picture book for children. The honored book sometimes targets an older audience, as with the 2004 winner, Mordicai Gerstein for *The Man Who Walked Between the Towers*, but there are some wonderful winners and honor books (the runners-up) for babies and toddlers. Look for the familiar gold medal or the silver honor shield. Here are some honorees we love:

- *A Ball for Daisy*, Chris Raschka
- *Ella Sarah Gets Dressed*, Margaret Chodos-Irvine
- *Freight Train*, Donald Crews
- *Hondo and Fabian*, Peter McCarty
- *The House in the Night*, Susan Marie Swanson, Beth Krommes (illus.)
- *Hush! A Thai Lullaby*, Minfong Ho, Holly Meade (illus.)
- *In the Small, Small Pond*, Denise Fleming
- *Joseph Had a Little Overcoat*, Simms Taback

- *Kitten's First Full Moon*, Kevin Henkes
- *Knuffle Bunny* and *Knuffle Bunny Too*, Mo Willems
- *The Polar Express*, Chris Van Allsburg
- *A Sick Day for Amos McGee*, Philip C. Stead, Erin E. Stead (illus.)
- *Sleep Like a Tiger*, Mary Logue, Pamela Zagarenski (illus.)
- *The Snowy Day*, Ezra Jack Keats
- *When Sophie Gets Angry—Really, Really Angry...*, Molly Bang

The Charlotte Zolotow Award

The Charlotte Zolotow Award, recognizing outstanding writing in a picture book, is relatively new. Although the award is for the writing, all of the books honored offer wonderful illustrations as well, leading us to conclude that the committee is wisely looking at the whole book. (Similarly, you won't see the Caldecott go to a beautiful book with poor writing.) It's administered by the Cooperative Children's Book Center, a children's literature library of the School of Education, University of Wisconsin–Madison, and appears as a gold seal with a rose on it. Molly Bang's *When Sophie Gets Angry—Really, Really Angry...* won this award as well as the Caldecott Honor medal in 2000. Other winning books, honor books, and highly recommended titles we like for babies and toddlers:

- *Apple Pie ABC*, Alison Murray
- *Birds*, Kevin Henkes, Laura Dronzek (illus.)
- *Dance with Me*, Charles R. Smith Jr., Noah Z. Jones (illus.)
- *Farfallina and Marcel*, Holly Keller
- *Five Creatures*, Emily Jenkins, Tomek Bogacki (illus.)
- *Moon Plane*, Peter McCarty
- *The Night Worker*, Kate Banks, Georg Hallensleben (illus.)
- *No Go Sleep!*, Kate Feiffer, Jules Feiffer (illus.)
- *Oh, No!*, Candace Fleming, Eric Rohmann (illus.)
- *Pouch!*, David Ezra Stein

- *Sleep Like a Tiger*, Mary Logue, Pamela Zagarenski (illus.)
- *Snow*, Uri Shulevitz (also a Caldecott Honor book)
- *Thank You Bear*, Greg Foley
- *The Twins' Blanket*, Hyewon Yum
- *What Can You Do With a Paleta?*, Carmen Tafolla, Magaly Morales (illus.)

The Coretta Scott King Award

The Coretta Scott King Award is presented annually by the Coretta Scott King Task Force of the American Library Association's Ethnic & Multicultural Information Exchange Round Table. Recipients are American authors and illustrators of African descent whose distinguished books promote an understanding and appreciation of African American culture and universal human values. Winning books display a pyramid over a circle on a black and gold seal. These awards aren't limited to children's books, but a few stand-outs for our age group have been honored, like *Uptown* by Bryan Collier, *My People* by Langston Hughes and illustrated by Charles R. Smith Jr., and *Let It Shine* by Ashley Bryan.

The Kate Greenaway Medal

The Kate Greenaway Medal is awarded for distinguished illustration in a book for children published in the United Kingdom. Many of these books are also available in the United States. Unfortunately, for some reason (British reticence?) there's no outward display of the medal on winning books, although it's often mentioned in the back cover copy. Look for *I Will Never Not Ever Eat a Tomato* by Lauren Child and *The Baby Who Would Not Go to Bed* by Helen Cooper.

The *New York Times* Best Illustrated Children's Books of the Year

Every year for over sixty years a small committee of illustrators, authors, librarians, and other experts has gathered at the *New York Times* to choose several of the best illustrated books of the year. Titles that have won have been everything from picture books to graphic novels. Here are a few honored titles that have something for little ones: *Grandpa Green* by Lane Smith, *A Penguin Story* by Antoinette Portis, *Ghosts in the House* by Kazuno Kohara, *Red Cap Girl* by Naoko Stoop, and *Every Friday* by Dan Yaccarino.

Pura Belpré Award

Named after the first Latina librarian at the New York Public Library, this award is presented to a Latino / Latina writer and illustrator whose work best portrays, affirms, and celebrates the Latino cultural experience in literature for youth. It is co-sponsored by the Association for Library Service to Children and REFORMA (the National Association to Promote Library and Information Services to Latinos and the Spanish-Speaking). A few Belpré honored books for the very young include *The Cazuela that the Farm Maiden Stirred* by Samantha R. Vamos and illustrated by Rafael López, *Fiesta Babies* by Carmen Tafolla and illustrated by Amy Cordova, and *Papá and Me* by Arthur Dorros and illustrated by Rudy Gutierrez.

Appendix B
RESOURCE BOOKS AND WEBSITES

◆◆◆

The following books and websites are excellent resources. The list includes potentially useful links and supports for parents, care providers, and all those wishing more information about books for babies, toddlers, and twos.

Books, Magazines, and Publications

- *A to Zoo: Subject Access to Children's Picture Books*, Carolyn W. Lima, Rebecca L. Thomas. Look for this reference book at your local library to find picture books on any topic imaginable.
- *Artist to Artist: 23 Major Illustrators Talk to Children About Their Art*, Eric Carle Museum of Picture Book Art. World-renowned illustrators, such as Maurice Sendak, Ashley Bryan, and Rosemary Wells, give us an inside look into their craft.
- *Baby Rhyming Time*, Linda L. Ernst. A great reference book for librarians and child-care professionals with tons of information on brain development and early literacy, programming ideas, and book lists galore.
- *The Best Children's Books of the Year*, issued annually by the Bank Street College of Education, www.bankstreet.edu. A wonderful list of great books for babies and toddlers up through the teen years.

- *CCBC Choices*, education.wisc.edu/ccbc. An annual guide to the best children's books of the year, University of Wisconsin's Cooperative Children's Book Center.
- *Every Child Ready to Read: Literacy Tips for Parents*, Lee Pesky Learning Center. This work has chapters that focus on special interests and children with learning disabilities.
- *Family Literacy from Theory to Practice*, Andrea DeBruin-Parecki (ed.), Barbara Krol-Sinclair (ed.). Full of academic and practical ideas for reading to children. Chapter 9 is Susan's contribution. Currently out of print.
- *A Family of Readers: The Book Lover's Guide to Children's and Young Adult Literature*, Roger Sutton (ed.), Martha Parravano (ed.). This guide features essays from the pages of *The Horn Book* magazine to help you inspire a lifelong love of reading.
- *From Cover to Cover: Evaluating and Reviewing Children's Books*, Kathleen T. Horning. A how-to book for those wishing to delve deeper into the world of children's literature.
- *Great Books for Babies and Toddlers: More Than 500 Recommended Books for Your Child's First Three Years*, Kathleen Odean. While this work has not been updated recently, there are some wonderful titles recommended.
- *The Horn Book Magazine*, www.hbook.com. A bimonthly magazine featuring book reviews, articles about literature for children and teens, and more.
- *How to Get Your Child to Love Reading: For Ravenous and Reluctant Readers Alike*, Esmé Raji Codell. This guide, from the renowned educator, is chock-full of tips and tricks to make reading fun and interactive.
- *Inside Picture Books*, Ellen Handler Spitz. This is a thought-provoking look at the meanings books have for children
- *The Read-Aloud Handbook*, Jim Trelease. The go-to guide on reading aloud. Make sure to look for the latest edition.

- *Reading Magic: Why Reading Aloud to Our Children Will Change Their Lives Forever*, Mem Fox, Judy Horacek (illus.). A manifesto from a passionate and prolific children's author.

Websites

- 100 Picture Books Everyone Should Know, New York Public Library (New York, NY): kids.nypl.org/reading
- American Library Association, Born to Read: www.ala.org/alsc/issuesadv/borntoread
  A program to promote reading with babies.
- Birth to Six, Hennepin County Library (Minnetonka, MN): www.hclib.org/BirthTo6
  A library site with lots of wonderful selections for books and read-aloud tips, and further nursery rhyme and story websites.
- *¡Colorín Colorado!* (in Spanish): www.colorincolorado.org
  Information on literacy for parents and professionals.
- Dolly Parton's Imagination Library: www.imaginationlibrary.com.
  Check to see if this free book give-away program exists in your community.
- First Five Years, Brooklyn Public Library (Brooklyn, NY): www.brooklynpubliclibrary.org/first-5-years
  For reading tips, videos of songs and rhymes performed by librarians, book recommendations, and more.
- First Book: www.firstbook.org
  For information and help getting books into the lives of families who need them.
- Goodreads: www.goodreads.com
  A fun site, with social networking capability, to track what you and your baby have read and get recommendations from friends and other users.

- The Literacy Site: www.theliteracysite.com
- Reach Out and Read: www.reachoutandread.org
  This national program in which pediatricians promote reading offers reading tips and titles of note.
- READ TO ME: www.readtomeprogram.org
  Susan's website for the READ TO ME Program that gets young families reading with their babies.
- Reading Is Fundamental (RIF): www.rif.org
  A fun and interactive site with lots of literacy tips in Spanish and English from one of the nation's largest literacy organizations.
- Reading Rockets (WETA): www.readingrockets.org
- Tell Me a Story, King County Library System (Seattle, WA): https://wiki.kcls.org/tellmeastory/
  The Seattle area library system has created a very extensive collection of song, rhyme, and finger play videos performed by its librarians.
- We Give Books (Pearson Foundation): www.wegivebooks.org
  As you read picture books online, this organization distributes new books to needy kids.
- Zero-to-Three: www.zerotothree.org
  Developmental information and resources from one of the premier organizations to support babies and toddlers.

Online Bookstores

- Abe Books: www.abebooks.com
  A great source for used and hard-to-find titles
- Amazon Books: www.amazon.com
- Barnes & Noble: www.BN.com
- Black Books Galore, Toni Trent Parker: www.blackbooksgalore.com
  Features books for and by African Americans, starting with pre-school titles.

- The Book Vine for Children: www.bookvine.com
  A good source for recommendations and for packaged collections
- Books of Wonder: www.booksofwonder.net
  An excellent NYC-based independent bookstore
- Powells Bookstore: www.powells.com
  Excellent Oregon-based bookstore for new and used books.
- Strand: www.strandbooks.com
  The famed New York City used bookstore sells many children's books online.

Often, your favorite author or illustrator has a website. Rather than list them all, we suggest putting his or her name into a search engine and see what pops up. Write to let them know how valuable their work is in your life with your youngsters.

Appendix C
OUT-OF-PRINT GEMS

❖❖❖❖❖❖❖❖❖❖❖❖❖❖❖❖❖❖❖❖❖❖❖❖❖❖❖❖❖❖❖

Many children's books go out of print very quickly. This may be the fate of several of the titles we suggest in these pages, or you may discover that a favorite from childhood is no longer available. Don't despair! It can be easy to find out-of-print books via online sellers large and small. Also, the title you seek may be available from the library, although check the online catalog or call before you make the trip. And, every so often, great books come back into print (ebooks may give titles a longer "shelf life"). Here are a few of our favorites that are worth going a little out of your way to track down:

- *Baby Says*, John Steptoe. Susan and Rachel's favorite sibling story—a baby in a crib communicates with his brother via teddy bear. Simple, realistic illustrations. This classic is currently out of print in a stand-alone edition, but it is included in the still in print *HarperCollins Treasury of Picture Book Classics: A Child's First Collection*, Katherine Tegen (ed.).
- *Blackboard Bear*, Martha Alexander. A chalk drawing of a bear climbs down and accompanies a small boy, helping him feel more powerful.
- *Come Along, Daisy!*, Jane Simmons. A duckling becomes so engrossed in play that she temporarily loses her mother.

- *Five Trucks*, Brian Floca. An up-close look at the five different trucks that help get an airplane ready for takeoff. Perfect for trips with long airport layovers, since you'll see the pages in action.
- *Goodnight Lulu*, Paulette Brogan. Mama chicken reassures Lulu at bedtime that all sorts of things *won't* happen.
- *Guji Guji*, Chih-Yuan Chen. A crocodile hatches amidst a brood of ducklings, but no matter how different he grows, he's loved by his mama duck and stays true to his family.
- *Happy Birth Day*, Robie H. Harris, Michael Emberley (illus.). A mother tells the story of her child's very first day in the world. Emberley's illustrations are realistic and warm.
- *I Will Not Go to Market Today*, Harry Allard, James Marshall (illus.). A big chicken, Fennimore B. Buttercrunch, endures endless catastrophes trying to obtain more jam for his morning toast.
- *Max's First Word*, Rosemary Wells. Max's first word isn't what Ruby was expecting.
- *Miffy*, Dick Bruna. When Miffy is born, all the animals come to visit the new little bunny.
- *My Aunt Came Back*, Pat Cummings. A young girl's globe-trotting aunt brings her souvenirs from several countries in this delightful rhyme. One of the few books to feature the aunt / niece relationship.
- *Papa's Song*, Kate McMullan, Jim McMullan (illus.). Papa Bear takes his sleep-resistant baby to hear the sounds and feel the gentle rhythms of the river.
- *Pat-A-Cake and Other Play Rhymes*, Joanna Cole, Stephanie Calmenson, Alan Tiegreen (illus.). With hand claps, finger wiggles, and bouncing motion, you'll both trot to Boston or ride a cockhorse to Banbury Cross.
- *The Saucepan Game*, Jan Ormerod. The baby uses her pot for everything imaginable…except, of course, to cook.

- *Sleepytime Rhyme*, Remy Charlip. A mother reassures her baby with a lullaby that details her love from lip to tippy toe.
- *Splash!*, Flora McDonnell. It is Baby Elephant who discovers a way to keep the animals cool on a blistering hot day.
- *What James Likes Best*, Amy Schwartz. James is thrilled by the mundane on trips in and around the city.
- *When Will Sarah Come?*, Elizabeth Fitzgerald Howard, Nina Crews (photos). A little boy waits for his big sister to come home from school.
- *Where Have You Been?*, Margaret Wise Brown, Leo and Diane Dillon (illus.). A brilliantly illustrated book answering the classic questions posed by both toddlers and parents: where have you been?

Appendix D
BILINGUAL BOOKS AND MULTILINGUAL RESOURCES

❖◦❖

Libros, Livres, Vitabu: Bilingual Books

To give your child a strong foundation, research shows that you should speak and read to your child in the language you know best. More and more books are being published bilingually to make it easier for you. When available, we have recommended bilingual Spanish / English or Spanish-only editions throughout the book, but here are a few more in a multitude of other languages:

- *Carry Me*, Rena D. Grossman. Learn how parents carry their babies around the world. Bilingual editions are available in Amharic, French, Portuguese, Somali, Spanish, and Vietnamese.
- *Hip Hop*, Catherine Hnatov. In Arabic, Hmong, Portuguese, Spanish, and English too, playful black-and-white animals share their antics.
- *A Nest in Springtime: A Bilingual Book of Numbers*, Belle Yang. In Mandarin Chinese and English, a goose and a gander count their eggs while they are hatching in this celebration of spring. Also available: *Summertime Rainbow: A Bilingual Book of Colors*.
- *Toddler Two / Dos años*, Anastasia Suen, Winnie Cheon (illus.). Two

toddlers explore all things that come in twos, such as hands, feet, and ears. In English and Spanish.

- *Row, Row, Row Your Boat*, Annie Kubler. This delightful version of the classic song is available in a dizzying array of languages: Arabic, Bengali, Cantonese, Farsi, French, Italian, Mandarin, Polish, Portuguese, Russian, Somali, Spanish, Tagalog, Urdu, and Vietnamese.
- *We're Going on a Bear Hunt*, Michael Rosen, Helen Oxenbury. Whether you speak Albanian, Czech, Farsi, Gujarati, Serbo-Croatian, or Turkish, you can go through the grass and river in search of the bear.

Multilingual Book Resources

Looking for more or can't find your native tongue? These publishers, vendors, and resources may help:

- ChinaSprout: www.chinasprout.com
- International Children's Digital Library: en.childrenslibrary.org
- Lectorum: www.lectorum.com
- Mantra Lingua: www.mantralingua.com
- Star Bright Books: www.starbrightbooks.org
- World of Reading: www.wor.com

INDEX

◆◆◆◆◆◆◆◆◆◆◆◆◆◆◆◆◆◆◆◆◆◆◆◆◆◆◆◆◆◆◆◆◆◆